Huts and History

UNIVERSITY PRESS OF FLORIDA

Florida A&M University, Tallahassee
Florida Atlantic University, Boca Raton
Florida Gulf Coast University, Ft. Myers
Florida International University, Miami
Florida State University, Tallahassee
University of Central Florida, Orlando
University of Florida, Gainesville
University of North Florida, Jacksonville
University of South Florida, Tampa
University of West Florida, Pensacola

Huts and History

The Historical Archaeology of Military
Encampment During the American Civil War

Edited by

CLARENCE R. GEIER

DAVID G. ORR

MATTHEW B. REEVES

University Press of Florida
Gainesville/Tallahassee/Tampa/Boca Raton
Pensacola/Orlando/Miami/Jacksonville/Ft. Myers

Copyright 2006 by Clarence R. Geier, David G. Orr, and Matthew B. Reeves
Printed in the United States of America on acid-free paper
All rights reserved

11 10 09 08 07 06   6 5 4 3 2 1

Library of Congress Cataloging-in-Publication Data
Huts and history: the historical archaeology of military encampment during the
American Civil War / [editd by] Clarence R. Geier, David G. Orr, Matthew B.
Reeves.
p. cm.
Includes bibliographical references and index.
ISBN 0-8130-2941-4 (alk. paper)
1. United States—History—Civil War, 1861–1865—Antiquities.
I. Geier, Clarence R. II. Orr, David Gerald, 1942–. III. Reeves, Matthew B.
E646.5.H88   2006
973.7'3—dc22   2005058572

The University Press of Florida is the scholarly publishing agency for the State
University System of Florida, comprising Florida A&M University, Florida At-
lantic University, Florida Gulf Coast University, Florida International University,
Florida State University, University of Central Florida, University of Florida,
University of North Florida, University of South Florida, and University of West
Florida.

University Press of Florida
15 Northwest 15th Street
Gainesville, FL 32611-2079
http://www.upf.com

The editors dedicate this volume to the professional and amateur historian and preservation communities who have committed themselves to merge their common interests to insure the preservation and interpretion of the cultural resources that speak to the military history of North America. In particular we recognize the efforts of private individuals such as D. P. Newton of Falmouth, Virginia. For decades, he and his father documented military encampments in Stafford County, Virginia. Their understanding of the historic importance of these sites convinced them to share their knowledge in the establishment of the outstanding White Oak Museum, whose interpretations of camp life attract both professional researchers and the public.

This volume is also personally dedicated to:

My parents, Clarence R. Geier, Sr., and Dorothy Elizabeth Confer Geier, both deceased. Their love and unwavering support provided me the education and opportunity to pursue a career that I dearly love.
C. R. Geier

Linda—for her support, love, and courage.
D. G. Orr

My children, Cole and Tess.
M. B. Reeves

Contents

Figures

Tables

Foreword

Nearly a third of a century ago I arrived in Fredericksburg, Virginia, to assume responsibility for historical activities at the four Civil War battlefields that surround that old town. The battle sites had enjoyed only sparse preservation attention by that time. Many of their important landmarks, even on protected ground, remained unidentified. Energetic preservation initiatives over succeeding years saved substantial tracts of historic ground, and skilled professionals steadily located house sites and other landmarks.

Two of the editors of this volume played a leading role in the professional studies that threw new light on the battlefields. David G. Orr, an archaeologist widely and justly renowned for his expertise, led the campaign to identify and explore battlefield sites. From his post as National Park Service regional archaeologist, Orr launched projects that accomplished immense, lasting good—not just around Fredericksburg but also all across the mid-Atlantic littoral. In an agency indifferent (or far worse) at its higher levels to historic resources, most especially those with any military-history cachet, Orr carved out a dramatic record in protecting such places. Clarence R. Geier of James Madison University carried out some of the most significant projects in the field in recent years.

Between them, Orr and Geier unmistakably have become the leading historical archaeologists for Virginia-theater Civil War battlefields, as well as unsung heroes to the millions of Americans who care deeply about those places. This book provides a glimpse of the important and fascinating work in which the two distinguished scholars have set the standard.

Across the past thirty years, Orr has managed projects that located or examined these Civil War landmarks around Fredericksburg, and Geier has executed several of the projects investigating them: Fairview house, Catharine Furnace, the Bullock-Kyle house, and the eponymous inn at Chancellorsville; Bernard's Cabins, Chatham, Marye's Heights, the deadly Sunken Road, and the Innis, Ebert, and Stevens houses at Fredericksburg; Ellwood, the Widow Tapp's farm, and the Higgerson house at Wilderness; the Landrum, Spindle, and Harrison houses at Spotsylvania Court House; and the Chandler property at Guinea Station, where General Thomas J. "Stonewall" Jackson died.

That sampling of famous sites in just one locality conveys some idea of the ground broken, both figuratively and literally, by the modern wizards of trowel, whisk broom, and remote sensors. They have made similar progress simultaneously at Manassas and Petersburg and Appomattox and elsewhere across Virginia. Development of new techniques, especially in the field of remote-sensing technology, has made their work steadily more effective over the years.

Huts and History, of course, reports not on battlefield archaeology but rather on exploration of places in which armies encamped between battles and through the winter lulls. The editors' opening chapter applies anthropological methodology to the study of Civil War encampments. Two further essays, one by the accomplished Colonel Joseph W. A. Whitehorne, discuss broad tendencies and trends. The rest examine specific locations and report on completed field investigations, most of them in Virginia but one in Kentucky.

The average Civil War student spends most of his time visiting battlefields. The more dedicated among that throng, whose number fortunately is legion, raise money to help preserve battle sites. Encampment scenes are, understandably but not entirely fairly, further down the average enthusiast's checklist. Everyone knows that the typical soldier of that war spent only a minuscule portion of his military service in battle, but the sheer extent of the disproportion is astonishing, especially by comparison to warfare as reconfigured a very few years later.

A typical Southern youngster, coming of military age in the winter of 1862–63 and entering Robert E. Lee's Army of Northern Virginia as either a volunteer or a conscript, faced the daunting prospect of imminent fighting in two of the most famous battles in American history: Chancellorsville and Gettysburg. He also faced, in marked contrast, months on end without any cause to load his musket. A recruit coming on duty at the beginning of March 1863, for example, would be engaged in battle no more than a dozen days during the 431 days reaching forward to the beginning of the Battle of the Wilderness ('twas a leap year in 1864, if someone is keeping score). That total counts four days each during the Chancellorsville and Gettysburg campaigns, when in fact two days each would be far more typical; two days at Mine Run; and one day each for Bristoe Station, Rappahannock Station, or one of the small actions in the Shenandoah Valley or along the Rapidan River. In the cliometric rage of some years ago, an ardent historical mathematician might have attempted a precise average for days in battle. I am content to suggest, confidently but without formulae, that the average soldier's experience of fighting through those 431 days did not reach ten days of combat.

The typical Civil War enlisted man spent a great many more than ten days during that 431-day period marching and otherwise engaged in military activities. Such maneuvers took him far from his encampments but usually without leading to battle action. He spent his nights under those circumstances in quickly constructed bivouacs, abandoned after a few hours or a few days. Once late fall rains and early winter snows shut down campaigning, though, Civil War units typically built reasonably sturdy encampments, and thousands of hard-used troops occupied them for long periods. Most soldiers spent about nine of the sixteen months from January 1863 through April 1864 living in substantial winter encampments.

In the immemorial style of the human species, soldiers usually come to view their primitive camps with a warmth bred of familiarity. Erich Maria Remarque, in his World War I classic, *All Quiet on the Western Front* (1929), wrote feelingly of "dark, musty platoon huts" becoming somehow "the object of desire; out here you have a faint resemblance to home." Men bound together by years of daring and hardship in the 1860s, far more familiar with (and comfortable around) their comrades than with nearly forgotten family and friends at distant homes, lived for weeks or months on end in these ersatz communities. Devilment inevitably abounded, in keeping with Rudyard Kipling's apt line: "Men in barracks don't grow into plaster saints." Ennui replaced bullets—what "Stonewall" Jackson called "the treadmill of the garrison." Soldiers played baseball, without either steroids or $9 hot dogs; they played cards with greasy, homemade pasteboards; they cooked scanty rations with clumsy utensils; they wrote letters (amazingly, without any hint of censorship); and they left behind traces of their lives as grist for the modern archaeological mills.

Anywhere the Army of Northern Virginia bivouacked became instantaneously a community larger than any prewar Virginia city. In the entire Southern Confederacy, only the population of New Orleans outnumbered the temporary cities that encamped armies made whenever they paused.

As the Civil War ended, changing modes of transportation and more sophisticated weaponry were altering forever the face of warfare. Never again would contending armies break contact for months at a time (except in amphibious campaigns covering vast watery expanses). A half decade after Appomattox, as the Germans routinely gave the French another thorough thrashing in the Franco-Prussian War, combatants remained in motion for extended periods with only limited quiet interludes. Many Prussian lads carrying breech-loading needle guns fought more days within a few months than some American boys toting Springfields had through four years.

The campsites in which hundreds of thousands of Americans lived for millions of man-months during the 1860s are being destroyed even more rapidly than the battlefields. As the snorting bulldozer inexorably replaces the bison and the bald eagle as America's national symbols, historic sites crumble to make way for bedroom communities, video stores, and nacho emporiums. Other campsites fall prey to swarms of relic hunters who go on "safari" together and hold "Grand National Relic Shoot-Outs." Professional archaeology of the sort described ably in this book stands as the last bulwark against permanent loss of the historical evidence that survives in such threatened sites.

At this writing, Geier is hard at work on new projects around Fredericksburg, in a broad archaeological survey of that battlefield. One week he tentatively identified more than four hundred tent platforms on wooded slopes near Fredericksburg Battlefield, surviving landmarks in an area casually bulldozed by the National Park Service in August 2000. The work pioneered by David Orr and Clarence Geier continues apace, to the benefit of Civil War history and for the edification of ua all. These two skilled pros have served as an advanced detachment—videttes, skirmishers, pickets—on the front lines of the search for the traces of surviving resources associated with the American Civil War.

Robert K. Krick
Fredericksburg, Virginia
April 2004

Part I

Introduction and Background

CLARENCE R. GEIER, DAVID G. ORR, AND MATTHEW B. REEVES

A theme common to the majority of chapters presented in this volume addresses efforts to understand those factors that influenced or determined the structure or plan of Civil War–era military encampments in physical space. To the historical archaeologist, this is no little matter, as military-social construct can vary dramatically in scope. Some encampments may be a product of a few hours of activity reflecting the actions of a small number of persons. Others can be of multi-month or multi-year occupations manned by forces numbering in the thousands and tens of thousands. An encampment can be revealed by a simple and minimal scatter of artifacts, perhaps associated with hearth circles. Or it can take the form of a site covering hundreds of acres and revealed in the spatial patterning of structures of different function and permanence and representing the diverse support and residential needs of an army at rest. To the soldier, virtually every day placed him in some type of encampment, whether it be an overnight bivouac or a winter encampment occupied for six to seven months.

For the military historian and archaeologist, encampments of diverse kinds may represent the most common site types, revealing in their nature the greatest insights into the lifeways of soldiers of all ranks. Despite this, they are among the least protected, understood, and interpreted of military sites.

This book is an effort to provide a fundamental introduction to the study and interpretation of these historically significant Civil War sites. To that end, chapter 1 by Clarence Geier, David Orr, and Matthew Reeves presents an introductory overview of the reality of camp life to the common soldier during the Civil War. It seeks to introduce the reader to certain of the established military and practical factors that combined to influence camp placement and plan. Issues impacting camp life—such as regimen, health, boredom, housing and supply—are considered.

In chapter 2, Joseph Whitehorne presents a "blueprint" for nineteenth-century camps. This discourse is instructive in that it presents the history and evolution of guidelines for encampments, as used and taught by the U.S. military in the mid-nineteenth century. These models were available to Union and Confederate officers, many of whom had been trained in the same traditions. The logic of these plans is discussed as they relate to the needs of different military groups such as infantry, artillery, and cavalry.

Of additional importance to the historical archaeologist, however, is the practical reality of encampment. As Whitehorne notes: "It is axiomatic that as soon as military units take to the field under combat conditions, circumstances, environment, unit discipline, and individual ingenuity will generate numerous variations from the norm." Training and personal idiosyncrasies of commanding officers, available housing, season and/or duration of encampment, the desire of individuals to maximize their comfort, size of force, threat of attack, terrain conditions, and availability of resources and supply can all contribute to defining the qualities and characteristics of a particular encampment. In effect, the challenge confronting the field archaeologist is that, despite established guidelines or protocols, each encampment must be addressed as a unique expression whose internal plan and the lifeways of the soldiers it supported needs to be discovered. While some encampment plans closely follow established standards, others vary significantly. The value of understanding the "standard," however, is summarized by Whitehorne when he states, "When visiting their campsites today, one should never be surprised to be surprised. However, an awareness of the regulations and confidence that good soldiers will adhere to their principles, if not their particulars, should provide substantial help in learning how these long-gone warriors lived."

Part I presents a thematic introduction to the study of encampment. The remainder of the text addresses four sets of issues: part II, survey and management of encampment sites; part III, encampment plan and layout; part IV, encampment architecture and material culture; and part V, summary and new initiatives.

Part II is a consideration of diverse strategies available to the archaeologist to locate and interpret encampment remains. It also points out problems of managing and preserving what are often extensive cultural resources. This section highlights the importance and value of collaboration among professional archaeologists and the collecting community in meeting goals of site identification. An example is also provided of an instance in which that collaboration failed, producing an unfortunate strain in this relationship.

Part III focuses on the manner in which encampment features are arrayed in and across space, producing often extensive cultural landscapes. Building on observations introduced in part I, these chapters present examples of the work of historical archaeologists as they have interpreted variation in the plan and layout of Union and Confederate encampments.

To pose models of encampment plan requires the ability to identify and interpret the architectural nature of specific encampment features that make up the larger whole. Further, through the analysis of associated material culture, what may appear as structurally similar features can be differentiated in terms of their individual use and purpose and/or with respect to the rank and ethnicity of the individuals occupying or using them. Part IV is presented to discuss examples of known encampment architecture and to consider the factors that determine variations in their form. In addition, examples of the use of material culture in considering camp life are provided.

Part V summarizes topical and research themes introduced in the preceding chapters. While this volume advances the emerging interest in encampment issues by focusing on Civil War examples, the study of the life of the American soldier transcends that one era of military history. The breadth of this larger area of inquiry and some of the themes emerging in that study are introduced in this section.

"I Am Now Very Comfortably Situated for the Winter Having a Very Nice Chimney Attached to My Tent, and Everything That Tends to Make This Unhappy Life Pleasant and Agreeable"

CLARENCE R. GEIER, DAVID G. ORR, AND MATTHEW B. REEVES

The topic of military encampment has become increasingly important to the study of American military history. To students of the French and Indian War through the recent war in Iraq, the encampment is a proper topic of study in that, for a soldier, virtually every day began or ended in some sort of camp setting. Indeed, despite the battlefield image of men at war, for most soldiers, far more time was spent in camp-related activities than in any other aspect of their military career.

Contributing to the growing interest of the historical archaeology community in encampment are both popular and practical issues. Certainly the fascination of a large segment of our society with military reenactment has spurred public support for encampment studies. On a more practical level, however, the dramatic and ongoing residential and industrial development in areas of past, historically significant military activity has stimulated cultural resource management and environmental impact research. Once considered a limitless and perhaps insignificant historic resource, military encampments from the continuum of American history are becoming increasingly threatened and, in some areas, very scarce resources. On the verge of being almost too late in some areas, a growing number of professional historical archaeologists and members of the preservation community are discovering the significance of these resources and alerting the larger community their protection and study. The increasing professional and academic interest in the study of military encampment is evidenced by the increasing numbers of papers and sessions presented at recent annual conferences of the Society for Historical Archeology. In fact, this volume was partially drawn from presentations given at the 2002 and 2003 Annual Conference on Historical and Underwater Archaeology.

The battle to manage, preserve, and understand encampment sites that date from before the French and Indian War to those of World War II and Vietnam is of growing national and international importance. While archaeology on America's battlefields has some legal and financial support when such resources are threatened, research on the military encampments of the same troops commemorated for their sacrifice lacks comparable support and recognition. Some federal agencies (National Military Parks, National Park Service, U.S. Forest Service) and private institutions (Montpelier Foundation and National Trust for Historic Preservation) have begun to research and inventory encampment complexes on their properties. Despite this, the greater amount of substantive excavation on such sites is conducted under the aegis of cultural resource management (CRM) studies that often place limits on the amount of background research and interpretation conducted.

The study of military encampments must be more than just applying traditional archaeological technique to the excavation of encampment features and artifacts. The fact is that, with some exceptions, most professional archaeologists are very poorly trained in both the material culture and architecture of encampment and understanding the human communities such sites supported. In many cases, members of the amateur or lay-historical community are significantly more advanced in their knowledge of such sites and in their dedication to their interpretation. What is also the case is that several recent studies have shown that many of the traditional archeological testing strategies do not reliably reveal many artifacts or ephemeral structural features associated with military sites. The use of traditional methods and experimentation with new techniques of historiography and archaeology that allow for the identification, assessment, and interpretation of sites is essential. While the majority of the articles presented in this volume include comments on field methodologies, chapter 3 by Brian Corle and Joseph Balicki and chapter 4 by Brandon Bies are of direct relevance. Corle and Balicki focus their attention on the issues of identifying encampment sites, discuss limitations of certain field methodologies, and argue for a closer working relationship with the amateur archaeology community. Bies, in turn, provides an example of archival and field strategies used in defining the Union's Camp Hooker, established at the Baltimore and Ohio Railroad crossing of the Monocacy River.

It is the purpose of this text to nurture a discussion of the factors that shape and determine the material and cultural nature of encampments as a phenomenon to be interpreted by historical archaeologists. We believe that historical archaeologists must become aware of the political, social, legal, functional, technological, support, ecological, health, and other demographic factors that combined to shape the most complex and long term, to the most short term and ephemeral of military encampments. Until we understand how such issues are illustrated in the variation and placement of structural features and material culture within encampment complexes, the ability to interpret or determine the cultural significance of archaeological findings will be significantly limited.

By definition, encampment refers to "the act of setting up or occupying a camp," or the "ground on which temporary shelters (as tents) are erected" (Merriam-Webster 1986:409, 199). More specifically, a military camp is "the place where troops are established in tents, in huts, or in bivouac" (Jensen 2000:172). These definitions conjure images of events and material culture that are temporary, transient, and ephemeral. While such descriptors have a degree of accuracy, the scope, significance, and material expression of military encampments vary dramatically from small, temporary bivouacs for a few men occupying an area for a few hours, to more permanent camps designed to support tens of thousands of troops for often much longer periods of time—months in the case of winter camps, and years in the case of training camps.

Joseph Whitehorne in chapter 2 discusses the efforts to standardize the protocols of the emerging American army to the time of the American Civil War. Differences over time in the political nature of a war, the technologies available for its conduct, and the mobilization and support of deployed troops prevent one-to-one analogies in the study of American military encampment in history. Nonetheless, certain common factors do exist that have a bearing on determining the nature of encampments across time. In considering these, the circumstances of the Union and Confederate armies during the American Civil War are referenced as example.

A first factor to consider is the structure, organization, and political hierarchy of the military unit under study. Whether in a defensive or an offensive posture, an army, during peace or conflict, is inherently intended to anticipate and/or engage in warfare or battle. While the focus of historical consideration is often on particular military engagements and their outcomes, in fact, the commanding general of an army is also the legitimate head of a government. He is the head of a large transient community of many parts in which corps or division, regiment, company, and platoon commanders serve as extensions of his authority and reciprocally inform him on the state and circumstances of their troops. Supplementary elements such as the quartermasters corps, engineers, medical corps, the U.S. Sanitary Commission, and provost officers provide special support services for what is a massive, transient, multicomponent society/town designed to move across cultural landscapes of both friend and foe. What is of immediate relevance is the fact that, if understood, these governmental and societal functions can be visible in camp disposition and hence, potentially, in the archaeological expression of that deployment. Often, however, a problem for an archaeologist in documenting evidence of these functions is the scope or size that certain types of encampment can assume.

An example of this scope and complexity can be seen in the encampment of General Philip Sheridan's Army of the Shenandoah in October 1864, in the Shenandoah Valley of Virginia. Following the successful "burning" of the valley, Sheridan's army moved into what was anticipated to be its winter camp on high ground north of Cedar Creek. The army included three infantry corps—the VI Corps commanded by Major General Horatio G. Wright with three divisions and an artillery brigade; the XIX Corps of Major General William H. Emory with two divisions and a section of reserve artillery; and the VIII Corps commanded by Major General George Crook—and three cavalry divisions and a section of horse artillery commanded by Major General Alfred A. Torbert. On the morning of October 19, Sheridan had approximately 32,000 combat infantry or cavalrymen and ninety pieces of artillery (Mahr 1992:362–72) at hand.

The deployment of combatant forces along Cedar Creek extended for over five miles (figure 1.1). Instead of being concentrated in space, the army was deliberately dispersed to take advantage of the rugged Cedar Creek topography to accommodate encampment needs and create a formidable natural/military barrier to any force moving down the valley. To the south, on narrow shale ridges above the junction of Cedar Creek and the North Fork of the Shenandoah, Crook's VIII Corps was encamped. Between the Valley Turnpike and a principal tributary stream known as Meadow Brook stood Emory's XIX Corps, and on the high uplands north of Meadow Brook was Wright's VI Corps. At the far right of the line were the cavalry divisions of Brigadier Generals Wesley Merritt and George A. Custer, the cavalry of Brigadier General William H. Powell being deployed south of the VIII Corps. Along the west wall, the sharply sloped walls of the valley of Cedar Creek served as a natural defense, though the troops of General Emory had constructed substantial earthworks and batteries above the descending slopes. Along with the east-west–trending Valley Turnpike, a set of local farm roads provided access and contact between units to the north and south (Geier and Whitehorne 1994:19, 20).

The camp was far more complex than a simple deployment of troops. General Sheridan, with his headquarters staff, was at the Belle Grove mansion near

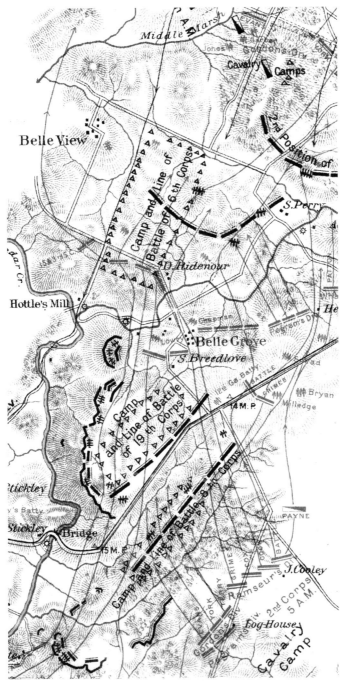

Figure 1.1. Encampment of army general Philip Sheridan (Hotchkiss 1864:Plate LXXXII, p. 9).

the center of the encampment. General Torbert, his cavalry commander, established his headquarters in a grove east of the mansion. In the fields between Torbert's position and the Valley Pike was a makeshift prison corral containing three hundred Confederate prisoners. On the high ground north and northwest of the mansion were a horse line and artillery park. The open fields north of the mansion and east of Meadow Brook provided pasture to a herd of several thousand head of cattle and other livestock that were being maintained for the support of the army. In addition, the extensive train parks for the army—including supply wagons, ambulances, and other support elements—stood in large camps to the rear of the infantry camp. One such train park stretched along the sides of the Valley Turnpike to the outskirts of Middletown, one and one-half miles to the north. A second camp extended along a small roadway along the valley floor of Meadow Brook (Geier and Whitehorne 1994:24).

While the actual construction of a tent and more substantial encampment structures during the American Civil War was typically the responsibility of enlisted men, the selection of campsites and the nature of their plan was not the concern of the common soldier. Reconnaissance normally preceded encampment; a camping party for a company of troops typically consisted of the regimental quartermaster, a quartermaster-sergeant, a corporal, and two men per company to select the disposition of the site. The general in command would decide whether his brigade's regiments would camp separately or together. When an advance party was sent to prepare a camp, instructions were given to the brigade's Quartermaster Department, which called on the regiments for their camping parties and, as appropriate, an engineer to propose appropriate defenses and lines of communication. If a camping party did not precede the company, the regimental quartermaster attended to these matters as soon as the regiment reached the campsite. For troops on the march, campsite selection typically considered the comfort and safety of the troops, the facility of communications between the military units involved, and the availability of critical supply needs such as firewood, water, and forage. For camps of longer duration and those under threat from an enemy, these and other factors consistent with their particular circumstances were considered in deploying the camp, as well as its communications and defenses (Jensen 2000:172, from United States War Department 1863:74–82).

The company quartermaster involved with establishing a camp was not left without guidance. In 1861, the War Department published its *Revised United States Army Regulations of 1861,* which outlined the procedures to be followed in laying out campsites. Military experience and requirements had been transformed into a series of detailed, step-by-step regulations for camp composition, with an expectation that such regulations were to be adhered to. The guidelines also anticipated the varying needs for different types of military units, providing different models for the infantry, cavalry, and artillery (Jensen 2000:27–30). The detail of these plans was extensive, addressing spatial patterning reflecting differences in military rank, as well as functional and support needs of both the men and the livestock upon which they depended. In addition, the regimented organization of camps reinforced the manner in which troops who fought and moved together, lived together and formed bonds that carried them together into battle.

Despite these standards, however, terrain and topography were often the determining influences that shaped camp deployment and plan. Using the infantry model in the 1861 regulations for a company as an example (see figure 2.5), the plan addressed differences in rank as well as functional needs. Infantry regiments were aligned, by company, on streets in ranks facing each other. Kitchens were placed in front of company streets. In front of the kitchens was a line of structures for noncommissioned officers, sutler, and police guard. Tents for company officers stood forward of this line, with those of support personnel (including the surgeons, quartermaster, company colonel and majors, and so forth) standing to their front. Baggage trains were in line to the front of this group, with the latrines or sinks for the enlisted men and officers being set at opposite ends of the encampment. These guidelines were presented with very specific directions: for example, "Each company has its tents in two files facing onto a street perpendicular to the color line. The width of the street depends on the front of the camp, but should not be less than 5 paces. The interval between the ranks of tents is 2 paces: between the files of tents of adjacent companies 2 paces; between the regiments, 22 paces . . ." (Jensen 2000:173; United States War Department 1863:515–16).

Examples of archaeological projects directed at defining camp plan and layout are presented in chapters 5, 6, and 8. In chapter 5, Joseph Balicki discusses archaeological evidence for the placement and plan for Camp French, a Confederate winter camp established in 1861/1862 to blockade the Potomac River. In chapter 6, Stephen and Kim McBride discuss the plan of Camp Nelson, Kentucky, a Civil War depot designed for long-term use that housed thousands of soldiers, civilian employees, and refugees. In chapter 8, Matthew Reeves and Clarence Geier provide an example of troop deployment implemented by General Samuel McGowan's Brigade of South Carolinians, who were encamped south of the Rapidan River, Virginia, in the winter of 1864.

Certainly, as noted in chapters 5 and 8, circumstances of terrain had to be accommodated in the deployment and plan of camps. In the spring of 1862, Confederate General Edward Johnson was commanded to move his four-thousand-man army to the apex of Shenandoah Mountain to defend a western approach to the Shenandoah Valley from an anticipated Union assault. In the midst of terrible late winter weather, the army converted the mountain peak into a strong defensive position and went about establishing a network of camps for its support. While an upland camp was established to house troops deployed at the fortification (Geier 2003), the remaining infantry camps were deployed to the rear in a series of narrow, deeply entrenched headwater valleys that lay almost a thousand feet below the fort and extended as far as three and a half miles to the east of the earthworks. Johnson's cavalry was encamped to the west, in front of the fortification at the foot of Shenandoah Mountain in a valley with access to substantial water and open ground for horses. Preliminary studies (Geier, Nash, and Dewan 1999) showed strong evidence of planned layout and some evidence for the political and functional diversity of the encamped troops; however, because of the very mountainous terrain, there was no effort to establish tent files or streets. Instead, tent platforms tended to be clustered on mountain slopes with footpaths joining them to what appeared to be important activity areas, such as officers' quarters, that had been placed on low benches along valley streams. The design of the fortification was such that when challenged, a cannon fired from the earthworks would alert the troops, who were then expected to march double time from their valley camps to man the defensive line.

As suggested earlier, the function of the encampment and the character of the group it supports can significantly influence a camp's placement and plan. Examples of differences have already been noted in government guidelines for establishing cavalry and artillery camps, which typically need to accommodate the forage and water needs of the substantial herds of horses that power them—often to a priority concern over troops involved. Camps associated with supply trains often require large areas of space, typically along existing roads, so as to address the needs of teamsters and draft animals. As noted earlier, trains were very much a physical presence in Sheridan's camp on Cedar Creek. At the same time, because of limited water supply and an absence of fodder, they were not present in Johnson's camp on Shenandoah Mountain. Instead, they were deployed as needed from the military depot at Staunton, Virginia, twenty miles southeast of the camp.

Baggage and supply trains were critical to the mobility of any army carrying ammunition, food, water, tents, medical facilities, and other support needs of the army. To the frustration of some, their importance often required the deployment of troops and cavalry to guard them. The massiveness, complexity, and problems created by such entities is illustrated by a description provided by Quartermaster Rufus Ingalls of the Union Army of the Potomac as it advanced to what would become known as the Battle of the Wilderness in May of 1864. On May 3 he reported that the army had

> 3,476 wagons and 591 ambulances; 4,076 horses and 20,184 mules were needed to draw these 4,067 vehicles. In addition to these animals, the army had 16,311 cavalry and 5,158 artillery, and 4,107 "private," that is, officer's horses. To provide the regulation of grain and hay for these nearly 50,000 animals would have required the daily delivery of 477 tons of feed to the army. To do this many miles from the railroad over execrable roads without impairing the flow of ammunition and food for the men was a manifest impossibility. (Starr 1981:87)

Despite these supply trains' visible support of troops at rest and in battle, to the best of our knowledge no instance of the intentional archaeological evaluation of a train camp has been undertaken.

A growing interest in Civil War medicine has drawn attention to field hospital sites. While such facilities commonly took advantage of houses, barns, and outbuildings on or near the field of battle, in some instances massive tent hospitals were established to meet short- and long-term needs. One such facility was established by General Philip Sheridan at Winchester, Virginia, following his successful defeat of the army of General Jubal Early in the third battle of Winchester. This massive encampment enclosed the southeastern side of the town, focusing on the principal water source of Shawnee Springs. The camp existed for four months and processed thousands of Union and Confederate wounded, including all of the physical elements needed to feed and care for the wounded and support the large number of doctors, staff, and troops required to ensure the defense and protection of the facility. Preliminary mapping and excavation at the site revealed unusual military features believed to be hospital wall tents placed end to end to form tent structures designed to house recuperating wounded. These linear structures, some of which attained lengths up to forty-eight feet, were spaced less than five feet apart and were arranged perpendicular to a camp street (Whitehorne, Geier, and Hofstra 2000:148–65).

Focusing more directly on encampment, it is a fact that in the four years of the Civil War, while more than 60,000 men died of wounds received in conflict, perhaps six times that number (360,000) died in camp from diseases

(Robertson 1984:78). Tuberculosis, smallpox, diphtheria, typhoid, malaria, dysentery, measles, pneumonia, and threats posed by them resulted in a set of regular army regulations that addressed strict cleanliness in living quarters and food-preparation areas, personal bathing, the regular airing of tents and bedding, careful placement and use of latrines and garbage pits, and the protection of water supplies. Unfortunately, the lessons learned from disease came hard to many soldiers and their officers, and the protocols put in place for their health were often ignored. To archaeologists, the high rate of disease and efforts to respond to illnesses can be seen archaeologically in the number and dispersal of cemeteries, the presence of camp hospitals and dispensaries, the spatial separation between encampments, the placement of latrines within the camps and relative to water sources, the presence of medicine bottles in dumps or waste areas, and the general cleanliness of some encampments.

In a paper presented in Providence, Rhode Island, Todd Jensen introduced the attendees to Report 19 of the United States Sanitary Commission, titled "Camp Inspection Return" (Jensen 2003). From the onset of the Civil War, inspectors of the Sanitary Commission visited military encampments and reported in depth on their circumstances. In all, 179 questions were to be assessed (appendix 1.1); these included the makeup of the group encamped, the plan and placement of the encampment including types of tents and structures, the conformity of the plan to army guidelines, and the presence of sutlers. Information on camp life and support, including problems with alcoholism and crime, are noted. Particular attention was paid to issues involving health. These latter questions focused on questions such as the nature and quality of the medical staff, access to vaccines and preventative medicine, availability of medicines, camp cleanliness and hygiene including the position and character of latrines, nature and placement of hospital facilities, and quality of food and its modes of preparation. This document, if available for an encampment under study, can generate a tremendous amount of very important and specific data concerning the support network available to the encamped military community.

Additional variables that influence the character of an encampment and its archaeological expression include seasonality, duration of occupation, and the size of the group involved. The physical character of an encampment established to support a military group for a day or two as it moves in space will be significantly different in the complexity, permanence, and material culture left behind as compared to a camp structured to meet the needs of troops in place for weeks and months at a time. Seasonality is a determining factor in that tent camps with structures that can be opened to allow the passage of air during hot summer months are replaced with more substantial and permanent barracks or huts and, potentially, stables to protect troops and livestock from what can, in some areas, be intensely cold winters. Certainly, the number of troops involved will influence the archaeological footprint they leave. The character of an outlying picket, for example, as compared to the temporary deployment of a regiment, company, or army, as modified by factors noted above, all take different forms.

The material culture found at encampments can reflect the ethnic and political origin of troops (for example, Irish Brigade, African American companies, German troops) as well as the idiosyncracies of individual troopers. The type and quality of housing, privacy, and personal life of officers, varying with rank, was generally greater than that of common soldiers. Indeed, some officers had personal servants or assigned staff who had to be accommodated. Historical evidence indicates that from the time of Valley Forge, individuals or teams of individuals down to the level of the common soldier had some leeway with respect to the dwellings they occupied and constructed. In a recent study, Todd Jensen observed that despite established guidelines, officers often allowed deviation from the military regulations dealing with encampment (Jensen 2000:30–32). With respect to winter camps in particular, he noted that in the shantytowns that were erected, varying with the tolerance of commanding officers, the huts that stood side by side could vary significantly in design with the resources, construction skills, creativity, and desire for personal comfort of their occupants.

The issue of camp architecture and material life is addressed in virtually all of the chapters, but is highlighted through material evidence in chapters 6 through 10. Stephen and Kim McBride (chapter 6) introduce the plan of the depot site of Camp Nelson and also address the types of architecture used to meet the needs of the resident community. Matthew Reeves and Clarence Geier (chapter 8) and Garrett Fesler, Matthew Laird, and Hank Lutton (chapter 9) present data on architecture and material culture from recently excavated Confederate encampments. In yet another chapter (chapter 10), David Orr discusses the nature and placement of the headquarters cabin of Ulysses S. Grant at City Point, Virginia. In chapter 7, in a presentation that includes several previously unpublished photographs along with accounts from individual soldiers' letters and diaries, Dean Nelson provides a discussion of the wide diversity of encampment architecture.

While most military histories focus on military engagements, to the greater number of soldiers, war—as described by Oliver Wendell Holmes—was an "organized bore" (Woodhead 1996:27). Oliver W. Norton, a Pennsylvania private, stated that "soldiering was a very slow business" in which "the stronger mental faculties are unused and of course they rust" (Newton 1996:27). The realities of a monotonous life filled with drilling, guard duty, details, and so forth, made boredom a feature of military life that was a detriment to the morale of the individual soldier and a major concern for officers who had the responsibility for maintaining their troops. In more permanent camps, drilling fields and firing ranges were established to maintain the discipline and fighting skills of the soldiers.

While having a practical training function, these ongoing events also kept the troops active. Guard duty, cleaning patrols, woodcutting teams, and other details also helped pass the time, but boredom continued to be a problem left to an individual soldier's resolve. On the downside, fights were not uncommon, particularly when regiments of different ethnic or national background were camped nearby. Despite prohibition, drinking and alcoholism were major activities and social problems, as were gambling, gaming, and (where available) womanizing. One fairly common response to military life was desertion. This option was so prevalent that extreme measures were often taken to curtail it, including branding and execution. In fact, issues of law and order, the existence of stockades, and matters of both civil and military justice were common issues of camp decorum.

More "moraley uplifting" pursuits included the formation of theatrical groups that gave plays to the units; choral groups, bands, or the personal playing of musical instruments; and organized group competitions between companies and regiments. The existence of a postal service, organized dances, and religious services and study groups were also common. Archaeological evidence of both the dark and the more positive side of camp life is common information that adds to our knowledge of camp life.

Certainly, a closer scrutiny of military encampment is warranted by any student of military history and especially by those who concentrate their labors toward interpreting material culture. Searching for a more holistic understanding of war leads us to examine all of the physical manifestations of such activity. In this sense, the field of battlefield archaeology has embraced military camps as clear manifestations for the understanding of battle and war. The chapters in this text serve us well in understanding war in all its guises.

APPENDIX 1.1: DRAFT OF SANITARY COMMISSION REPORT NO. 19, CAMP INSPECTION RETURN

The draft is an exact copy of form No. 19, altered only with respect to spacing and the removal of text lines.

Sanitary Commission
No. 19
Camp Inspection Return

Abbreviations.—Y, "yes;" N, "no;" n. e., "not exact;" Q? "So reported, but Inspector doubts if correctly." The answers are supposed to express the fact as believed by the Inspector, unless otherwise indicated. Where one subdivision of a question is answered, the others may be disregarded.

1. Name and locality of site.
2. State.
3. Military department.
4. Date of conclusion of inspection.
5. Name of inspector.
6. Designation of body inspected?
7. Name of its commanding officer?
8. Where recruited?
9. Predominating nativity?
10. When recruiting began?
11. When mustered into U.S. service?
12. At what places stationed since, and how long at each?*
13. How strong when mustered in?
14. Present strength?
*Stations of less than one week may be disregarded if the list would otherwise be long.
p. 2
15. Who selected present camp site?
16. Had the site been occupied shortly before for same purpose?
17. Was the selection mainly influenced by military considerations?
18. Situation of camp:
    upon a hill-top?
    " " hill–side?

" " hill-foot?

in a glen?

on a plain?

19. Is the site slightly elevated?

" " unshaded?

" " in the shade of woods?

20. Is it sheltered by higher land?*

" " sheltered by wood?*

21. From what quarter is the prevailing wind?

22. As to malaria, what is the reputation of the site?

unknown?

good?

bad?

very bad?

23. Local conditions presumptive of malaria

Near a swamp?

Near a river delta?

Near a pond?

*If so, show on what side: by letters, as, S. W.

p. 3

24. Soil of camp site:

sandy?

loose gravel?

loose loam?

firm loam?

agglomerated pebbles, gravel, or sand, (hardpan)

impervious clay?

25. Sub-soil:

sandy?

loose gravel?

loose loam?

firm loam?

agglomerated pebbles, gravel, or sand, (hardpan)

impervious clay?

26. Is the site favorable for surface drainage? (as to inclination)

27. Is the camp arranged mainly in accordance with the "army regulations?"

more crowded?

more open?

28. How far apart are the tents in the rows?
29. How is the artificial drainage?
    systematic and complete?
    partial, and with no general system?
    Entirely neglected?
30. Are the drains straight?
p. 4
    are the drains very sinuous?
31. About how deep are the drains generally?
32. About how wide at the top are the drains generally?
33. Are the drains kept clean?
    " " foul or clogged?
34. Is there a good outlet for the drains?
35. Condition of the camp streets:
    very clean?
    moderately clean?
    dirty or neglected?
36. Edges of tents and spaces between tents:
    very clean?
    moderately clean?
    neglected and littered?
37. In what sort of tents are the privates mostly?
    Sibley, or conical, with ventilator at top?
    Regulation wall-tents?
    Regulation "servant's," "common," or "wedge-shape?"
    Wall?
    Wedge?
    What is the size* (in feet)?
38. Average number of men to each tent?
    Thus: "6x9x9 (high.")
p. 5
39. Is the ventilation of the tents looked after by any officer at night?
40. Are the tents struck on certain days for the purpose of a thorough cleansing
    and airing?
    if so, how often? . . .
41. On what do the men sleep?
    Rubber blankets?
    Wooden tent floor?

Straw, hay, or leaves?

Blankets laid on the bare ground?

42. Do the men generally make any change of clothing at night?

43. Are the men supplied with two shirts each?

44. Have they blankets?

1 each?

2 each?

45. Of what quality are they?

Regular U. S. A.?

Not regular, but good?

Not regular, poor?

46. Have they overcoats?

47. Is the overcoat of fair quality, and in good condition?

48. Is the body coat or jacket of fair quality, and in good condition?

49. Is the pantaloons of fair quality, and in good condition?

50. Are they required to regularly wash their underclothing?

p. 6

51. Are they required to remove dust from and otherwise cleanse their other clothing?

52. Is a careful and systematic inspection with reference to these matters undertaken?

53. Do you think it efficient, (judging by the appearance of the men)?

54. Do the men bathe regularly?

55. Are they required, to bathe under the eye of an officer?

If so, how often each man?

56. Does each man, (as a rule) wash his head, neck, and feet once a day?

57. Is evidence of neglect of this looked for at inspection?

58. Are the men infested with vermin?

59. If so, has any application been made to remove them?

60. Do you observe scraps of food, bones, or rubbish collected in the edges of tents?

In the drains?

In the camp streets?

Between the tents?

61. Are refuse slops and food disposed of systematically, so as not to be offensive?

62. Do you observe odors of decay in the camp?

63. Do the men void their urine within the camp?

at night?

both day and night?

64. How far is the privy from the tents of the body of the camp?

p. 7

65. Is there a sufficient pit, or trench for the purpose?

66. Is it provided with a sitting rail?

67. Is it provided with a screen?

68. Is earth regularly thrown in it daily?

69. Are disinfectants used in it?

70. Are the men forbidden to ease themselves elsewhere?

71. Do you find this prohibition to have been enforced?

72. Is there a separate sink for officers?

73. At what distance from the tents are the cattle and horses picketed?

74. What number?

75. Is their dung daily removed, or so placed or covered as to be unobnoxious?

76. From what source is water procured?

    Surface springs?

    Wells?

    Stream?

    Pond?

    Ditch, slough or puddle?

77. Is the water clear?

78. Does it seem to be of unwholesome quality?

79. Has it a reputation of being of unwholesome quality?

80. Do the captains make requisitions for the rations of their companies?

    See form 13, page 228, Army Regulations

p. 8

81. Do the captains generally look after the supplies of their companies, to see that they are not used to[o] rapidly, and that they are properly served and cooked?

82. Is any officer required to examine and taste the food of the men before it is served at any meal, or is this done generally by the captains or other officers, either by order or voluntarily?*

83. Are the rations found in sufficient quantity?

84. Are they generally considered good in quality, each of its kind? If not, mention what is alleged to be poor.

85. Are you satisfied of the justness of this allegation?

86. About how often is fresh meat served?
    Fresh vegetables?
    Dessicated vegetables?
    Dessicated meats or soups?
    Dried fruits?
87. Is the cooking in most instances done with portable stoves?
    with earth flues?
    in trenches?
    on the unbroken ground?
88. Is "the greatest care observed in washing and scouring cooking utensils?"
89. Is most of the food of the regiment prepared by cooks who perform that duty regularly, or by men taking short terms at it, and who generally have no skill?
90. How is it probable that the food is generally cooked—well, or very badly?
    *See Army Regulations, par. 111, page 15. Army Regulations, par. 113, page 15.   See Army Reg., par. 112, p. 15.
    p. 9
91. Is the last question answered with the more confidence from personal observation?
92. Is tea sometimes drawn in the ration instead of coffee?
93. Is fresh bread served?
94. Is soft bread served?
95. Is it baked in the regiment at a general bakery?
96. Is it generally of good quality?
97. Has the company fund arrangement* been successfully established in any case?
    With several companies?
    With all?
98. Is there a regimental sutler?
99. Who appointed him?
100. Are the prices of articles on sale fixed in accordance with the army regulations?
101. Is ardent spirits sold?
102. Do the men obtain spirits otherwise?
103. Is there much intoxication?
104. What is about the average daily number of men sent to the guardhouse?
105. Are these cases chiefly from intoxication?

106. Are pedlars of eatables or drinks allowed access to the men in camp?

107. Are the men strictly and effectively kept within the camp, except those having leave of absence?

See Army Regulations, Par. 197, page 27 Par. 207, p. 23.　　*** See Army Regulations, Par. 208. See also Articles of War, art. 29, p. 6, end of volume Army Reg.

p. 10

108. What is the largest number of the men ever allowed to be absent from camp except on duty?

109. What is the ordinary number of absences?

110. Are the men generally in good spirits?

111. Are means systematically used to promote cheerfulness, by games, entertainments, & c?

112. Is there a regimental band?

113. Is it maintained from a regimental fund to which the men contribute?
by the officers?

114. Are there any provident or mutual benefit societies within the reg't.?

115. Do the men generally save or send home a part of their wages?

116. Does the general discipline of the camp appear better or worse than usual?

117. Was there a medical inspection of the men on their enlistment?

118. If so, state by what official it was made?

119. Was it thorough?

120. Has there been any subsequent medical inspection?

121. If so, state by what official it was made?

122. Was it thorough?

123. Has the regiment been systematically vaccinated?

124. Name of surgeon?

125. When appointed?

126. By whom?

127. At whose nomination or suggestion?

p. 11

128. Was he previously examined and approved of by a State or other medical board?
superior medical officer?

129. If so, state by what?

130. What had been the nature of his preparation or previous experience?
general country medical practice? (a)
general town medical practice? (b)

Limited hospital experience? (c)

Extensive? (d)

" surgical practice? (e)

Qualified as a student? (f)

No valuable experience or preparation? (g)

131. Name of assistant surgeon?

132. By whom appointed?

133. Qualifications: (Answer by repeating the letter opposite the appropriate suggestion after question 130)

134. Is a camp hospital organized?

135. Non-combatant regimental nurses?

male?

female?

none?

136. Is there a moderate supply of medicines?

137. What important articles are wanting, if any?

138. How long since requisitions have been made for these?

p. 12

139. Is there a case comprising the most essential field instruments?

140. What important surgical articles are wanting?

141. Is there a regimental ambulance, or more than one?

142. Are there any field stretchers?

143. How long since requisition has been made for any of the above articles which are wanting?

144. Is the large (regulation) hospital tent appropriated to its proper purpose?*

145. Is the regimental hospital in a house, (temporary structure) or tent?

146. If in a house or temporary structure, is it fairly adapted to its purpose?

147. Is it fairly well ventilated?

148. If in a tent, is it well drained?

149. Is it well ventilated?

150. Is there a separate sink for hospital patients?

151. Is it well arranged?

152. Is it carefully and adequately deodorized?

153. Are there a few sheets and suitable hospital dresses?

154. Are there any special hospital stores, (delicacies and cordials?)

155. What are the prevailing diseases?

156. How many patients from the regiment are now in general hospital?

157. How many patients are in the regimental hospital?
   *In some instances it has been found misused for the colonel's headquarters, or a mess-room.

p. 13

158. How many "sick in quarters?" (slight cases in their own tents)
159. Are there any serious cases in the regimental hospital?
160. If so, has it been impracticable to remove them to the general hospital?
161. Are there any contagious or infectious cases?
162. Are they kept in a separate tent or house from the others?
163. Are the discharges from the latter placed in the privy used by others?
164. What has been the daily average number on the sick list during the last two weeks?
165. Have there been any deaths in that time?
166. If so, are the dead buried near the camp, and at what depth?
167. Is the general health of the regiment improving or deteriorating?
168. Does the surgeon understand that he is responsible for all conditions of the camp or regiment unfavorable to health, unless he has warned the commanding officer of them?
169. Does the surgeon make a daily inspection of the camp with reference to its cleanliness?
170. Does he inspect the food, and see how the cooking is done?
171. Does he report on these matters, and urge remedies upon the company officers, and, when necessary, upon the commanding officer?
172. Is anything administered to the well men to guard against the effects of malaria?
173. Is there a drill before breakfast?
174. If so, does the surgeon approve of it?

p. 14

175. If not, has he remonstrated against it with the commanding officer?
176. What is the length of time the men are on drill daily?
177. What is their arm?
178. Is there any limit placed upon the weight of the knapsack for heavy marching order?
179. If so, what?

No. 19
Sanitary Commission

NOTE

Chapter title is from Robertson 1984:9.

REFERENCES CITED

Geier, Clarence R.

1995   An "Immense Lilac Hedge in Full Bloom": The Archaeological Definition and Assessment of the Belle Grove Plantation. Department of Sociology and Anthropology, James Madison University, Harrisonburg, Va. Report submitted to Belle Grove, Inc., Middletown, Va.

2003   Confederate Fortification and Troop Deployment in a Mountain Landscape: Fort Edward Johnson and Camp Shenandoah, April 1862. *Historical Archaeology* 37(3):31–45.

Geier, Clarence R., Carole Nash, and Bill Dewan

1999   A Preliminary Historical-Archaeological Assessment of the Fort Edward Johnson–Camp Shenandoah Military Complex with Comments on the Staunton-Parkersburg Turnpike. Department of Sociology and Anthropology, James Madison University, Harrisonburg, Va. Report submitted to George Washington and Jefferson National Forest, Roanoke, Va.

Geier, Clarence R., and Joseph Whitehorne

1994   Archaeological Assessment of Cultural Resources South of the Confluence of Meadow Brook and Cedar Creek in Frederick County, Va. Department of Sociology and Anthropology, James Madison University, Harrisonburg, Va. Report submitted to Belle Grove, Inc., Middletown, Va.

Hotchkiss, Jedediah

1864   A Sketch Map of the Battle of Belle Grove or Cedar Creek. In *Atlas to Accompany the Official Records of the Union and Confederate Armies*. Edited by Maj. George B. Davis, Leslie J. Perry, and Joseph Kirkley, Map LXXXII, No. 29. United States War Department, Washington, D.C., 1891–95.

Jensen, Todd L.

2000   "Gimme Shelter": Union Shelters of the Civil War, a Preliminary Archaeological Typology. Master's thesis, Department of Anthropology, College of William and Mary, Williamsburg, Va.

2003   X Marks the Spot: What Camp Inspection Returns Tell Us about Civil War Encampments of Union Forces. Paper presented at the 36th Annual Conference on Historical and Underwater Archaeology, Providence, R.I.

Mahr, Theodore C.

1992   *The Battle of Cedar Creek*. The Virginia Civil War Battles and Leaders Series. H. E. Howard, Lynchburg, Va.

Nelson, Dean E.

1982   "Right Nice Little House[s]": Impermanent Camp Architecture of the American Civil War. In *Perspectives in Vernacular Architecture*. Edited by Camille Wells, vol. 1, pp. 79–94. Vernacular Architecture Forum, Annapolis, Md.

Newton, John (editor)

1996   *Soldier Life*. Voices of the Civil War Series. Time-Life Books, Alexandria, Va.

Orr, David G.

1982   The City Point Headquarters Cabin of Ulysses S. Grant. In *Perspectives in Vernacular Architecture*. Edited by Camille Wells, vol. 1, pp. 195–200. Vernacular Architecture Forum, Annapolis, Md.

1994   The Archaeology of Trauma: An Introduction to the Historical Archaeology of the American Civil War. In *Look to the Earth: Historical Archaeology and the American Civil War*. Edited by Clarence Geier Jr. and Susan Winter, pp. 21–36. University of Tennessee Press, Knoxville.

Robertson, James I., Jr.

1984   *Tenting Tonight: The Soldiers Life*. The Civil War Series. Time-Life Books, Alexandria, Va.

Starr, Stephen Z.

1981   *The Union Cavalry in the Civil War*. Vol. 2, *The War in the East from Gettysburg to Appomattox, 1863–1865*. Louisiana State University Press, Baton Rouge.

United States War Department

1863   *Revised United States Army Regulations of 1861*. George W. Childs, Philadelphia.

Whitehorne, Joseph W. A., Clarence R. Geier, and Warren R. Hofstra

2000   The Sheridan Field Hospital, Winchester, Virginia, 1864. In *Archaeological Perspectives on the American Civil War*. Edited by Clarence R. Geier and Stephen R. Potter, pp. 148–65. University Press of Florida, Tallahassee.

Woodhead, Henry (editor)

1996   *Soldiers Life*. Voices of the Civil War Series. Time-Life Books, Alexandria, Va.

2

Blueprint for Nineteenth-Century Camps

Castramentation, 1778–1865

JOSEPH W. A. WHITEHORNE

The art of war has no traffic with rules, for the infinitely varied circumstances of combat never produce the same situation twice.

George Marshall 1939:34

BIVOUACS, CAMPS, AND CANTONMENTS

Army tradition has long held that regulations are rules to be broken, just guidelines to help with each unique situation (Heinl 1966:270). This should be kept in mind when encountering military encampments. The tendency of many persons is to take regulations literally in analyzing a possible site, overlooking the need for flexibility. This could lead to unnecessary confusion because the dictates of terrain, combined with the multiple sources of information and guidance used by military leaders, caused many variations in actual camp layout. Individuality, technology, and doctrinal confusion ensured differences, although procedures for encampment remained perhaps the least changed of any aspect of military activity in the early republic.

By the time of the Civil War, United States Army Regulations defined a camp as any place where troops were housed for a relatively short period in tents or huts, or were in bivouac (USWD 1861:74). Camps, although temporary, involved using regular shelters of some sort. "Bivouac" refers to situations in which troops on the march without equipment were obliged to stop for the night. Sometimes, if enemy contact was imminent, even if equipment was available, it would not be used and the men would sleep in the open, ready for action, as in bivouac. The layout and dispersal of units is the same whether a unit is in bivouac or is encamped (Wheeler 1879:312). When troops were in "cantonment" they occupied permanent or semipermanent structures for what was anticipated to be a longer time. Cantonments were normally established during the winter but occasionally appeared during periods of prolonged inactivity owing to unusual weather or a lengthy truce (Wheeler 1879:308).

All camps, as well as winter quarters, were tactical positions; consequently, they included advanced posts established well out from them along likely avenues of approach, which were sometimes supported by intermediate strong points. When a large combined arms force went into cantonment, tactical capabilities and requirements of its components determined the placement of particular type units. For example, artillery was closest to roads so that it could move quickly to support the infantry in case of an attack. In rough country, roads and bridges might even be made to ensure the guns' deployment. Cavalry, by contrast, was sufficiently mobile that roads were not a factor; however, it had to be placed as close as possible to substantial water and forage points.

If a unit received orders to defend an area or position for a short period, it established a so-called entrenched camp that often included extensive fortifications in addition to shelter for the troops. Camps more often were established to provide a resting place after a day's march while on campaign. Under such conditions, they might not be fortified with anything more than hasty abatis but still were expected to allow the resting unit to defend itself if it was attacked. The decision to bivouac instead of going into camp could be dictated by the tactical situation or because the unit commander chose not to move with tentage, to reduce the size of his trains and perhaps to increase his unit's speed or range (Wheeler 1879:309, 1882:201).

Tactical considerations also determined unit placement in a bivouac. Forces had to be positioned so they could go into battle formation quickly. A Civil War infantry regiment going into bivouac first formed a line of battle facing in the direction of the enemy. It then broke into companies that each camped on lines perpendicular to the battle line. Unit campfires, about one for every eight or ten men, were located where the company tents would be were they in use, and the men contrived whatever shelter they could. Often the men just lay down in squad clusters, the only sign of a system being spaces that in other conditions would have been the streets between companies. Cavalry formed to the rear of the infantry and similarly broke into companies. The company horses were picketed behind the fires area in a single line with the unit arms stacked behind them. Forage was placed to the right of each company horse line. Artillery could not follow such a precise routine because of the larger amount of space it needed and the normal vagaries of terrain and tactics. The men formed in battery groups along a line of fires with a single officer's fire to the front. The battery horses, usually in four ranks, formed a line behind them.

A third line composed of the forage wagons came next. The guns, caissons, limbers, and wagons formed the rearmost line. The only firm rule in the artillery was to keep all fires far away from the forage, caissons, and limbers (Wheeler 1879:310).

Terrain and tactical circumstances meant that no encampment site of any type could be exactly the same as any other. There were, however, some universal considerations regardless of the final layout. The site had to be defendable and located near adequate water for men and animals with grazing for the latter. Additionally, troop comfort and sanitation mandated that the site be as well drained as possible. Any camp had to be sufficiently spacious to allow the unit using it to form quickly for battle, meaning that the camp front had to be as long as the unit's battle line. Finally, by the time of the Civil War, regulations showing preferred camp layouts had become virtually second nature to every veteran. The roots of this standardization extended back to the American Revolution.

Von Steuben's Legacy

One of George Washington's greatest problems in the first years of the American Revolution was the absence of uniformity and standard procedures throughout his army. At the outbreak of hostilities, American leaders, many of whom were British Empire veterans of the Seven Years' War, dusted off a variety of European military publications to serve as guides. *The Manual Exercise, as ordered by His Majesty in 1764* was among the most popular, with at least twenty-six American editions between 1766 and 1780. Nine American imprints of Sir William Windham's *Plan of Discipline, Composed for the Militia of the County of Norfolk* (1759) appeared in the colonies between 1768 and 1774. The new state of Massachusetts adopted, for all its militia to use, Timothy Pickering's *Easy Plan for the Discipline of Militia,* published in Salem in 1775. Any one of these, or many other works available, could have been adequate for basic drill and procedures—but not all of them simultaneously (Riling 1966:1–3).

General Washington correctly reasoned that the absence of uniform guidance and practices contributed significantly to his overall lack of battlefield success. This was never clearer than after the series of humiliating defeats his army experienced trying to defend Philadelphia in the summer and fall of 1777. Even before his battered units limped into winter camp at Valley Forge, he pressed the Congress to identify and appoint an officer capable of helping him rectify the situation (Clary and Whitehorne 1987:27).

His request eventually resulted in the arrival of Frederick W. A. Von Steuben at Washington's headquarters in February 1778. The affable Von Steuben had served in the Prussian Army during the Seven Years' War. Part of his service had been unusual in that his commander, King Frederick the Great, used him at times as a troubleshooter to analyze and improve units that were not performing well. Such work was rarely done by Europe's professional officers and gave Von Steuben a unique perspective on organizing and training units successfully (Clary and Whitehorne 1987:33–34; Palmer 1937:36).

Von Steuben applied these skills at Valley Forge, training Washington's officers and men while concurrently writing a manual destined to be of lasting influence. Formally designated *Regulations for the Order and Discipline of the Troops of the United States,* the color of the little book's covers gave it the nickname of "Blue Book." The first half of the manual prescribed a system of drill and tactics starting with the individual and continuing up through the regiment. The second part prescribed camps, marches, inspections, and individual duties. Although influenced by French and Prussian practices, most of the book's inspiration came from the British 1764 *Manual Exercise* and a few other British sources (Graves 1991:230). Von Steuben tailored his language, drill, and guidance to American forms and tastes, rendering a manual immediately popular and comprehensible to Washington's officers and soldiers when it was published in 1779. By 1812, most of the tactical part of his treatise was supplanted owing to changing military fashions and technology; however, his guidance on marches and encampments remained in effect for many more years (U.S. National Archives and Records Administration 1814).

Von Steuben's prescription for camp layouts reflected the view that any camp or bivouac was a tactical position. It had to be on defendable terrain with access to supplies delivery. Units camped so that they could react quickly with minimum interference from impedimenta such as wagons and animals. Sanitation, cleanliness, and police of the camp (before, during, and after occupation) was a constant expectation. The Blue Book designated specific unit members' duties in vacating a camp area, properly loading and positioning the wagons in convoy, and cleaning up the area, as well as the procedures for entering and establishing a new camp (Von Steuben 1779:84).

Von Steuben specified that the unit quartermaster was the officer responsible for quartering or encamping his force and guiding it to the site. The adjutant had the responsibility to detail (levy from subordinate units) the parties necessary to work for the quartermaster to clear the camp ground; gather wood, water, and forage; and "dig the vaults or sinks" (Von Steuben 1779:135–36). The quartermaster instructed and supervised his sergeant and the work parties

Plate VIII

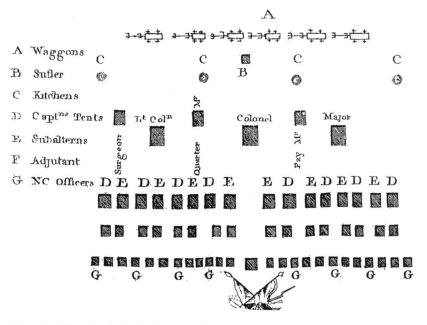

Figure 2.1. Von Steuben's plan for a single-battalion regimental camp (Von Steuben 1802 [1779]:Plate VIII).

in the actual camp layout based on the manual. Oversight included issues of cleanliness and sanitation and ensured the siting of fires only at kitchen locations. The quartermaster further ensured that the camp occupied only the area necessary for the troops on hand. Camp size depended on the number of men available for duty. Knowledge of unit strengths thus could be helpful to later site analysis.

Von Steuben directed that the first thing a quartermaster did upon arrival was to fix the encampment line (figure 2.1), equivalent to the length of the unit's front. He then moved along the line, assigning appropriate space to subordinate units' representatives. These men, in turn, marked out places for their unit tents, kitchens, and so on, along the prescribed lines parallel to the encampment line. Twenty paces between each battalion (equal parts of the regiment) were allowed, with an additional eight paces for each piece of artillery placed on line if required by the tactical situation. The front of each unit was calculated on the basis of two feet for each file (row) of men with sixteen-foot intervals between platoons (equal parts of each company). One tent was allowed for company

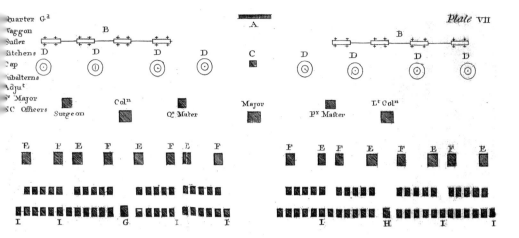

Figure 2.2. Von Steuben's plan for a two-battalion regimental camp (Von Steuben 1802 [1779]:Plate VII).

noncommissioned officers with an additional tent for every six men. These were pitched in two ranks with six paces between ranks and two paces between tents. The sergeants' tent was on the left or right flank of each rank. Each tent fronted along nine feet. If the regiment formed a single battalion, twenty feet in the center of the line was allocated for the adjutant's tent. If the regiment was broken into two battalions (figure 2.2), the adjutant set up in the center of the first (right) battalion while the sergeant major did the same in the second (left) battalion (Von Steuben 1779:76–77).

Company officers' tents occupied a line twenty feet behind the troops' tents, with the company commander's tent to the left or right depending on battalion organization. Field officers' tents were set up on a line thirty feet behind that of the company officers. The regimental commander's tent was in the center, with his deputy's on the right and the major's on the left. However, if there were two battalions, the colonel set up behind the center of the first battalion while the lieutenant colonel moved behind the second battalion, and the major's tent occupied the interval between the two battalions. Starting on the right, the front of the tents of the surgeon, quartermaster, and paymaster were on a line with the rear of the field officers' tents. Kitchens were "dug behind their respective companies, forty feet from the field officers' tents" (Von Steuben 1779:79).

Any sutlers camped at the center of the line, between the kitchens (figure 2.3). Horses and wagons occupied the rearmost line, twenty feet behind the kitchens. Sinks (latrines) and guard posts were established three hundred paces

BATTALION LOG HOUSE CITY

Companies or "platoons" of infantry were composed of twenty-five to fifty men. A standard number of companies formed a battalion of about two hundred soldiers (as sketched). Two battalions were combined into a regiment, the basic infantry unit of the Continental Army. A brigade was made up of two or more regiments.

The following buildings were to be found on a well-drained hillside:

A. Hospitals – small units separated from camp.
B. Artillery Park – all ammunition issued here.
C. Supply Trains – food rations issued here every few days.
D. Kitchens – ovens for baking bread.
E. Officers' Cabins – large, less crowded and varied construction.
F. Soldiers' Huts – identically built in two or more rows and divided by camp roads of varying widths.
G. Color Line – Regimental flags planted here, as well as stacked muskets in good weather. When the "Alarm" was beaten, the army formed on this line, ready for action.
H. Parade Ground

A.

B.

C.

D.

E.

E.

F.

F.

G.

H.

CABINS OF NOTE –

1. Adjutant ⎫ behind regimental colors
2. Sergeant Major ⎭
3. Captain
4. Subalterns (lieutenants and ensigns)
5. Colonel
6. Paymaster
7. Major
8. Quartermaster
9. Surgeon
10. Sutler
11. Slaughter House

Figure 2.3. Revolutionary War battalion log-house city (Wilbur 1969:64).

to the front and rear of the camp, and the quarter guard (reaction force)—composed of men drawn from throughout the regiment—was posted forty feet behind the wagons in the interval between the two battalions (Von Steuben 1802[1779]:35).

Von Steuben's Blue Book quickly became the standard throughout the American forces. Between its issue in 1779 and 1815, at least eighty editions or variants were printed, and its principles are evident in other, later, efforts published to accommodate new developments (Riling 1966:27–31). Washington acknowledged Von Steuben's contribution and training success by ensuring that Congress commissioned Von Steuben inspector general of the army, with the rank of major general, a position in which he served throughout the remainder of the war (Clary and Whitehorne 1987:44).

The Blue Book's guidance on tactical formations underwent a gradual transformation as writers tried to incorporate new procedures derived from the changing nature of warfare in Revolutionary Europe. The growing success of the French Republic's mass armies dealt a blow to rigid linear tactics. Many authors urged adoption of its *Reglement concernant l'exercise et les manoeuvres de l'infanterie Du 1er Aôut, 1791* (Paris 1792). William Duane, later a colonel in the army, obtained Secretary of War Henry Dearborn's support in publishing *The American Military Library, or, Compendium of the Modern Tactics* (in two volumes, Philadelphia 1809), which, among other things, included an English translation of the French regulations. Other efforts soon followed, including Inspector General Alexander Smyth's *Regulations for the Field Exercises, Manoeuvres and Conduct of the Infantry* (Philadelphia 1812), which was adopted briefly by the United States Army (Heller and Stofft 1986:37).

These manuals and regulations, like those before them, and their later modifications, showed very heavy French influences in their tactical portions but virtually replicated the Blue Book's paragraphs on administration and encampment. During the War of 1812, many officers even continued to use the Blue Book's tactical guidance because of the mix of publications emerging, all with some form of government sanction. The confusion was not ended until after hostilities ended, when the army produced in 1816 *Rules and Regulations for the Field Exercise and Manoeuvres of Infantry,* modified slightly by a revision in 1825. In the revision, Von Steuben's encampment guidance survived largely intact, influenced only by changing the size of unit fronts (Graves 1991:225).

Brigadier General Winfield Scott translated a later French manual that appeared in 1834 as *Infantry-Tactics: or Rules for the Exercise and Manoeuvres of the United States Infantry* (in three volumes, New York). This so-called *Scott's*

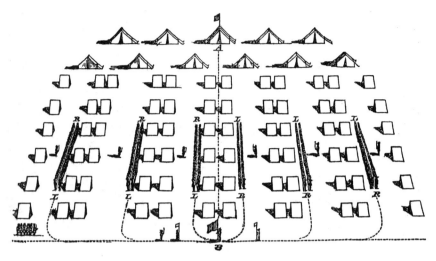

Figure 2.4. Civil War–era battalion forming on color line (Butterfield 1862). "B" is the color line. "R" and "L" refer to the "left" and "right" of the company lines before tents preparatory to going on color line.

Tactics dominated the army well into the Civil War. It experienced some competition from *Rifle and Light Infantry Tactics* (Philadelphia 1855), translated from the French by a committee headed by Lieutenant Colonel William J. Hardee (Heller and Stofft 1986:86–87). Starting with Scott, Von Steuben's encampment procedure changed somewhat. For rapid deployment, the company streets were set up perpendicular to, rather than parallel to, the unit front as shown in the diagram from Daniel Butterfield's (1862) *Camp and Outpost Duty for Infantry* (figure 2.4). A newspaper reporter described such a camp in this new configuration in 1839:

> The soldiers' tents are pitched facing streets that run at right angles with the line of encampment, so that, to the spectator in front, the sides of the tents are presented; and those of adjoining companies are, of course, back to back. In each tent there are, we believe, seven men. At some distance behind the soldiers' tents, and in line parallel with the front, are the wall tents, as they are called, of the company officers; the captain's in rear of the right, the lieutenant's in rear of the left, of the company. On another parallel line, in the rear, are the tents of the field and staff officers, and in rear of the center of the line, that of the Colonel. (Crimmins 1954:62)

Encampment and administrative procedures also became a matter for army regulations at this time, rather than appendages to tactical manuals. As a consequence, modern students must consult both sources as aids when examining possible campsites.

1861 Regulations

The regulations in effect at the outbreak of the Civil War outlined in considerable detail camp models for each of the combat arms. Additionally, guidance for the disposition of supply and materiel convoys, "trains," could be found as well. Unit quartermasters and their staffs continued to be responsible for selecting campsites. If their regiment was part of a larger force, the senior unit quartermaster held the overall authority to allocate areas to each subordinate unit and to arrange the necessary site security with unit provosts and adjutants (USWD 1861:75).

When a regimental advanced party reached its assigned area, it selected the color line (that is, the regimental front), on which all other parts of the camp layout were based (figure 2.5). Ideally, companies set up ten paces behind the color line on streets at least five paces wide running perpendicular to the line. Tents faced each other across each street. Two paces separated each tent along the street as well as from the rear of adjacent units facing on the next streets. Kitchens were twenty paces behind the left file of each company. Noncommissioned officers on the regimental staff and the sutler set up tents another twenty paces back. The police guard's tent was in the center of this line. Company officers were another twenty paces to the rear, their tents aligned on their company's files with the commander's on the right. Field officers and commissioned staff had their tents twenty more paces behind those of the company officers. Staff officers' horses and unit baggage with wagons and personnel were set up twenty-five paces behind the field officers. Latrines ("sinks") for the troops were dug 150 paces to the front of the camp while officers' sinks were dug 100 paces beyond the trains line. The advanced guard post and a tent for any prisoners was another 50 paces to the front. The approximate depth of a camp was about 480 paces, with a variable front of about 400 paces. If the regiment was not full strength, or a narrower front was desirable, the tents could be pitched in a single file (USWD 1861:77).

The arrangement of a single file of tents was normal in the cavalry (figure 2.6). Camp selection required finding sufficient space to set up horse lines by company. Each company then moved a little to the rear of the line along which its horses were to be secured, and the men dismounted. The men fixed the picket rope, attended to the horses, and then set up a single row of tents three to six

Camp of a Regiment of Infantry.

Cl.—*Colonel.*
Lt. Cl.—*Lieut. Colonel.*
M.—*Major.*
Surg.—*Surgeon.*

Ast. Surg.—*Asst. Surgeon.*
Adjt.—*Adjutant.*
Q. M.—*Quarter Master.*
n-c-s.—*Non.-Com.-Staff.*

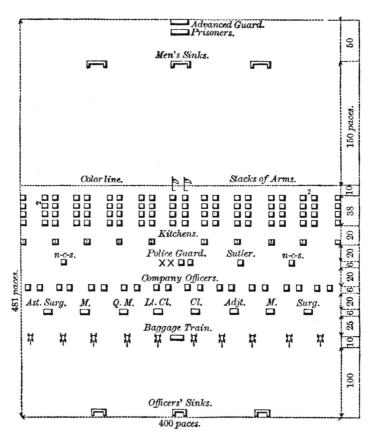

Figure 2.5. Civil War camp of regiment of infantry (U.S. War Department 1861: Plate 1).

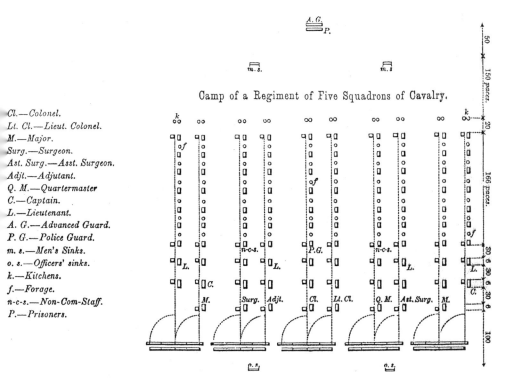

Figure 2.6. Civil War camp of regiment of five squadrons of cavalry (U.S. War Department 1861:Plate 2).

paces behind the picket line, forming a company street with all tents facing to the left of the camp (USWD 1861:79–80). The space between each company's tents had to be wide enough to accommodate the company mounted in column, that is, the unit's length in formation on the march. The depth of a camp was determined by the number of horses, each of which represented two paces.

In the cavalry company, kitchens were placed twenty paces in front of each tent file, with the unit noncommissioned officers' tent being the first in the file. Noncommissioned regimental staff and sutlers set up as the last tents behind the company files. Thirty paces rearward were the lieutenants' tents, with the captains' another thirty paces back. The regimental commander's tent was centered thirty more paces to the rear, flanked by tents of his commissioned staff. All the headquarters' horses were picketed to the left of the tents on a continuation of a line from the company pickets. Sick horses and their attendants set up on either flank in the same arrangement as a company but with the forges and wagons along the same line. The trains and their horses and men set up similarly behind either the right or the left squadron of the regiment. The troopers' sinks were 150 paces to the front while the officers' were 100 paces to the rear. The advanced guard and any prisoners were to be 50 paces beyond the men's sinks (USWD 1861:78–79).

If a cavalry regiment went into bivouac, it shifted from order of battle to platoon groups and set up picket lines perpendicular to the color line. Sufficient space was left between platoons so they could mount and face to the front or rear. Each platoon could have a fire near the color line, about twenty paces behind its horse line. There, the men sheltered as best they could. Officers set up similarly at the opposite end of the picket line (USWD 1861:80–81).

Artillery camped where it could best support, and be supported by, the infantry. A Union six-gun battery broke down into three sections, each forming a file of tents fifteen paces from those of the next section. Section horses were picketed in one or two files ten paces to the left of their respective section's tents. The battery kitchen was twenty-five paces forward of the first rank of tents. The unit guns and rolling stock were posted forty paces behind the officers' tents, centered on the camp. They were aligned in files with four paces between each carriage and in ranks sufficiently far apart to allow rapid hitching up. Men's sinks were 150 paces to the front, and officers' 100 paces to the rear (USWD 1861:80).

Trains

Frederick the Great once observed that "without supplies no army is brave"; however, few modern researchers take much note of the wagons and horses forming the trains that kept Civil War armies in the field (Heinl 1966:315). At the start of the war each infantry regiment was allocated as many as twenty-five wagons just for its own cargo. By 1863 this figure dropped to six wagons per thousand men. Nevertheless, the requirements of a large force in the field remained immense. The campaigns of 1862 and 1863 proved the value of organizing and controlling logistics trains centrally. For example, by autumn 1863, the Army of the Potomac's chief quartermaster, Colonel Rufus Ingalls, implemented a well-organized system that General Grant later praised as one of the best features of the eastern army. Trains specializing in ammunition, subsistence, and so on were established at army level. All movement was directed by the chief quartermaster, who designated roads, destinations, and times, thus minimizing congestion, confusion, and unnecessary delays. Division trains were consolidated under the supervision of their respective corps quartermasters, who received their direction from Colonel Ingalls (Stern 1961:255).

Trains were organized so that each wagon was marked with its corps badge and a symbol denoting what type of material it carried. Empty wagons never were allowed to follow the army or stay with it. Once unloaded, they promptly returned to the depot containing material they were marked to haul. Issues usually were made at night, allowing wagons to return when the roads were least congested and when draft animals could be fed in the rear, obviating the need to carry as much forage (Grant 1885:2:189–90).

Despite these efforts, an army's trains remained substantial and had to be carefully considered. For example, the leaner 800-wagon baggage train of General Winfield S. Hancock's 27,000-man II Corps, Army of the Potomac, was only a part of the army trains that penetrated the Virginia Wilderness in May 1864. The aggregate probably approached approximately 4,300 wagons; 835 ambulances; 29,945 artillery, cavalry, medical, and quartermaster horses; 4,046 private mounts; and 22,528 mules. This total of 56,499 animals required 20,000 men to handle them and 26 pounds each, daily, of fodder and forage (USWD 1865:32). General William T. Sherman's 60,000-man force in Georgia, in even more austere circumstances, required 2,500 wagons and 600 ambulances for its March to the Sea (Stern 1961:259).

Careful attention thus had to be given to convoy organization. All subordinate trains were consolidated at division level. Only a few wagons with ammunition and material needed to be moved immediately with the regiment. All other components (supply, subsistence, ordnance, and forage) were at division level under the control of the division quartermaster officers. Even division and corps wagons replenished from the forwardmost depots. The convoy halted once an hour to rest the horses and to close up. The entire convoy was protected by designated cavalry or reserve infantry units (Shrader 1988:274).

Ideally, a convoy had some pioneers or work parties assigned to it to work the road, remove obstacles, and help construct defenses. An advanced guard preceded the convoy, noting and reporting obstructions and searching for enemy activity. It also looked for suitable resting places and the site at which the wagons would park overnight. The wagons were never supposed to halt unless they were at a defendable location. If an overnight park was necessary, that site should be defendable and preferably far from "inhabited places" to enhance security and, at a minimum, reduce pilferage. Wagons were parked axle to axle, poles all in the same direction with sufficient space between each rank to hitch up the teams. If attack was feared, the wagons were formed into a square, poles

to the inside, corralling the horses and mules. Otherwise, the animals were picketed to the rear of the wagon park. Teamsters bivouacked near their wagons
while the escort set up as prescribed by the regulations (USWD 1861:108–11).

Variations on the Ideal

It is axiomatic that as soon as military units take to the field under combat conditions, circumstances, environment, unit discipline, and individual ingenuity will
generate numerous variations from the theoretical norm (Heinl 1966:239). This
is certainly the case with the various encampments and any vestiges they might
leave. Perusal of correspondence and memoirs indicates that most commanders
tried to adhere as closely as possible to regulatory guidelines as far as camp layout
went. This was the case especially early in the war, before they evolved their own
idiosyncrasies and unit strengths had shrunk as a result of combat and illness. At
the individual level, greater variation could be found from tent to tent, depending upon the energy and initiative of the men in each squad.

Consequently, units could leave a variety of vestiges, especially if they remained in the same place for any length of time. Soldiers were quick to make
themselves as comfortable as possible, using whatever was at hand. However,
the better-disciplined and -led organizations left behind fewer material items
because of the emphasis on daily area police and supply accountability. Junior
leaders of these units, no doubt inspired by their colonel, could be relied upon
to adhere more closely to regulations, keeping their areas clean and not losing
property. Veteran units additionally would have discarded most of their impedimenta before as a result of experience. There certainly could be remains of unit
streets, leveled parade ground, ditching, latrines, trash, and so on regardless of
how well run a unit was, especially early in the war.

Each type of tent left a different footprint because of its shape, the ditching done around it, and vestiges of housekeeping in its interior. More elaborate
traces might be made in permanent winter camps. Early in the war the Sibley
tent was popular. Called a "bell tent" because of its shape, it resembled a tepee
and was erected around a twelve-foot-high center pole. Its circular imprint measured eighteen feet in diameter. A metal stove named for the same designer, if
used, passed its smoke by way of a metal chimney through an adjustable vent
at the tent's peak. Although it was intended to accommodate eight to twelve
men, frequently more were packed in. Its weight and cost caused it to go out of
general use by early 1863. The wedge, or "A," tent was common early in the war
and remained in use in rear areas throughout. Shaped like an inverted "V," it

was a canvas sheet stretched over a six-foot-long pole supported by two vertical poles of about the same height. This tent was staked out so that its front on the ground also was about six feet. Often as many as six men crammed into it. These "A" tents passed out of general use by early 1863 because of their bulk (Stern 1961:23).

A wall tent, so called because it had four sides beneath its sloping roof, came in various sizes. A prewar model used by hospitals was twenty-four feet long, fourteen feet six inches wide, and eleven feet six inches high at its center. It was covered by a fly, a canvas sheet used to give shade, which was twenty-one feet six inches by fourteen feet. Including poles and pins, the wall tent weighed 217 pounds. Each wall tent had a flap that allowed it to be connected to other tents to make a larger ward. Sometimes the fly would be used as a shelter by itself. Each hospital wall tent could "comfortably accommodate" eight patients. In 1860 the length of the hospital wall tent was reduced to fourteen feet, its height and width staying the same (within inches). This tent's wall was four and a half feet high. It used the same size fly. Regulations authorized regimental surgeons the use of three wall tents, one Sibley tent, and a wedge tent (USWD 1883, vol. 12:919).

The smaller wall tents also were issued to senior officers and staffs. But by 1862, company officers and all soldiers used the shelter tent. Because it looked like a kennel when erected, the troops called it a "dog tent." The ancestor of the modern shelter half, it was a piece of canvas about seven feet long and four feet wide. It had buttons and buttonholes along three sides and two holes for stakes at each corner. Two soldiers were expected to combine their canvas pieces ("halves") to create a miniature "A" tent, using poles or branches as the center stakes (Stern 1961:29).

Camps of newly mobilized units could be highly irregular. A 36th Illinois Volunteers soldier recalled that his first camp was an "unmilitary jumble" until the unit colonel arrived and "referred us to Hardee for instructions" (Eisenschiml and Newman 1956:40). An officer from the 3rd New York Volunteers wrote home that his company streets were thirty feet wide and ten rods long, spaced to catch the few breezes in a hot Tidewater Virginia summer. He added that the men cut bushes to make bowers to shade the tents as well (Babcock 1922:17, 19). Many soldiers reported leveling their camp area, grubbing out roots and filling in holes. A large space always was cleared to the front of the camp to provide a parade ground. Part of the daily camp police entailed sweeping and scraping the ground along officers' row (Babcock 1922:27; DeForest 1946:4).

Terrain often dictated departures from the norm. The 75th New York Volunteers on Santa Rosa Island, Florida, made one long street between two parallel sand dunes. Kitchens were at one end while headquarters and staff built a large brush shed at the other end, where they placed their tents in shade from the relentless Gulf sun. The winds were so strong in their camp that the tents were secured to the ground by wire cables (Babcock 1922:21, 22).

A visitor to Grant's army during the Vicksburg operations observed an unusual form of camp never considered by the regulations. The water table in northwestern Mississippi was so close to the surface that often merely ditching brought up water. Consequently, entire units cut terraces on the sides of the levees and pitched closely packed tents. From a distance, the white rows of tents seemed to be floating between the river and the low-lying fields (Censer 1986:565, 571).

Senior headquarters quickly banned carrying tents on campaign because of the demands on horses or mules and the need to reduce the number of wagons. Consequently, when in the field, veteran units just wrapped up in blankets while tent flies were put up for the officers. Fires and sleeping areas were placed in accordance with regulations to make clear streets to allow movement through the sleeping formations. Dog tents would be pitched if conditions merited doing so and if it was assumed that the unit might be there for more than a night. If the enemy was close, the men made abatis and dug shallow earthworks and artillery lunettes. Often, troops made the shelter tents more comfortable by building annexes with fence rails and roofing them over with branches. If enough rails or logs were available, crude sidewalls were built and the dog tent parts used as a roof (Babcock 1922:24, 29; Benedict 1895:44).

Veterans quickly learned to ditch tents to keep dry. Daniel Butterfield's advice was to dig a six- to eight-inch-deep trench around each shelter. Sometimes, each little moat had to be linked to a larger ditch running down the company street or to the nearest slope (Butterfield 1862:45). In addition to ditching, many regiments routinely contoured the camp area to improve drainage and leveled where tents were to be pitched (Bauer 1977:11, 12).

A soldier from the 12th Vermont Volunteers observed that whenever his unit remained beyond a night, each company kitchen prepared a fire pit "whose patent that is, I cannot say. It is composed of a trench, four feet long and two deep, dug in the ground. In the bottom of this the fire is kindled. Forked sticks at the corners support a couple of stout poles, parallel with the sides, across which are laid the shorter sticks on which hung the kettles" (Benedict 1895:62–63). A soldier from the 17th New York Volunteers commented that no matter how elaborate these bivouacs became, when it was time to move, "we leave these and everything and take our little shelter tents" (Jackson and O'Donnell 1965:48). The next group coming into the area often broke up their predecessor's handiwork to use the wood for fuel or to remake it to their own satisfaction (Benedict 1895:105).

Techniques learned in the field during good weather contributed to making comfortable winter quarters. Some men stockaded their tent walls, placing logs in the ground vertically. Others salvaged boards or logs and laid them parallel to resemble a log cabin. Although it was discouraged because of drainage problems, many dug a pit around whose edge they built a low wall of rails and logs, covering the whole structure with their tents. This technique saved having to search for a lot of wood to make the walls. One regiment considered making large log cabins, each holding an entire company, but never was in a place long enough to justify the effort (Benedict 1895:74).

Units with sedentary missions often went to elaborate lengths to improve their situation. For example, when the 14th West Virginia Volunteers established a base to guard the railroad at New Creek (modern Keyser), West Virginia, one member wrote,

> We established the most beautiful and picturesque camp I ever saw. It was laid out along the B&O Railroad on a piece of ground in regular military order. Then we graded all the streets and avenues as nicely as the paved streets of Wellington. We then set cedar trees along the company streets, one to each tent, making eleven to the company. The trees were about twelve feet high and all the same size and height. Still larger trees were set along the company officer's avenue, three to a company, or thirty-one to the avenue. The regimental headquarters, which was in the center of the regiment in the rear of the company officers, was set to large cedar trees, eighteen feet high, completely surrounding the headquarters in a square. The quartermaster's and commissary's headquarters were set likewise, except the cedar forest in this instance was set circular and very dense. (Johnson 2002:3–4)

Although units rarely modified forests as these West Virginians did, they often did more than trim foliage to make shady bowers. A first sergeant of the 2nd Ohio Cavalry stated that bushes and "evergreens" were transplanted to help build a windbreak to shield the horse lines. His unit further dug postholes in the rocky soil to set in "stout poles," against which the men made a wall of cedar and pine bushes piled six to twelve feet high and covered the base of the wall with earth to anchor it. This not only made a formidable windbreak but also was "handy for other purposes, easily understood by veterans," implying that his unit was not fastidious about latrine use (Starr 1978:323, 332).

Staying warm was an expression of individual choice. The Ohio first sergeant noted that some men did not bother to make any kind of fire in their tent and sponged off other, more energetic, comrades. Many men described building some kind of fireplace using scavenged bricks or stones from fence walls or buildings (Starr 1978:328). Chimneys could be of the same material or be made of mud-covered sticks or barrels. Others used some version of the so-called California system to heat their tents. This entailed making a pit about two and a half feet deep in front of the tent entrance, from which a trench extended longitudinally, ending outside on its rear. A chimney of some sort was built over this rear portion. The trench in the interior was covered over—rarely with sheet metal, more often with stones—and the occupants enjoyed a crude form of radiant heat (USWD 1883, vol. 12:921).

Some 1st Vermont Volunteers evolved a hasty California version by digging a pit inside their tent and connecting a pipe made of tin cans with their tops and bottoms removed that extended from the outside to the bottom of the pit. They then placed a curved piece of sheet metal or tin plate over the top of the tin can pipe, leaving enough space to insert another section of improvised pipe to serve as a chimney, and claimed it worked fine. Twelfth Vermont soldiers developed a more elaborate version while serving in Fairfax County, Virginia, in November 1862:

> We excavated a hole in the firm and adhesive clay which forms the floor of our tent, its top was a little less in circumference than our tin plate, its bottom, a foot or more below the surface, was somewhat larger. A hole was then dug outside the tent, sloping inward till it nearly met our excavation inside, and the bottoms of the two were connected by a passage two inches in diameter, worked through with the knife. From the top of our circular cavity within, a trench was made extending outside the tent, and covered by a brick bat—the tin plate was placed over the hole, [the ground] forms the body of our stove. The tin plate is both door and top of the same. The small hole at the bottom is the draft, the trench at the top is the flue! We fill it with hardwood chips, light a fire, and it works quite as well as expected. (Benedict 1895:56–57)

In conclusion, the ingenuity of soldiers to achieve their comfort is a constant, and their choices vary almost as much as there are individuals. Another constant is the virtual certainty that with experience they and their leaders will modify official guidance to accommodate unit procedures, comfort, and local conditions. When visiting their campsites today, one should never be surprised to be surprised. However, an awareness of the regulations and confidence that good soldiers will adhere to their principles, if not their particulars, should provide substantial help in learning how these long-gone warriors lived as well as they could while in harm's way.

References Cited

Anonymous

1863　*Instructions for Officers and Non-Commissioned Officers on Outpost and Patrol Duty and Troops in Campaign.* United States Government Printing Office, Washington, D.C.

Babcock, Willoughby M., Jr.

1922　*Selections from the Letters and Diaries of Brevet–Brigadier General Willoughby Babcock of the Seventy-Fifth New York Volunteers.* University of the State of New York, Albany.

Bauer, K. Jack (editor)

1977　*Soldiering: The Civil War Diary of Rice C. Buell, 123rd New York Volunteer Infantry.* Presidio Press, San Rafael, Calif.

Benedict, George G.

1895　*Army Life in Virginia: Letters from the Twelfth Vermont Regiment and Personal Experiences of Volunteer Service in the War for the Union.* Free Press Association, Burlington, Vt.

Brinkerhoff, Roeliff

1865　*The Volunteer Quartermaster.* D. Van Nostrand, New York.

Butterfield, Daniel

1862　*Camp and Outpost Duty for Infantry.* Harper and Brothers, New York.

Censer, Jane T. (editor)

1986　*Defending the Union: The Civil War and the United States Sanitary Commission, 1861–1863.* Vol. 4 of *The Papers of Frederick Law Olmsted.* Johns Hopkins University Press, Baltimore, Md.

Clary, David A., and Joseph W. A. Whitehorne

1987　*The Inspector Generals of the United States Army, 1777–1903.* Office of the Inspector General and Center of Military History, Washington, D.C.

Craighill, William P.

1863　*Army Officer's Pocket Companion.* Van Nostrand, New York.

Crimmins, Martin L. (editor)

1954   Camp Washington, Trenton, New Jersey, 1839. *Military Collector and Historian* 6:62–64.

Cross, Trueman

1825   *Military Laws of the United States.* Edward de Krafft, Washington, D.C.

DeForest, John W.

1946   *A Volunteer's Adventures: A Union Captain's Record of the Civil War.* Yale University Press, New Haven, Conn.

Dempsey, Janet

1987   *Washington's Last Cantonment: "High Time for a Peace."* Literary Research Associates, Monroe, N.Y.

Eisenschiml, Otto, and Ralph Newman

1956   *Eyewitness: The Civil War as We Lived It.* Grosset and Dunlap, New York.

Gilham, William

1861   *Manual of Instruction for the Volunteers and Militia of the United States.* Charles Desilver, Philadelphia.

Grafton, Henry D.

1861   *A Treatise on the Camp and March . . . For Use of Volunteers and Militia in the United States.* Van Nostrand, New York.

Grant, Ulysses S.

1885   *Personal Memoirs of Ulysses S. Grant.* 2 vols. Charles L. Webster, New York.

Graves, Donald E.

1986   Dry Books of Tactics: United States Infantry Manuals of the War of 1812 and After, parts 1 and 2. *Military Collector and Historian* 38:50–61, 173–77.

1991   From Steuben to Scott: The Adoption of French Infantry Tactics by the United States Army, 1807–1816. *International Commission of Military History* 13:223–33.

Heinl, Robert D.

1966   *Dictionary of Military and Naval Quotations.* United States Naval Institute, Annapolis, Md.

Heller, Charles E., and William A. Stofft (editors)

1986   *America's First Battles, 1776–1965.* University Press of Kansas, Lawrence.

Jackson, Harry F., and Thomas F. O'Donnell (editors)

1965   *Back Home in Oneida: Hermon Clarke and His Letters.* Syracuse University Press, Syracuse, N.Y.

Johnson, Mary E. (editor)

2002   *From a "Whirlpool of Death . . . to Victory": Civil War Remembrances of Jesse Tyler Sturm, 14th West Virginia Infantry.* West Virginia History, Charleston, W.Va.

Lord, Francis A.

1957   Army and Navy Textbooks and Manuals Used by the North during the Civil War, parts 1 and 2. *Military Collector and Historian* 9:61–67, 10:95–102.

Maltby, Isaac

1811   *The Elements of War.* Thomas B. Wait, Boston.

Marshall, George, et al.

1939   *Infantry in Battle.* 2nd ed. Infantry Journal, Washington, D.C.

Murray, Robert A.

1981   *The Army Moves West: Supplying the Western Indian Wars Campaigns.* The Old Army Press, Fort Collins, Colo.

Palmer, John M.

1937   *General Von Steuben.* Yale University Press, New Haven, Conn.

Rees, John U.

1997   Soldiers' Shelter on Campaign during the War for Independence, part 2. *Military Collector and Historian* 49 (winter 1997):156–68.

2001–2 Soldiers' Shelter on Campaign during the War for Independence, part 3. *Military Collector and Historian* 53 (winter 2001–2):161–69.

2003   Soldiers' Shelter on Campaign during the War for Independence, part 4. *Military Collector and Historian* 55 (summer 2003):89–96.

Riling, Joseph R.

1966   *Baron Von Steuben and His Regulations.* Ray Riling Arms Books, Philadelphia.

Risch, Erna

1981   *Supplying Washington's Army.* Center of Military History, United States Army, Washington, D.C.

Scott, H. L.

1861   *Military Dictionary.* Van Nostrand, New York. Reprint 1864.

Shrader, Charles R.

1988   Field Logistics in the Civil War. In *The United States Army Guide to the Battle of Antietam: The Maryland Campaign of 1862.* Edited by Jay Luvaas and Harold W. Nelson, pp. 255–84. Harper and Row, New York.

Starr, Stephen Z. (editor)

1978   Winter Quarters near Winchester. *Virginia Magazine of History and Biography* 86:320–38.

Stern, Philip V. D. (editor)

1961   *Soldier Life in the Union and Confederate Armies.* Bonanza Books, New York.

United States Army, Adjutant and Inspector General's Office

1813   *Military Laws and Regulations for the Armies of the United States.* Washington, D.C.

United States National Archives and Records Administration

1814   Record Group (RG) 98, vol. 442, AG Orders, Northern Army, 9th Military District, 14 May.

United States War Department (USWD)

1841   *General Regulations for the Army of the United States, 1841.* J. and G. S. Gideon, Washington, D.C.

1847   *General Regulations for the Army of the United States, 1847.* J. and G. S. Gideon, Washington, D.C.

1857   *Regulations for the Army of the United States, 1857.* Harper and Brothers, New York.

1861   *Regulations for the Army of the United States, 1861.* Harper and Brothers, New York.

1865   *Annual Reports of the Quartermaster General, 1861–1865.* United States Government Printing Office, Washington, D.C.

1883   *Medical and Surgical History of the War of the Rebellion,* vol. 12. 12 vols. United States Government Printing Office, Washington, D.C.

Viele, Egbery L.

1861   *Handbook for Active Service.* Van Nostrand, New York.

Von Steuben, Frederick W. A.

1779   *Regulations for the Order and Discipline of the Troops of the United States, Part 1.* Styner and Cist, Philadelphia. Reprinted 1802, William Norman, Boston.

Wheeler, Junius B.

1879   *A Course of Instruction in the Elements of the Art and Science of War For the Use of the Cadets of the United States Military Academy.* D. Van Nostrand, New York.

1882   *The Elements of Field Fortifications.* D. Van Nostrand, New York.

Whitehorne, J.W.A.

1986   Inspector General Sylvester Churchill's Efforts to Produce a New Army Drill Manual, 1850–1862. *Civil War History* 32:159–68.

Wilbur, C. Keith

1969 *Picture Book of the Continental Soldier.* Stackpole Co., Harrisburg.

Wiley, Bell

1951   *The Life of Billy Yank.* Bobbs-Merrill, Indianapolis.

Part II

Survey and Management
of Civil War Encampments

MATTHEW B. REEVES, CLARENCE R. GEIER, AND DAVID G. ORR

Part II of this volume discusses two issues that are extremely sensitive and pertinent for archaeologists investigating Civil War encampments: the first is the ability of archaeologists to locate encampments; the second, how to manage these sites as cultural resources once they are located. Since the mid-twentieth century, the types of Civil War resources most likely to be protected are those associated with battles and the tactical maneuvering of troops. As a result, within states such as Virginia, Maryland, Pennsylvania, and Tennessee, there are numerous national and state parks that protect battlefields. Such sites have traditionally been seen as having an important role in our historic identity. What has been left out of this picture are the sites where soldiers spent the vast majority of their time and were at greater risk to perish from disease or malnutrition; that is, the encampments where troops awaited arduous overland campaigns and the carnage of battle.

The emphasis on battlefields as representing Civil War history is similar to how plantation life has traditionally been presented to visitors at Southern house museums. For years, plantation homes that served as visitor destinations have presented the glory and richness of the plantation owner's home. What was lost or diminished in this presentation of history were the lives of the individuals who made this wealth and prosperity possible—the enslaved community. Similarly, in presenting the history of the Civil War, many national and state parks have presented the glory and intrigue of particular battles, where enlisted soldiers are portrayed as a fighting machine led into battle by their brave officers. What has been forgotten and overlooked in this history is the overwhelming sacrifice that soldiers made in leaving their homes for an extended time and subjecting themselves to the miseries of soldier life. The majority of an enlistment was spent in camps where soldiers faced endless hours of loneliness and worry for their families while at the same time being deprived of adequate shelter and food. It was this sacrifice, most often faced in camp, and not the fear of dying, that often inspired men to desert the camps and head back to their families.

This oversight in Civil War history has been extended to public and government attitudes toward the historic importance of and to the interest in the preservation and management of such cultural resources. This is particularly evident in efforts to protect encampment sites through cultural resource management practices; that is, they have been ignored in surveys and cultural resource management (CRM) planning. This lack of regard has stemmed from two factors: (1) the historic perception of these sites as not contributing to meaningful or significant Civil War history, and (2) the difficulty of locating and interpreting these sites using standard archaeological survey techniques. Unfortunately, over the past twenty years, many areas of intensive military encampment, such as those enclosing historic Civil War–era towns and communities like Richmond, Fredericksburg, Atlanta, and Washington, D.C., have witnessed phenomenal growth and development. The oversight in managing these resources has resulted in countless sites being lost to developers' bulldozers. While this loss occurred, the individuals charged with the oversight responsibility in managing these resources, including staff of many state historic preservation offices and members of the professional archaeological community, largely ignored the importance of these sites as historic and cultural resources. The one group that has taken an avid interest in pursuing these has been the relic-hunting community. For years, responsible members of the relic-hunting community have published articles and books on Civil War encampments, petitioned for protection of these sites as cultural resources, and spent untold hours researching and documenting many of these sites prior to their destruction at the hands of developers. As Bryan Corle and Joseph Balicki discuss (chapter 3), rather than archaeologists' seizing upon the destruction of these sites and assisting relic hunters in their efforts to record them, many in the discipline chose to condemn the role that relic hunters played in using improper excavation and documentation techniques in their hunting activities in these camps.

The identification and survey of Civil War encampments by professional archaeologists, as Corle and Balicki discuss, has been hampered by standard archaeological survey techniques that are tailored to locate domestic scatters from long-term occupations, such as house sites, rather than the low-density artifact scatters that typically characterize camps. In their chapter, Corle and Balicki apply techniques employed by relic hunters to identify camp locations (see also Balicki, chapter 5). They convincingly show that these techniques can be easily employed by archaeologists to ensure that these resources are more readily identified during surveys.

As professional archaeologists begin to document and study military camps, many find themselves in a situation familiar to many relic hunters who discover a particularly good camp: not wanting to disclose the location for fear others may come in to "share." In many cases, the campsites that archaeologists are trying to protect are on lands where relic hunting is prohibited. Disclosing information on the location of such sites presents a serious problem, as there are some relic hunters who choose not to seek permission to hunt sites and do so clandestinely and illegally, for no motive other than profit. Little can be done to protect resources from this small portion of the relic-hunting community, other than disclose as little as possible about site location and information. This situation's unfortunate result is that valuable and compelling information cannot be published, for fear of site location reaching the wrong hands. In his article on Camp Hooker at Monocacy, Maryland, Brandon Bies (chapter 4) presents a case study of how the contrasting interests of illegal relic hunting and resource protection can be at odds.

The chapters in this section present the complex and often contradictory position in which archaeologists and cultural resource managers of Civil War encampments are placed. We rely upon the generosity of responsible relic hunters to show us site locations, share information on artifacts, and provide insights into locating this often elusive set of sites. At the same time, we must face the reality that some individuals within the relic-hunting community seek only material gain from Civil War encampments. For many in this latter group, the only tactic that can be successful in protecting sites is to avoid disclosing site information. Cost is a major limitation to educating the public about the importance and historic information that these sites have to offer. Our job as students and managers of these resources is to strike a balance between these two extremes and develop partnerships based on common historical interests and respect that will ensure the preservation and proper management of our shared cultural heritage. We hope the chapters in this section will provide insight into how some have approached this dilemma.

3

Finding Civil War Sites

What Relic Hunters Know, What Archaeologists Should and Need to Know

BRYAN L. CORLE AND JOSEPH F. BALICKI

INTRODUCTION

Over the past four years, we have spent the majority of our time researching five years of northern Virginia history. Initially, even though we had some interest in the archaeology of military sites and Balicki wrote an article on Fort C. F. Smith, one of the Civil War fortifications of Washington, D.C., we never fully realized the complexity of researching the war. We wouldn't say our research became an obsession, although sometimes hearing us talk you would think otherwise. It was as if we were filling a cup from a stream while watching most of the water run by. Researching the Civil War can be like that, and that's probably why it can be so seductive. During this time, we met a lot of people and learned a great many things. Some of what we learned led us to question how archaeologists view the past, how they employ methodologies to identify evidence of past activity, and even how they interact with individuals and groups with far different agendas. In addition, we learned—and present here—practical field methodologies that have proven useful in locating and interpreting military encampment sites.

In our discussion we address the dichotomy that exists between professional archaeologists and relic hunters. On one hand, professionals who should know how to find, research, and interpret encampments, cannot; on the other hand, amateurs have devised realistic approaches to locating these site types. The opinions presented here should not be taken as either a validation of relic hunting or unduly harsh criticism of archaeologists. Illicit relic hunting and bad archaeology result in the same end: a failure in the ability to interpret the past. Relic hunters have made significant contributions, mainly in material culture studies, and some have successfully collaborated with archaeologists (Buttafuso

2000:15; Espenshade et al. 2002:43; Geier and Winter 1994:13; Scott and Fox 1987:21). However, the negative aspects of relic hunting (such as widespread trespassing on private and public lands, destruction of known archaeological sites, and reluctance to work with archaeologists) often overshadow the many positive contributions made by some relic hunters. At the same time, archaeologists cannot take the higher moral ground. Through ignorance and indifference, many Civil War archaeological sites are not found or, if found, are not adequately evaluated.

It has been ten years since Clarence Geier and Susan Winter published *Look to the Earth: Historical Archeology and the American Civil War* (1994). In the intervening decade, a growing number of archaeologists have turned their attention to the war, and several other studies have been published (for example, Espenshade et al. 2002; Geier and Potter 2000). Some archaeologists have made significant contributions toward understanding military archaeology and the study of conflict, particularly battlefields, but research into the most common sites, habitations, or encampments and the wealth of data they contain is sorely lacking. Moreover, mainstream archaeology has not embraced the study of the War or, generally, altered standard operating procedures to find encampments. As a result, encampments continue to be overlooked and an important aspect of the past is lost.

Historical archaeology, particularly that driven by the cultural resources management (CRM) industry, is not routinely using methods that would increase the chance of identifying Civil War encampments. Locating and interpreting Civil War encampment sites is difficult archaeology. Encampments vary widely in their nature and expression. Many are characterized by low artifact density, with artifacts clustering in discrete areas rather than being randomly or broadly distributed across the site. A growing mass of field experience indicates that these site types are often not readily identified using the standard CRM archaeological field methodologies that rely heavily on shovel testing. It must be recognized that part of the problem are state guidelines for CRM survey, which emphasize the role of shovel-testing strategies rather than the (at times) more costly eclectic approach needed to find Civil War encampments and other military sites. By addressing some of these methodological shortcomings and incorporating the successful strategies employed by relic hunters, archaeologists stand a greater chance of locating and evaluating Civil War resources.

SPANNING THE GREAT DIVIDE

The Civil War has been described as a Rubicon in the nation's history (Geier and Potter 2000:xxvii; Smith 1994:4). In a mere five years, the nation changed socially and economically. Its people went in a different direction, and in many areas the physical landscape of the nation was scarred. On a national scale, the dynamic flow of the war, the intensity of the occupations, and the accompanying devastation caused by military conflict resulted in the creation of large numbers of archaeological sites and the discard of countless artifacts. The Civil War remains one of the most popular and most studied periods in United States history, as evidenced by the number of popular shows on the History Channel, reenactment attendance, the interest of professional historians, the popularity of relic hunting, and the market for all things Civil War. Archaeologists have not capitalized on this popularity, but relic hunters have. It is curious that a cultural event (more like a cultural supernova) of such magnitude would have not drawn more interest from archaeologists. Why have many practitioners of historical archaeology marginalized the study of the Civil War? The answer goes beyond research specialization and may be found in the social and historical context of historical archaeology.

Historical archaeology developed into an accepted field, and most of its practitioners grew up and were educated, during the Vietnam War and the civil rights movement. Within a cultural environment that was predominately anti-military and antiwar, much archaeological inquiry focused on subgroups, such as the oppressed, minorities, and women. Indeed, telling the stories of those who did not write their own histories is one of our greatest contributions as a field. However, the focus on limited subsets of American history has left, and continues to leave, its mark on the field. Other worthy areas of study are ignored or marginalized. Yes, the Civil War was bloody, violent, and dominated by men organized in groups, things that make many archaeologists uncomfortable. Not acknowledging that conflicts are part of the historic fabric, create archaeological records, and are mechanisms of change, however, creates a biased, unrealistic view of the past. This approach will not lead to a better understanding of our history.

On various levels, relic hunters find significance in the Civil War and the objects associated with the war. They view their hobby as a way of commemorating the ideals of military service, duty, and patriotism. Further, some use relic hunting as a way to honor and perpetuate their heritage. The majority of relic hunters are men. In Virginia, the relic hunters we have met tend to have conservative political views, emphasize Confederate heritage, and are outdoorsmen. Within their group they have developed a relic-hunter mystique, where the allure of treasure hunting, secretiveness, and the outdoors all play a big role in their hobby. They also do not have a high opinion of most archaeologists. As archaeologists who openly attend relic-hunter shows and club meetings and try to engage relic hunters in meaningful discussions, we have heard the general feeling many relic hunters have for archaeologists. A great many relic hunters view archaeologists as irrelevant, untrustworthy, arrogant, and elitist. We are lumped as a group of academically elitist, liberal socialists who want to legislate away their hobby and are biased against Civil War history in general. That sentiment was from the relic hunters who cared to share an opinion: many just turned away when the "arkies" approached them, some used us as a sounding board for past grievances against other archaeologists, and some waited to see if we were just there for the money. Initially some wanted to send us to Russia or better yet Afghanistan, where in the summer of 2001 "we arkies" could protect statues of Buddha from the Taliban. Relic hunters saw hypocrisy between the preservation communities' pleas to save these world heritage landmarks, and the preservation communities' silence or ineffectiveness over the uncontrolled destruction of Civil War battlefields (places where Americans shed blood and died) here at home. Of all the comments, the questions concerning archaeologists being in it just for the money were the most interesting, because it's the relic hunters whom we generally equate with making money off the past.

Civil War relic collecting dates back to the soldiers themselves and has developed into a local tradition in many areas (Donald 1975; Nevins 1962:21; D. P. Newton, personal communication 2001; Sylvia and O'Donnell 1978). Veterans returning to the scene of battles often brought home souvenirs, and people who lived near battlefields and camps often collected scrap metal to supplement their income (Buttafuso 2000:3; Crouch 1978:2, 1995:1; Sylvia and O'Donnell 1978). With the acquisition of metal detectors after World War II, and the Civil War's centennial, modern-day relic hunting became an established hobby (Buttafuso 2000:5). At that time, many unprotected battlefields were collected. Today, the Archaeological Resource Protection Act legislation applies only to federal lands. It does not matter whether you like relic hunting or not. If it is practiced on private property and with the landowners' permission, it is not illegal.

Relic hunters and archaeologists are on two diametrically opposed sides of "who owns the past." Relic hunters want to possess, collect, trade, and often sell objects from Civil War sites, whereas archaeologists want to possess, collect, trade, and share or sometimes sell information from sites. Relic hunters cannot be faulted for their desire to own material objects from the past but can be faulted for their indiscriminate destruction of archaeological sites. Archaeologists, for their part, have failed to synthesize much of their work into a form relevant to the general population and have not developed realistic methods to find and investigate Civil War sites. Within the past forty years, relic hunters have developed effective methods of identifying encampments. In contrast, archaeologists have continued to use and to an extent formalize standard operating practices that almost ensure that many military site types will not be found.

In many jurisdictions, archaeological studies are limited by legislation that requires survey only under certain conditions. Further, in an atmosphere in which many developers and politicians will not voluntarily allocate funds to protect or investigate historic properties, relic-hunter collections and their site-specific observances may be the only remaining evidence for destroyed sites. Unfortunately, many archaeologists will not actively engage in discourse with the relic-hunting community (Buttafuso 2000:5; Espenshade et al. 2002:42). This reluctance to communicate has inhibited accurate recording of Civil War military activities on a local and regional basis.

For the past twenty years, increased development in Washington, D.C., and adjacent suburbs of northern Virginia has resulted in the destruction of countless Civil War (and other) archaeological sites. In many instances, because of the absence of local, state, and federal CRM ordinances, locations containing archaeological sites were not investigated. In 1997, Camp Knox, the land housing the 1861–62 winter encampment of the 4th Maine Volunteers, was developed for residential housing (O'Donnell and Wilder 1999). No archaeological assessment was required as part of the permitting process. Relic hunters had known of Camp Knox since the 1960s, but it was assumed to have been "hunted out" (O'Donnell and Wilder 1999:42–44). After heavy equipment cleared vegetation and removed the humus, relic hunters once again searched the site. One was a local relic hunter, historian, and writer who had spent years finding sites and talking to other relic hunters as they collected. He wrote an article about Camp Knox (O'Donnell and Wilder 1999). Many archaeologists would dismiss this article for its praise of relic hunting. However, the article contained a detailed camp history, artifact photographs, and relic-hunter accounts. Interpretations on camp layout, artifact density and patterning, features, and camp activities such as policing were also touched upon. These interpretations were used to explain why only certain types and quantities of artifacts were found.

Based on the information, it was clear that the site had retained integrity, contained numerous features, and had the potential to address numerous research questions. If relic hunters had not shown an interest, the site would have gone totally unrecorded and unreported.

Northern Virginia is home to the oldest and one of the largest relic-hunter clubs in the United States. The Northern Virginia Relic Hunters Association (NVRHA) was founded thirty years ago by some of the first relic hunters to use metal detectors. Currently, club membership is about three hundred. The club's members have published twenty-seven books on Civil War material culture or history. These references are often used by archaeologists to identify artifacts. In the past, the club assisted the Smithsonian Institution in the excavation of unexpected soldier burials and the National Park Service at Manassas Battlefield (London 1998; Reeves 2001:viii). Many members provided information to archaeologists in the past, but having been rebuffed or not taken seriously, they have come to view archaeologists with suspicion.

Their views are based on experiences with archaeologists who dismissed their overtures. We, however, grew weary of hearing comments such as "the archaeologists said that they would rather see all the artifacts bulldozed than let the relic hunters get them." One day a relic hunter came to see us. He had tried to work with archaeologists but had been continually turned away. He recounted to us an incident in which an archaeologist wouldn't come out of the office to meet him, even though he came to share detailed histories, historic photographs, and information on what had been found on a site the archaeologist was investigating. This potential information was lost because the relic hunter used what the archaeologist called "the devil's stick," better known as a metal detector. Relic hunting at the site had not been illegal, as the property owner had given permission for it to take place. The archaeologist's response caused a valuable contact to be lost; what is worse, pertinent information (which probably would have led to a better understanding of the site) was not collected. Our experience with this gentleman was different. We spent a day with him visiting unrecorded sites, and later he introduced us to several other people whom he encouraged to share information. As a result, over twenty Civil War camps on public and private property were formally recorded.

We began going to the relic-hunter meetings with no illusions of turning relic hunters "from the dark side," as some colleagues had suggested we try. Relic hunting happens and will continue to do so; in most cases collecting is legal. Some relic hunters are extraordinarily knowledgeable amateur historians. By attending meetings, we began to recognize that relic hunters have a vast body of information about local and regional Civil War sites that, at present, is not documented. By simply asking questions and listening, we were able to tap into an alternative source of knowledge that continues to provide us with significant information on the region we work in.

WHY TRADITIONAL METHODOLOGIES DO NOT WORK

The nature of certain military camps renders them difficult to reliably locate and evaluate using established CRM methodologies that rely on the extensive use of systematic subsurface testing. Further, military encampments, though habitations, often do not conform to established predictive models commonly used to locate domestic habitations that are based on terrain slope or proximity to natural resources.

Military camps differ from most domestic historic occupations or prehistoric sites in that they can be highly maintained landscapes. Further, unlike other site types, artifacts in military camps are often few in number and are sparsely distributed (Espenshade et al. 2002:42). Part of the daily routine of the soldiers was "police duty," during which the camps were cleaned up and refuse removed. Policing resulted in a majority of the artifacts associated with a camp life being redeposited in discreet locations (Balicki 2001:136–37). The absence of artifacts from policed areas has often been misinterpreted as an indication of relic-hunter activity, when the paucity of artifacts could as easily reflect the occupants' policing activities. The absence of large numbers of artifacts presents an interpretive problem for archaeologists who rely heavily on the presence of material culture when evaluating encampment sites for eligibility for the National Register of Historic Places. Examination of the distribution of artifacts across encampment sites can provide useful information on camp conditions and maintenance of the landscape (Balicki 2001:136–37). When camps are being investigating, attention must be given not only to where artifacts are found, but also to where there are noticeable absences of artifacts. Only then can camps and the activities that occurred within them be evaluated.

It is only through the use of an understanding of the types of camp activities and how these activities shaped the archaeological record that realistic methodological techniques and analysis can be applied. In northern Virginia, Civil War campsites are located in a variety of settings that range from optimal settings to inhospitable locales, such as steep-sided stream valleys and north-facing hillsides. Although needs such as food, water, and shelter were basic requirements for the Civil War soldier, this does not mean that camps were always sited on well-drained landforms close to water sources. The location of encampments may reflect response to orders, a lack of available space, or the necessity to defend a crucial tactical area. In these situations, water and other supplies could be transported to the camps as needed. For example, a camp at Quantico, Virginia, was located on a hillside with a slope of over 20 percent (Balicki, Farnham et al. 2002:269). Usually, such steep terrain is not routinely investigated during CRM studies because some state guidelines consider these locations as having no, to low, site potential (Shaffer and Cole 1994:13; Trader 2001:8; VDHR 2000:84).

Systematic shovel testing is not an appropriate strategy for finding camps. Relic hunters have said, "Finding Civil War sites by digging test holes, is like trying to find a needle in a haystack. In fact, we have found many artifacts in construction sites that were first searched by archaeologists who dug a few test holes and deemed that nothing existed on the site" (Buttafuso 2000:15). Espenshade and colleagues (2002) give numerous examples of the ineffectiveness of shovel tests and provide examples of how large, well-preserved camps were entirely missed.

Most state guidelines rely heavily on shovel testing and walk-over surveys to identify archaeological sites. Some states, such as Kentucky and West Virginia, do acknowledge that metal detectors should be used on known encampments but do not mention their use as a tool for discovering unknown sites (Sanders 2001:22; Trader 2001:3). Recently, the use of metal detectors to search for and investigate military sites has become an accepted archaeological tool, but it is not standard practice to use them during CRM studies. Often, when used, they are used inappropriately. Although these machines appear simple, they can be complicated and do require that a substantial amount of time be spent learning how to operate and use them effectively. Many relic hunters own several different kinds of metal detectors. Each machine operates differently, depending on numerous conditions such as mineralized soils, humidity, weather, time of day, soil moisture, and soil aridity. Given the factors that determine the quality of metal signals, it is unrealistic to expect satisfactory results if inexperienced people attempt metal detection. Unfortunately, this happens all too frequently when an untrained field crew is handed metal detectors during CRM investigations.

A preliminary review of established state guidelines for the proper conduct of field surveys and site testing in some states where the war occurred demonstrates the ineffectiveness of regulatory agencies to enact guidelines that consider military camps and the alternative field and historical research methods needed to find them (BHP 1991:15–18; Sanders 2001:22; Shaffer and Cole 1994:8; Trader 2001:3; VDHR 2000). Although some guidelines mention using metal detectors, no direction is given for appropriate historical research on military sites. Standard historical resources—such as deeds, chain of title, and property tax assessments—often will not reveal evidence a military occupation. If encampments and other military sites are suspected in an area, it is advised that additional historical research be undertaken at an early stage of the investigation. Resources such as local histories, the Official Records of the army and navy, and Civil War maps can provide general information. Reviewing primary resources such as regimental histories, military reports, and soldier's diaries likewise assists in locating Civil War sites and should be undertaken whenever feasible.

HOW RELIC HUNTERS FIND SITES

"Unlike the random antique collector, the relic hunter has researched his quarry; he has carefully studied a troop unit's movements to a given point, then sought out that specific camp site or skirmish area. Here, armed with a metal detector, if he is lucky enough to find and dig an artifact, he has an antique not just in the usual sense, but one that retells him the story" (Crouch 1978:1).

The information that relic hunters accumulate can be hard earned, and they usually keep their hunting areas secret. In most cases, they will not share information that would locate their specific hunting grounds. Many relic hunters will, however, trade information about various metal detectors, tips and techniques for finding sites, and locations of "hunted out" sites. General information on relic hunting is easily obtainable on World Wide Web relic-hunting forums (Buttafuso 2000:60). Relic hunters usually try to establish contacts with local landowners. Some will go out and knock on doors, not only to seek permission, but also to gain information about a locality's history. Unfortunately, some relic hunters will trespass, and landowners may not know that they have a Civil War site on their property or that the relic hunters are stealing their property. This leads to problems with landowners and to relic hunters' withholding information about sites on properties where they have trespassed. Many times relic hunters have withheld useful information because they did not receive permission to go on the private property and they know that what they did was illegal. This can also lead to problems with landowners who want to develop on a property but owing to past relic hunting have to undertake archaeological studies that otherwise may have been successfully avoided.

Knowing the history of a specific area helps relic hunters find sites. Much information can be gathered from the collective knowledge of local people (Buttafuso 2000:32; Espenshade et al. 2002:43; Poche Associates 2002:9). For example, local people may remember long-forgotten place names, specifics about an existing site's condition, and the locations where Civil War artifacts have been found in the past.

Successful relic hunters develop an ability to evaluate a landscape for its military potential (Poche Associates 2002:5). Many of them consider this research to be the most essential part of their hobby. Relic hunters do a lot of legwork. They will walk over areas specifically looking for potential sites. Additionally, successful relic hunters have an idea of what type of camp to expect. With a general knowledge of how Civil War camps are configured, relic hunters know where to concentrate their search to get the best results. Through research and past experiences, relic hunters understand typical camp layout and also have a good idea where in a camp to begin their search. They take into account factors such as wind direction and how it may have affected where trash pits and sinks were placed. Close examination of the local topography can provide insight into the location of picket posts, target ranges, privies, sinks, and other features.

Relic hunters find that an understanding of an area's historic transportation network is important because troop and supply movement was predominately along roads and railroads (Poche Associates 2002:5). Additionally, battles and skirmishes were fought to protect these routes. Homesites along roads were often stopping points for troops. Important crossroads, bridges, and river fords were frequently picketed (Poche Associates 2002:19). Railroad stops were important, and railroad beds were used as roads. Relic hunters ask questions such as what communities the transportation system connected and whether it went through a mountain gap that would have provided the only course of troop movement. If a road name was important enough to be mentioned in Civil War records, the probability of sites being located near it is high.

Historic maps are a commonly used resource for both archaeologists and relic hunters. Relic hunters use these maps the same way we do. Many historic maps identify Civil War period homesites and place names. These resources can be a good place to start site-specific research. The Official Records, damage claims, soldiers' diaries, regimental histories, and other resources can then be researched by property owner's name or by place name. If these homesites or place names were important enough to be mentioned, relic hunters have discovered that, if found, these sites often contain Civil War artifacts (Buttafuso 2000:33).

Relic hunters often search on construction sites. Modern construction methods commonly include clear-cutting and topsoil removal. These activities greatly increase the effectiveness of metal detectors in locating cultural remains by removing modern deposits and vegetation. It is common knowledge among relic hunters that, once an area has been cleared of vegetation and soil overburden, even sites once considered picked clean or collected for years can still yield artifacts and intact features (Buttafuso 2000:29).

Relic hunters do not necessarily rely solely on metal detectors. A majority of the better-known camps have been metal detected extensively, resulting in the removal of most near-surface artifacts. Relic hunters will then use alternative methods such as probes and the digging of test holes to locate trash pits and buried huts (D. P. Newton, personal communication 2001).

HOW WE HAVE INCORPORATED RELIC HUNTER INFORMATION INTO OUR WORK

In 2000, the Fairfax County Park Authority sponsored an inventory of county Civil War sites and events (Balicki, Culhane, et al. 2002). Fairfax County is approximately 260,000 acres. In the past thirty years, the county population has doubled, and undeveloped land dropped from 32 percent in 1980 to 9 percent in 2004 (Rein 2004:18). Like many jurisdictions, Fairfax County is pro-development and, in most cases, requires little in the way of cultural resource studies. Although thousands of sites have been recorded in Fairfax, the rapid transformation of the county's landscape has resulted in the destruction of an unknown number of archaeological sites, many of these dating to the Civil War.

Between May 1861 and March 9, 1862, northern Virginia was the major war front in the east. The Federal army established a foothold in Virginia, occupying an approximately twelve-mile front along the Potomac River bluffs overlooking the capital. After their victory at the Battle of First Manassas (Bull Run), the Confederate army established an approximately forty-two-mile front anchored on the Potomac River. The main Confederate army, approximately thirty-two thousand troops, established winter camps behind extensive earthworks at Centreville, approximately twenty miles west of the Federal camps in Alexandria. The area between the armies, comprising most of Fairfax County, was "no man's land." On March 9, 1862, the Confederates withdrew for logistical reasons.

Both armies swept across this region in the summer of 1862 when the Battle of Second Manassas and the Battle of Chantilly (Ox Hill) took place. For the remainder of the war, northern Virginia became the defensive outer perimeter for Washington. Strategic towns, villages, rail stations, road intersections, and bridges were guarded by Federal troops, and the Confederate presence consisted of groups of partisan rangers and bushwhackers.

The goal of the Fairfax project was to develop a Civil War site database to allow county planners to consider these resources during future planning projects. Although the area was intensely occupied during the war, no comprehensive history of either army's use of the region had been undertaken. In fact, few historians know much about the area's Civil War history. Accordingly, the project included development of a site database based on historic research, fieldwork, and community involvement. Public meetings were held, local Civil War roundtables were contacted, and the assistance of relic hunters was actively sought. The project team would not have recorded as many sites or gained as much insight into the dynamics of the war in this area without relic-hunter community input. At the beginning of the inventory, 2,625 archaeological sites were identified within the county, but only 80 were Civil War sites. By the end of the project, the number of recorded Civil War sites had increased to 650 (Balicki, Culhane, et al. 2002). Also identified were 200 locations where events had occurred but no archaeological resources could be expected.

Our role was to contact relic hunters and ask them for information. Prior to the Fairfax project, we had had few dealings with relic hunters. During the early stage of the project, local officials told us that we probably would be rebuffed, but they required us to attend a NVRHA meeting. The first meeting we attended was in the spring of 2001. The meeting hall was filled with over a hundred people who came to hear a talk about Federal camps in Stafford County, Virginia, given by a relic hunter who grew up exploring this area. Upon hearing the talk and listening to the questions, we realized that we were Civil War neophytes. We did not expect the level and quality of historic research, the adeptness at locating sites, the knowledge of Civil War material culture, and the general enthusiasm that individuals within this group showed for commemorating the war in their own way. When we presented the goals of the Fairfax project, we simply asked for their assistance. Given what archaeologists had been telling us, we didn't really expect much of a response. We were wrong. The dialogue that began that night continues, and we still attend monthly meetings and are better archaeologists for it. Not only did many members provide us with site information, they also provided primary and secondary historical sources to back up what they were saying.

How to Find Civil War Campsites

The focus of this section is on identifying Civil War campsites, not battlefields or skirmish sites. Some of the following information is based on how relic hunters find Civil War sites; the remainder is from archaeologists with experience in finding these site types. By using a combination of these sources, we have come up with ways in which archaeologists who have little experience and are working under the time constraints and budget limitations of CRM can improve their chances of identifying encampments. We have used some of these methods in a successful investigation of a 193-acre, well-preserved Confederate cantonment site (see chapter 5).

The most expedient method for finding out if a particular location contains a Civil War site is to ask local relic hunters. Locating relic hunters is not hard; contact a local relic-hunter club, local archaeologists who have relic-hunter contacts, metal detector dealers, and local historians. Where possible, relic hunters' information should be cross-checked using historic research and other relic hunters' accounts. If Civil War sites are suspected, in addition to talking with relic hunters, archaeologists should conduct more background research prior to initiating fieldwork. Whoever conducts the background research should have knowledge of using military history resources. The Official Records (O.R.) of the War of the Rebellion (O.R. 1997; O.R.N. 1999) and the Official Records Supplement (Hewett 1998) are an excellent resource and can be particularly useful, especially early in the war when recording was more detailed. However, the Official Records are not an end-all but only a first step (Buttafuso 2000:35). If specific troops can be identified, other good sources are regimental histories, historic maps, soldier's diaries, and damage claims.

- If known Civil War camps are within an area, identifying what troops were there and when can assist in defining research questions and methodology. This information will help identify what camp types and features to expect. Winter camps often contain subtle surface features and architectural artifacts while summer camps may contain only artifact scatters. Further, factors such as the effectiveness of policing, discipline, date of occupation, and how a camp was abandoned can affect artifact density. This information is invaluable for developing appropriate field strategies.

- When using historic maps, researchers should pay special attention to the transportation networks, historic place names, and people's names. This information can be cross-referenced with other resource materials.
- View historic maps with a general idea of military tactics. Armies defended and protected specific locations. At what places are there crossroads, river fords, or bridges? Where are the railroad stops, bridges, and stations? What was the strategic importance of the area when viewed regionally?

If research indicates that a camp or military site may be present, a field visit is recommended. During a reconnaissance visit, the following should be taken into consideration.

- What are the site conditions? Is the site in forest? Is the site covered in modern trash, is it in the vicinity of modern or historic structures? If the site has been disturbed, what are the levels of disturbance? Site conditions can be a very important consideration and will affect the best approach. For example, if a site is covered with modern metallic trash or thick vegetation, an intensive metal-detector survey will require a lot more time to attain successful results. Keep in mind, inexperienced metal-detector users will find it very difficult to discriminate between trashy signals and Civil War artifacts. If a site is covered in fill, the use of machinery or large block excavations may be a better approach.
- Are there visible surface remains such as hut depressions, tent platforms, paths, road traces, drainage features, and entrenchments?
- Is there obvious evidence that the site has been relic hunted? Relic hunters will often leave large iron artifacts such as horseshoes and cast-iron vessel fragments against the base of trees. Often, unwanted metal and trash are hung on branches. The relic hunters may have not filled in their holes or may have left behind a scattering of spent batteries.
- There is a distinct time of the year when Civil War campsites can be more readily identified. Many camps contain subtle, indistinct surface features. These features are best identified during the winter and early spring, when ground cover and leaf litter has had time to settle and become compacted. Many Civil War camp features, such as tent sites and drainage features, are shallow and are quickly rendered invisible when the ground cover begins to grow or newly fallen leaf litter covers them. A light snowfall often outlines features (see chapter 5).
- Civil War camps require differing methodologies at a Phase I level to attain successful results. Using mechanically assisted stripping at a Phase I level

should be considered, since military campsites often contain few artifacts or the artifacts are concentrated at discrete locations. In such cases, machine-assisted stripping may be the only way to find physical evidence of the site.

Field methodologies will vary depending on camp type, level of investigation, and field conditions. The following list contains some field methods that should be considered. None of the methods is particularly new to archaeology, but when the methods are put together in a commonsense approach, the chances of finding a camp increases.

- Conduct a walk-over survey to locate and then map surface features.
- Carefully evaluate depressions that might be considered tree falls. Archaeologists not familiar with camp layouts containing hut features will often interpret these features as tree falls, even when they are arranged in regular patterns and rows.
- Rake out all visible surface features. Raking helps expose the features in greater detail, exposing past relic-hunter digging, firebox and chimney remnants, visible surface artifacts, and drainage features. Raking away the leaf litter also helps increase the effective depth of metal detection.
- Personnel who are experienced with metal detectors should conduct the metal detection. An intensive metal-detector survey will not be successful if untrained or inexperienced crew members are used.
- Metal-detector hits should be mapped and recorded as one would record shovel tests. This will help the initial assessment of site stratigraphy and integrity.
- Shovel tests or test units should be excavated at metallic concentrations identified during metal-detector survey. Metallic concentrations can indicate the presence of trash pits, huts, and activity areas (Buttafuso 2000:62).
- If the site is covered in fill or a plowzone, machine stripping should be conducted to reach cultural deposits. Metal detectors can then be used and the stripped surface examined for features.
- If machine stripping is not an option, block excavation can be used effectively to identify features.
- Stripped areas and the resulting spoil piles should be metal detected; metal detectors have greater depth effectiveness in stripped areas. Spoil piles should be checked, as they may contain artifacts previously masked by concentrations of iron. Although out of context, these artifacts may contain information on the troops occupying the site.
- If the camp is located near a field edge, close inspection of an adjacent tree

line may indicate surface features such as hut depressions, tent platforms, entrenchments, and metal discarded by relic hunters that can guide excavations.

- After the camp layout and metal-detector survey results are recorded on the site map, it may then be possible to determine distances between hut features and the width and length of company streets. These measurements should then be used to project where buried features might be located.

- Based on projected locations of possible buried features, shovel tests should be used at areas that may contain buried features. Additional shovel testing should be done at metallic concentrations to sample for nonmetal artifact deposits.

- If features are identified as a result of stripping, they should be promptly excavated unless the site is guarded. It is not advisable to sample features or leave them partially excavated. If you are on a known Civil War site, if you dig it they (relic hunters) will come.

Conclusion

The attitude of noncooperation and general mistrust between relic hunters and archaeologists has resulted in numerous Civil War sites going unrecorded. As a result, many sites have been destroyed without being investigated. An archaeologist once put forth the argument that by talking to relic hunters we were condoning what they do and giving them legitimacy, and that including them in projects as volunteers set a bad precedent. We reject this notion and feel that it really misses the point. The relic-hunter community has valuable information. Granted, their view differs from ours in terms of the overriding emphasis on material culture, owning objects, and not recording context. However, both sides—archaeologists and relic hunters—can greatly benefit from mutual cooperation. Common ground can be found on shared issues such as battlefield preservation and limiting unregulated development. Communication will facilitate an understanding of federal and local laws concerning relic hunting; right now a lot of inaccurate information passes for truth, and some relic hunters may honestly not know they are on protected lands. In certain cases, the situation is made worse when federal and state employees who do not know, or choose to ignore, relevant legislation and permit relic hunting on protected lands.

The biggest threat to archaeological sites is not from relic hunting. The threats from uncontrolled development and lack of regulatory oversight are much more destructive. The accelerated pace of development in areas with past

Civil War activity is quickly destroying sites (Crouch 1978:ii, 1995:1). At locations that have been developed, the collective memory of relic hunters is often the only link to physical remains of the Civil War. In areas threatened with development, relic-hunter information can provide a clear indication of resources that may be present and can provide a starting point for historic research. To disregard or ignore a body of knowledge because individuals or groups outside of mainstream archaeology and history gathered the information is shortsighted (Espenshade et al. 2002:42).

The fact that the majority of relic hunters are better at locating Civil War sites than the majority of archaeologists should be alarming to the preservation community. Further, steps must be taken to ensure that Civil War site destruction does not happen as a result of generalizations in state guidelines. For a profession with an overriding goal of "preserving the past for the future," overlooking Civil War encampments owing to the use of inappropriate methods is indefensible and worth addressing.

ACKNOWLEDGMENTS

The authors of this chapter would like to extend their thanks to the following agencies, groups, and individuals: The Fairfax County Park Authority; Northern Virginia Relic Hunters Association (NVRHA); Jeff Gardner, Natural Resources Affairs Branch, Marine Corps Base Quantico; Kerri Holland and Charles D. Cheek, John Milner Associates, Inc.; Robert L. Jolley, Virginia Department of Historic Resources; John McAnaw, Bull Run Civil War Roundtable; D. P. Newton, White Oak Museum; and numerous relic hunters who, unfortunately, prefer to remain anonymous.

REFERENCES CITED

Balicki, Joseph F.
2001   Defending the Capital: The Civil War Garrison at Fort C. F. Smith. In *Archaeological Perspectives on the American Civil War.* Edited by Clarence R. Geier and Stephen Potter, pp. 125–47, University of Florida Press, Gainesville.
Balicki, Joseph, Kerri Culhane, Walton H. Owen II, and Donna J. Seifert
2002   Fairfax County Civil War Sites Inventory, Technical Report Version. John Milner Associates, Alexandria, Va. Report submitted to Fairfax County Park Authority, Fairfax, Va.

Balicki, Joseph, Katherine L. Farnham, Bryan Corle, and Stuart J. Fiedel
2002   Multiple Cultural Resources Investigations, Marine Corps Base Quantico, Prince William and Stafford Counties, Virginia. John Milner Associates, Alexandria, Va. Report submitted to EDAW, Inc., Alexandria, Va.

Bureau for Historic Preservation (BHP)
1991   *Cultural Resource Management in Pennsylvania: Guidelines for Archaeological Investigations.* Harrisburg, Penn.

Buttafuso, Robert A.
2000   *Civil War Relic Hunting A to Z.* Sheridan Books, Ann Arbor, Mich.

Crouch, Howard R.
1978   *Relic Hunter: The Field Account of Civil War Sites, Artifacts, and Hunting.* SCS Publications, Fairfax, Va.
1995   *Civil War Artifacts: A Guide for the Historian.* SCS Publications, Fairfax, Va.

Donald, David Herbert (editor)
1975   *Gone for a Soldier: The Civil War Memoirs of Private Alfred Bellard.* Little, Brown, Boston, Mass.

Espenshade, Christopher T., Robert L. Jolley, and James B. Legg
2002   The Value and Treatment Of Civil War Military Sites. *North American Archeologist* 23(1):39–67.

Geier, Clarence R., and Stephen R. Potter (editors)
2000   *Archeological Perspectives on the American Civil War.* University Press of Florida, Gainesville.

Geier, Clarence R., and Susan E. Winter (editors)
1994   *Look to the Earth: Historical Archeology and the American Civil War.* University of Tennessee Press, Knoxville.

Hewett, Janet B. (editor)
1998   *Supplement to the Official Records of the Union and Confederate Armies.* Broadfoot Publishing Company, Wilmington, N.C.

London, Don
1998   NVRHA http://www.nvrha.com/stnhouse.HTM

Nevins, Allan (editor)
1962   *A Diary of Battle: The Personal Journals of Colonel Charles S. Wainwright (1861–1865).* Harcourt, Brace and World, New York.

O'Donnell, Michael J., and Eddie Wilder
1999   Fort Knox Camp of the 4th Maine Volunteers. *North-South Trader's Civil War* 26(6):38–57.

Official Records of the Union and Confederate Armies (O.R.)
1997   *The War of the Rebellion: A Compilation of the Official Records of the Union and*

Confederate Armies. CD-ROM version, originally published 1880–1901. Guild Press of Indiana, Carmel.

Official Records of the Union and Confederate Navies (O.R.N.)

1999   *Official Records of the Union and Confederate Navies in the War of the Rebellion.* CD-ROM version, originally published 1894. H-Bar Enterprises, Oakman, Ala.

Poche Associates

2002   *Finding Civil War Campsites in Rural Areas.* Blue and Grey Book Shoppe, Independence, Mo.

Rein, Lisa

2004   Buying Spree Only the Beginning. *Fairfax Extra of the Washington Post* [Washington, D.C.], 29 January, pp. 18–19.

Reeves, Matthew B.

2001   *Dropped and Fired: Archaeological Patterns of Militaria from Two Civil War Battles, Manassas National Battlefield Park, Manassas, Virginia.* Occasional Report no. 15. Regional Archaeological Program, National Capital Region, National Park Service, Washington, D.C.

Sanders, Thomas N. (editor)

2001   *Specifications for Conducting Fieldwork and Preparing Cultural Resource Assessment Reports.* Revised from 1991 issue. Kentucky State Historic Preservation Office, Frankfort.

Scott, Douglas D., and Richard A. Fox Jr.

1987   *Archaeological Insights into the Custer Battle: An Assessment of the 1987 Field Season.* University of Oklahoma Press, Norman.

Shaffer, Gary, and Elizabeth Cole

1994   *Standards and Guidelines for Archeological Investigations in Maryland.* Technical Report No. 2. Maryland Historical Trust, Crownsville.

Smith, Steve D.

1994 Archeological Perspectives of the Civil War: The Challenge to Achieve Relevance. In *Look to the Earth: Historical Archeology and the American Civil War.* Edited by Clarence R. Geier, Jr., and Susan E. Winter, pp. 3–20, The University of Tennessee Press, Knoxville.

Sylvia, Stephen W., and Michael J. O'Donnell

1978   *The Illustrated History of American Civil War Relics.* Publisher's Press, Orange, Va.

Trader, Patrick

2001   *Guidelines for Phase I, II, and III Archaeological Investigations and Technical Report Preparation.* West Virginia State Historic Preservation Office, Charleston.

Virginia Department of Historic Resources (VDHR)

2000   *Guidelines for Conducting Cultural Resource Survey in Virginia.* Richmond.

4

Guarding the Junction

The Encampment of the 14th New Jersey Volunteer Infantry

BRANDON S. BIES

Throughout most of the American Civil War, the typical soldier spent only a few days out of the year engaged in combat. Instead, his time was mostly spent either on campaign or living at a long-term camp. For this reason, long-term encampments can provide a wealth of information, both through archaeological remains and through historical documents, about the common soldier's life. In the past, most scholars have attempted to tell the Civil War soldier's story through the details of combat. Instead, one must look at the historical and archaeological evidence of numerous military encampments to understand the war and its participants in a proper context. One such site, Camp Hooker, is located just outside Frederick, Maryland, adjacent to what is now Monocacy National Battlefield.

This chapter illustrates the importance of utilizing both historical and archaeological data to identify and interpret Civil War encampments. Unfortunately, owing to a serious and real risk of looting, only limited archaeological evidence is presented. Instead, the chapter focuses on historical accounts crucial to understanding encampments and also demonstrates the threat that exists to such resources. Through a combination of intensive development and relic hunting, few Civil War encampments retain a high level of archaeological integrity. While some tools utilized by relic hunters and Civil War archaeologists are identical, the methodologies, mentalities, and intentions of these two groups could not be more different.

THE FIRST DAYS AT MONOCACY JUNCTION

The 14th New Jersey Volunteer Infantry was formed on July 8, 1862, on the old Monmouth Battlefield near Freehold, New Jersey. For the next two months, roughly one thousand men were mustered, armed, equipped, and trained at Camp Vredenburgh (Terrill 1884:5–6). The camp earned its name from a prominent local judge, Peter Vredenburgh Sr., whose son was killed two years later leading the regiment at the Battle of Third Winchester (Martin 1987:200–201). Like members of regiments of both sides, many men of the 14th New Jersey were eager to face the enemy for the first time. With the Confederate advance into northern Virginia and then western Maryland in early September 1862, the regiment soon had its chance.

On Monday, September 1, 1862, orders were received to break camp and embark for Washington, D.C. The men boarded trains that took them to Philadelphia and then got into baggage cars to Baltimore. While the regiment was waiting for trains bound for Washington, D.C., the orders were changed and the troops soon found themselves on the way to Frederick Junction, on the Baltimore and Ohio Railroad, 58 miles west of Baltimore (Terrill 1884:7–8). The men camped near the junction overnight.

However, the following morning they received word that Confederates under the command of General Thomas J. "Stonewall" Jackson had crossed the Potomac into Maryland. Colonel William S. Truex knew that his "green" regiment would be no match for such a large contingent of the Confederate Army, so the 14th New Jersey quickly struck tents, boarded trains yet again, and traveled back toward Baltimore. By all accounts, the regiment had been gone no more than one hour when Confederate soldiers reached the junction. The Confederates destroyed the depot and burned the strategically important railroad bridge (8–9). When he learned of the news, Major Vredenburgh wrote: "The bridges over the Monacacy which we were sent to protect we have since learned from reliable authority have been blown up and we would have taken the same elevating tour if we had remained there" (Olsen 1993:32).

Approximately ten days later, on September 17, the regiment returned to find the place laid waste. Lieutenant Marcus Stults described the situation:

> We are at Frederick Junction yet, but do not know how long we will stay here. The chances are we will stay some time, to guard the Monocacy Bridge on the B&O R.R. The bridge I spoke of, I told you in my former letter the rebels had burned, but a new one has been erected. The bridge is 400 feet long and 60 feet above the water. It was rebuilt in about four days—quick work. Frederick Junction has been a busy place since the bridge was burned[,] for all army stores intended for Harpers Ferry have been transported by wagons from here. You can form no estimate and I but a poor estimate of the number of wagons employed. The road was filled with them and hundreds of ambulances were constantly employed in carrying the wounded off the battlefield bringing them here, to be sent home

and to hospitals in different parts of the country. . . . About 1000 rebel prisoners were also sent here. We kept them a day and night, and then they were sent to Fort Delaware—three companies of the 14th being sent with them as guards. They were a rough looking set of men, and as strong on the secession question as ever (Olsen 1993:42–43).

As it turned out, the regiment remained at Monocacy Junction longer than anyone had imagined. They immediately named their encampment Camp Hooker, in honor of General Joseph Hooker. From then until the regiment's departure the following June, the men continuously fortified and improved their position until it became a small, self-sufficient city, complete with a hospital, store, theater and church, and jail.

When the 14th New Jersey arrived at Monocacy Junction in September 1862, the majority of soldiers found it to be a rather agreeable spot. Major Vredenburgh wrote home,

> To refer to a more pleasant subject Mother, this country here is beautiful. Tell Henry, he would never get tired of scanning over the fields here, the country is so lovely and beautiful. The Monocacy reminds me a good deal of the Raritan as it appears between Uncle Van Dorn's & Sommerville. It is fordable in as many places and Bill [Vredenburgh's servant] takes great pleasure in bathing and washing the horses in it every day. On each side of the river particularly on the westerly side, the fields are fertile and rise gradually till they are lost in the mountains which run between us and the Potomac. (Olsen 1993:38)

Private William Burroughs Ross expressed similar sentiments in a letter to his cousin: "We are encamped on a hill alongside of Monocacy Creek. We have a splendid view from where we lay and it is very healthy here so far" (Olsen 1993:45).

ESTABLISHING THE CAMP

When the men realized that they would be remaining at Monocacy Junction for more than just a few days, they organized a more permanent camp set out according to strict military guidelines (U.S. War Department 1861:76). The standards allowed for a full regiment of one thousand men, as well as their accompanying horses and supplies, to be laid out in an area measuring 400 paces wide by 481 paces long (see figure 2.5). At the very front of the camp was placed the guardhouse, followed by the sinks, or latrines. These were then followed by a parade ground measuring 400 paces by 150 paces. Next were ten streets, one for each company, lined by the appropriate number of tents or huts for the regiment's enlisted men. Adjacent to these streets were ten company cookhouses, each one responsible for feeding a company of enlisted men. Beyond the company streets were the company officers, and behind this were the field and staff officers of the regiment. In the camp's rear were the support elements, such as baggage trains and stables, and then the officer's sinks. However, the regulations gave commanding officers some leniency in laying out their camp, specifically with regard to the terrain (U.S. War Department 1861:76–79).

A private soldier's detailed sketch illustrated the layout of Camp Hooker a few months after the regiment arrived at Monocacy Junction. The sketch, included in a letter written by Corporal James Bullman to George Bullman on January 18, 1863 (Bullman 1863), revealed many similarities to, and some inconsistencies with, the War Department regulations (figure 4.1). Bullman described the map:

> I have undertaken to make a sketch of our camp and its surroundings which you will find inside. It is new business to me therefore not a perfect work but near enough to give some idea of how things look, around yer (as a Marylander would have it). . . . The cross near the center of the camp is intended to represent the tent in which I reside. Those straddlesbugs which you see posted on the outside of the encampment are intended to represent the guards on their several posts. (Bullman 1863)

Bullman, who was declared missing in action and presumed dead at Cold Harbor, clearly stated that this was a sketch and not a perfect map. However, it is a crucial source for understanding Camp Hooker's layout.

The Bullman sketch was also important in understanding the camp layout with regard to the War Department regulations. Rather than ten company streets with each company's quarters on both sides, the living quarters at Camp Hooker were all arranged in single rows by company (figure 4.1). Also, rather than the entire camp being placed on one axis, a number of structures were placed to either side. The guardhouse, stables, and an additional structure appear on the eastern side, while the commissary and sutler appear on the western. While Bullman may not have illustrated every structure, there are no buildings indicated behind the officer's quarters. The sinks are not illustrated.

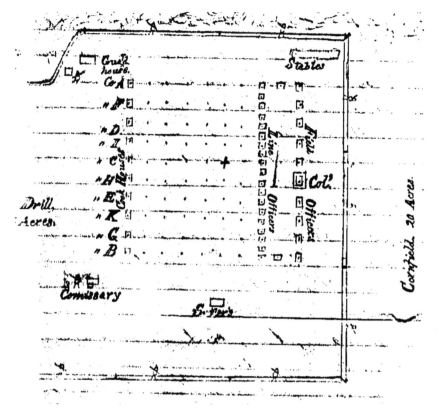

Figure 4.1. Portion of sketch map by Corporal James Bullman of Camp Hooker. The X in the center of the camp represents Bullman's hut (Bullman 1863).

LIVING QUARTERS

Letters written by a number of soldiers from Camp Hooker supported the sketch map's particulars and offer many additional details. When the regiment first reached Monocacy Junction, the soldiers made several references to sleeping in tents. These references continued for the first month or so that the 14th New Jersey was stationed at the junction. In all likelihood, the men did not know that they would remain here several months, so they did not bother to construct permanent structures. Instead, they were content with their government-issue shelter halves, also named dog tents, designed to be buttoned together down the center to form one small tent with two open ends. Shelter tents were approximately five feet square, with barely enough space for two soldiers. Some men, particularly the officers, may have used the more spacious

Figure 4.2. The officers' quarters at Camp Hooker would have been similar to this structure at Brandy Station, Virginia. The officers are in front of winter quarters at Army of the Potomac headquarters (February 1864) (photographer unknown, possibly Mathew Brady; Library of Congress, LC-B817–7161).

A-frame tents that gave soldiers significantly more room (Gaede 2001). In the end, neither tent style would have provided soldiers much protection from the elements.

There were some differences between the quarters of officers and those of the enlisted men, and there is evidence that the officers began to improve their tents earlier (figure 4.2). Perhaps the most detailed description of officers' quarters comes from Major Peter Vredenburgh. Writing home on October 20, 1862, he stated, "It is storming violently and consequently we are all confined to our tents, which are as comfortable under our present arrangement as a house. Some of the officers having brick fireplaces and chimneys while others, I amongst the latter, have stoves. I have a neat little cast iron one and Bill always keeps on hand a bountiful supply of hickory wood, so that it is really quite cheerful and cozy" (Olsen 1993:58).

Private Jacob R. Wolcott provided additional details about the officer's quarters. He wrote, "Today I have been putting a floor in the Col.'s tent and he treated me twice to good brandy, the first I have had since I left old Jersey" (Ol-

Figure 4.3. Sergeant Albert Harrison, Company G, 14th New Jersey Infantry (1862–63) (photographer unknown; taken in Frederick, Maryland; private collection, courtesy of Steve Meadow).

sen 1993:70). While these letters mention officers' tents, the term could refer to improved structures that utilized a tent as the roof but were built of wood throughout the remainder of the structure.

Although the officers may have had more spacious quarters, the enlisted men soon followed in improving their living conditions. By all accounts, the men realized by mid-November that they would remain at Monocacy Junction for the winter. While some may have waited for explicit orders from Colonel Truex, others may have had more unofficial methods of improving their quarters. Sergeant Albert C. Harrison (figure 4.3) offered a detailed description of how he set about improving his tent,

We have worked all day long stockading our tents. We cut logs five feet in length, then dug a trench around our tents two feet deep, leaving three feet above ground. We then chucked up the cracks and dabbed it with mud, that is as far as we could get with it. So God willing we will commence again in the morning and take down our tent and set it on the stockade, so it will give us more room. But the worst of all, we will have to tear down our chimney as it will come too far in the center of our tent, but we can soon stick it up again and then we can live like folks if Uncle Sam lets us stay here long enough to pay us for our trouble. (Olsen 1993:67–68)

Sergeant Harrison's description may be representative of other 14th New Jersey soldiers. Just before the regiment left Camp Hooker, Harrison wrote that "the men are at work carrying away the dirt from around the stockades so as to white wash them tomorrow morning. We expect the Governor of the little state of New Jersey to pay us a visit tomorrow and we want to have things in trim" (Olsen 1993:117). Presumably, Harrison was speaking about the stockades supporting each tent. This would indicate that from mid-November 1862 until June 1863, soldiers lived in semipermanent structures that should leave a substantial archaeological footprint.

Besides improving and insulating their tents, most soldiers constructed bunks rather than sleeping on the cold ground. There are multiple references to soldiers utilizing several blankets at once, an option not available to an infantryman on the march. Some men, particularly officers, designed various types of beds. In a letter to his mother, Major Vredenburgh stated, "I have fitted a board frame over my cot which keeps the straw and blankets on and prevents the cold wind from penetrating as it used to before I had it so fixed. About 11 or 12 at night Dash finds it too cold for him on the bricks by the stove and so he very quietly and gently gets upon my bed and immediately lies down on my feet and so we mutually warm each other" (Olsen 1993:73). Lieutenant Marcus Stults described a similar style of bed that he devised: "We got the boys to put us up a 'patent' bed—my patent, but still it won't sell in Jersey. It is made by driving crutches in the ground for posts and instead of bedcord, we use cross poles and then with a straw bedtick and four or five woolen blankets we sleep first rate" (Olsen 1993:49–50).

Other than great variation in structure types that the officers and men constructed at Camp Hooker, it is important to understand the camp's size. According to Lieutenant Marcus Stults, there were always at least 125 fires burning twenty hours each day, and wood was carried in at a price of five dollars per cord

(Olsen 1993:97). What is even more interesting is that this was at a time when several companies were on detached service and not living at Camp Hooker. At its peak, Camp Hooker likely consisted of over two hundred structures housing nearly a thousand soldiers.

GUARDHOUSE AND COOKHOUSES

The regiment's men were engaged not only in improving their living quarters, but also in improving the camp as a whole. Private Wolcott wrote home, "I think it looks very much like we will be staying here this winter. Your humble servant J. R. W. assisted to build 2 bake ovens and sheds to cover them. Time I get home, I will be able to build houses, dig ditches, carrying brick-stone, etc. which I have had a hand in last week—building log houses and stables" (Olsen 1993:64). Sergeant Harrison wrote his mother on November 9, 1862, "It is almost certain that we will stay here all winter. We will cart logs I think tomorrow for the purpose of building kitchens, also to finish our guard house. The colonel intends to have the church and guard house together. The building is forty feet by sixty. It will be a right smart building" (Olsen 1993:62). Another description is offered by Private William B. Ross, who stated, "We are preparing winter quarters here expecting to sojourn in this vicinity during the winter months. All the companies have log kitchens put up at the end of their row of tents and now the men are engaged [in] erecting a guard house, two stories high—upstairs will be all one room—will hold five hundred men, which will be used as a concert room for darkey performances, theatricals, etc. and I suppose on Sunday will be used for preaching" (Olsen 1993:63).

Additional evidence about constructing the guardhouse can be found at the National Archives and Records Administration (NARA). One such source is the Regimental Books, which include orders and morning reports. One order details a general court martial in which a soldier is accused of numerous violations: Private Jacob Kiefer "did willfully and maliciously break out and destroy by violence the window lights of the guard house" (NARA, RG 94, Regimental Books, March 23, 1863). This would indicate that the guardhouse was constructed with glass windowpanes.

Finally, as impressive as some accounts described the guardhouse to be, there is evidence that it may have not lived up to expectations. Following the departure of a section of Battery L, 5th U.S. Artillery (which had also been stationed at Monocacy Junction), Sergeant Harrison wrote, "We have taken one of their buildings for a guard house as it was far better than our old one" (Olsen 1993:95–96).

Other sources describe the regiment's cookhouses. Sergeant Harrison wrote his mother about one of his meals: "I have just finished my breakfast and a hearty one it was on roast beef, fresh bread and coffee. Our cook house is finished and you can hardly touch Joe Reeves with a ten foot pole now. He is as happy as any lord, although he is in a log cabin" (Olsen 1993:65).

Another description of the cookhouse comes from an unexpected source, a postwar pension record. Sergeant Jervis N. Bennett, of Company B, claimed a pension for having broken his leg while at Camp Hooker. In fact, Bennett's leg was broken so severely (in two places) that he was discharged from the army. However, the significance of this pension request is not in the injury but in the description of the incident. According to a noncommissioned officer who witnessed the incident, the accident occurred when Bennett "came in from picket duty (a time of 24 hours continuous duty) some time in the fore noon, in the midst of a storm of 'sleet.' He went into the cook-house to get his rations, and whilst so employed fell in such a way as to induce a compound fracture of his right leg . . . caused by slipping, the floor of the cook house being very slippery and muddy caused by the rain and snow, the roof being covered with brush" (NARA, RG 19).

While all company cookhouses may not have been identical, this pension record may describe a common style. It would appear to describe a structure with wood or log sides and a dirt floor. Rather than covering the structure with a tent fly, the men appear to have used brush, with pine boughs being the most obvious choice for this task.

OTHER CAMP IMPROVEMENTS

Besides building and maintaining structures, the men were constantly engaged in other camp projects. Perhaps the first and most important improvements involved fortifying the camp by constructing defensive entrenchments throughout much of the surrounding area. Just ten days after establishing Camp Hooker, Private Jacob Wolcott finished a letter to his friend by stating, "I must close this—the order is to dig trenches. I am going to sneak out of it if I can. Good many of our boys are taken suddenly sick—but the Colonel is a little too sharp for them—his advice—a lead pill" (Olsen 1993:47). A number of these trenches are still evident along the ridge overlooking the Monocacy River on National Park Service property.

Once immediate priorities were accomplished, other improvements were made. Some were practical, while others were purely decorative. Sergeant Harrison described one such task: "When it [the rain] held up in the afternoon the colonel set the men at work carrying slate stone to macadamize our avenues. . . . The work was to give them exercise more than anything else but after we get that job done it will be a good thing for us because it will keep us from tracking so much mud in our tents" (Olsen 1993:66). Private Ross wrote his mother shortly after Christmas and described the trimming of the camp with greenery (Olsen 1993:80). While these decorations would leave no archaeological evidence, they are important in that they remind us that the camp's appearance was constantly changing.

LIFE AT CAMP HOOKER

While the 14th New Jersey was continuously engaged in constructing fortifications and making other camp improvements, they also guarded and patrolled the surrounding countryside. Some guard details began immediately after settling at Monocacy Junction, when thousands of wounded men and prisoners flooded the area. At this time, letters home reflect pity for the maimed and suffering men of both sides, many of whom passed through the junction on their way to various hospitals and prisons. Lieutenant Marcus Stults wrote his parents about one such train: "It was an awful sight—thousands, shot & maimed in every possible manner. Some of them shot so badly one would think they could not live an hour. One man was shot between the eye and ear—the ball passing through the head and coming out in the same place on the opposite side" (Olsen 1993:43). Major Peter Vredenburgh described a similar scene to his mother, "The 800 rebel prisoners are still shivering on the bare ground within 100 yards of my tent. The wounded Union men are still moaning at the railroad not ¼ of a mile off, and yet all this misery & suffering must be endured" (Olsen 1993:38). It is likely that these sights and sounds left a lasting impression on the newly enlisted soldiers of the 14th New Jersey.

Time at Camp Hooker during late September and early October appears to have been spent guarding prisoners and assisting in the general cleanup of Monocacy Junction after its partial destruction by the raiding Confederates. Three companies were detailed to guard prisoners being transported to the new Federal prison camp at Fort Delaware (Olsen 1993:36–39). By early October, many men were occupied with improving both their personal quarters and camp structures such as cookhouses and a guardhouse. These duties occupied the regiment for much of October and November (Olsen 1993:49–68).

The relative peacefulness of the regiment's duty was suddenly interrupted on October 12, when news of a large body of Confederate cavalry was reported at Urbana, just four miles to the south. All but two companies were immediately dispatched toward Urbana, along with a section of Battery L, 5th U.S. Artillery, which was also stationed at the junction. Estimates of enemy troop strength varied wildly, from 250 to 5,000. Upon arriving in town, the men learned that the Confederates had escaped and that the force most likely numbered approximately 250 men. This experience raised the anxiety levels of many troops, who appear to have preferred to fight it out with the small band of Confederates (Olsen 1993:53–59; Terrill 1884:11–12).

In early December, there were additional run-ins with Confederate or guerilla forces, none of which involved a shot being fired. Except for these occasional scares and false alarms, the men appear to have become increasingly bored and depressed after months of relatively easy camp duty. Recently promoted Sergeant William Burroughs Ross wrote his mother of one such false alarm: "Capt. Conover's company went up to Urbana . . . with the expectation of seeing some Rebs and I only went along to see the fun, but we came back without seeing a Reb. It was the only time I have been out and only went there for a little excitement. For it nearly gives one the blues to stay here doing nothing" (Olsen 1993:74). Sergeant Albert C. Harrison wrote his mother just five days later on December 18, 1862, and described the departure of another regiment stationed at the junction: "The 29th Regt. has been taken to the front. But we still hang around old Camp Hooker and to tell the truth I don't think we will leave here this winter. But come what will we are prepared for the worst" (Olsen 1993:75).

The 14th New Jersey celebrated their first Christmas away from home with fine dinners and festivities. The majority of the men (with the exception of camp guards) were given passes to visit nearby Frederick or other places of interest (Olsen 1993:77). In addition, Camp Hooker itself was decorated for the holiday. Sergeant Ross wrote his mother on December 30, "You ought to see our camp now, all trimmed up in greens, every avenue has an arch of greens over it with the letter of the company on it in evergreen. We had a twenty pound Turkey on Christmas and on New Years we will have another. The Col. came in our mess tent the other day to see how we fared. He was surprised to see the style we had things, and told us we lived better than he did himself" (Olsen 1993:80–81).

Shortly into the new year, companies of the regiment were sent on detached service away from Camp Hooker. On January 7, 1863, Company K was sent to Monrovia, along the railroad, where they established a small camp. On April 28, Companies A, C, D, H, F, and I were dispatched to Harpers Ferry and returned to Camp Hooker in late May (NARA, RG 94, Regimental Books, 1863). There was little activity at Camp Hooker, and the remaining men continued their daily routine of guard duty and camp details.

The final days of the 14th New Jersey at Camp Hooker were marked by two special occasions. On May 26, the entire regiment turned out to present a sword to Colonel Truex from the company officers. Two weeks later, on June 11, the regiment again turned out when a set of regimental and national colors was presented to the unit (Olsen 1993:116–18). This was perhaps in anticipation of a shift in the duties of the 14th New Jersey. Four days later, the regiment left Camp Hooker to join the Army of the Potomac in its pursuit of advancing Confederate forces (Olsen 1993:118–19). Regiment historian J. Newton Terrill perhaps summed up the impressions of many men on this day: "Monocacy to us was a home, and with a sigh of regret we left, although anxious to move" (Terrill 1884:14).

After nine months of relatively dull and monotonous guard duty in and around Frederick, the 14th New Jersey rushed to Harpers Ferry in mid-June 1863 to join the Army of the Potomac. They would not return to Monocacy Junction until the evening of July 8, 1864. Now with the 1st Brigade, 3rd Division, 6th Corps, the 14th New Jersey was among the handful of veteran regiments hurried north to Maryland to meet invading Confederates under General Jubal Early. In early July 1864, the Confederate raiders were wreaking havoc across much of western Maryland. Union forces commanded by General Lew Wallace were primarily of untested home guard troops and "100 days" volunteers with little experience. Two brigades from the veteran 6th Corps were rushed to Wallace's aid, arriving at Monocacy Junction on the evening of July 8 (Bilby 1987:169–73).

The following day, the 14th New Jersey engaged the invading Confederates in the Battle of Monocacy (figure 4.4), later known as "The Battle that Saved Washington" (Cooling 1997). Greatly outnumbered and outgunned, the 14th New Jersey withstood three separate charges by Confederate forces and eventually retreated in good order. In this battle, the regiment suffered 140 casualties out of approximately 350 men engaged (40 percent casualties). Only one officer in the 14th New Jersey was unscathed. For its crucial role in this battle, as well as the nine months spent at Camp Hooker, the regiment would be known as "The

Figure 4.4. Union skirmishers retreating across the railroad bridge over the Monocacy River during the Battle of Monocacy (photographer and date uncertain, possibly Henry Bacon, ca. 1909; Monocacy National Battlefield Cultural Resource Library).

Monocacy Regiment" (Bilby 1987:176–89; Cooling 1997; Martin 1987:xxi). By the time they mustered out on June 19, 1865, over 1,300 men had served with the regiment, and 257 were either killed in battle or died of disease; the 14th New Jersey is listed on William Fox's list of "300 Fighting Regiments" (Martin 1987: xii, xxi, xxii; Terrill 1884:130).

Over forty years after the Battle of Monocacy, the State of New Jersey erected a monument to honor the 14th New Jersey (figure 4.5). The monument, while located adjacent to the Georgetown Pike (MD Route 355), is some distance

Figure 4.5. Postcard (circa 1908) of the monument of the 14th New Jersey Infantry at Monocacy National Battlefield (Monocacy National Battlefield Cultural Resource Library).

from where the regiment fought during the battle. Instead, it is closer to Monocacy Junction, which had been guarded by the regiment for such an extended period. The dedication of this monument demonstrated the impact that the months at Camp Hooker had on surviving members of the 14th New Jersey.

Archaeology and Camp Hooker Today

Today, Monocacy National Battlefield consists of 1,533 acres preserved because of their importance to interpreting the Battle of Monocacy. Located adjacent to the battlefield, Camp Hooker is not part of this land. While archaeological resources on National Park Service lands are protected by laws such as the Archaeological Resources Protection Act of 1979, Camp Hooker has no such protection. It is for this reason, and at the request of Monocacy National Battlefield, that specific site information is not discussed in this chapter.

The staff of Monocacy National Battlefield have long known about Camp Hooker and had a very general understanding of its location. For decades, relic collectors hunted within the camp's general vicinity and recovered a wide range of Civil War artifacts. In recent years, the site was largely left alone because local collectors understood it to be "hunted out" (Susan Trail, personal communication, 2002). With this in mind, the National Park Service partnered with the author to determine whether Camp Hooker's exact location could be established and whether the camp retained any archaeological integrity.

In 2002, an archaeological survey was conducted as a joint effort between the University of Maryland's Department of Anthropology and the National Park Service. This survey consisted of a systematic metal-detector survey and resulted in the recovery of a significant amount of material culture related to the occupation of Camp Hooker. By analyzing nail distribution across the site, as well as the data presented in numerous historical sources, archaeologists were able to identify the encampment's precise bounds. As a result of these findings, preparations were made to nominate Camp Hooker for listing on the National Register of Historic Places.

During a site visit in early winter 2002, an appalling discovery was made. Despite tremendous efforts by archaeologists and the National Park Service to safeguard the location and integrity of Camp Hooker, relic hunters illegally accessed the site and excavated approximately 300 holes. In their quest for an additional Minié ball or button, relic hunters compromised the remains of Camp Hooker to the point that its eligibility for listing on the National Register of Historic Places was placed in question. In addition, since the site is not managed by the National Park Service, little could be done to locate and prosecute the offenders. Despite claims to the contrary by advocates of relic hunting, this scene is all too familiar to archaeologists.

Because of the severity of the looting, additional survey was required during the spring of 2003 to determine whether portions of the camp remained intact. While the damage caused by relic hunters was severe and irreparable, additional archaeological fieldwork demonstrated that Camp Hooker still retained a relatively high degree of integrity. As a result, the nomination was completed, and as of this date the site is being reviewed for inclusion on the National Register of Historic Places. In addition, the recent looting prompted the National Park Service to consider adding this property to Monocacy National Battlefield. The looting demonstrated that this resource is highly threatened; ownership by the National Park Service is the only way by which the site can be protected. Until protection under federal law occurs, illegal looting will continue to threaten the site's integrity, and the archaeological evidence cannot be shared with the public. In addition, the staff of Monocacy National Battlefield intend to incorporate Camp Hooker's story into future visitor center exhibits. While many relic hunters would prefer to collect artifacts from sites like Camp Hooker, it is the duty of the National Park Service to manage and interpret these endangered resources for present and future generations.

Further research and archaeological fieldwork would greatly enhance our understanding of the 14th New Jersey. While living at Camp Hooker, these men wrote countless letters and deposited thousands of items, leaving historians and archaeologists a plethora of resources with which to study their lives. While this chapter briefly describes the physical appearance of Camp Hooker and the inhabitants' activities, it only scratches the surface of the social and cultural interactions of these men. By studying these interactions we can begin to better understand the individuals who fought the American Civil War.

References Cited

Bilby, J.
1987   9 July 1864: The 14th New Jersey Infantry at the Battle of Monocacy. In *The Monocacy Regiment: A Commemorative History of the Fourteenth New Jersey Infantry in the Civil War, 1862–1865.* Edited by D. G. Martin, pp. 167–92. Longstreet House, Hightstown, N.J.

Bullman, J.
1863   Map of Camp Hooker. Private collection; copy of map and letter on file at Monocacy National Battlefield Cultural Resource Library, Frederick, Md.

Cooling, B. F.
1997   *Monocacy: The Battle that Saved Washington.* White Mane Publishing Company, Shippensburg, Penn.

Frye, S. W., and D. E. Frye
1989   *Maryland Heights: Archaeological and Historical Resources Study.* Occasional Report no. 2. Regional Archaeology Program, National Capital Region, National Park Service, Washington, D.C.

Gaede, F. C.
2001   *The Federal Civil War Shelter Tent.* O'Donnell Publications, Alexandria, Va.

Martin, D. G., ed.
1987   *The Monocacy Regiment: A Commemorative History of the Fourteenth New Jersey Infantry in the Civil War, 1862–1865.* Longstreet House, Hightstown, N.J.

National Archives and Records Administration (NARA), Washington, D.C.
n.d.   Record Group 19. Records of the Veterans Administration. Pension Case Files.
n.d.   Record Group 94. Compiled Military Service Records. Regimental Records. Modern Military Records Division, Records of the 14th New Jersey Volunteer Infantry.

Olsen, B. A., ed.

1993   *Upon the Tented Field.* Historic Projects, Inc., Red Bank, N.J.

Terrill, J. N.

1884   Campaign of the Fourteenth Regiment New Jersey Volunteers. In *The Monocacy Regiment: A Commemorative History of the Fourteenth New Jersey Infantry in the Civil War, 1862–1865.* Edited by D. G. Martin, pp. 1–165. Longstreet House, Hightstown, N.J.

Trail, S.

2002   Park Superintendent, National Park Service, Monocacy National Battlefield. Personal communication to author.

U.S. War Department

1861   *Revised Regulations for the Army of the United States, 1861.* J.G.L. Brown, Philadelphia.

Part III

Encampment Plan and Layout

CLARENCE R. GEIER, DAVID G. ORR, AND MATTHEW B. REEVES

Chapter 1 presents an overview of camp life during the Civil War that introduces the reader to certain established military and practical factors that influenced camp placement and plan. This overview is important in the identification and interpretation of military encampment archaeology. On a more regulatory note, Joseph Whitehorne (chapter 2) introduces readers to the history and evolution of guidelines for encampment used and taught by the United States military in the mid-nineteenth century. While the existence of these guidelines suggests the imposition of normative patterns of structure, Whitehorne concludes his chapter with an appropriate and highly relevant caution noting numerous factors of function, taste, training, and circumstance that impact the actual camp nature and design. While seeking absolute standards, the archaeologist is confronted by the reality that despite the existence of guidelines or protocols each encampment must be addressed as a unique expression whose internal plan and the lifeways of the soldiers it supported needs to be discovered.

In Part II the presentation by Bryan Corle and Joseph Balicki (chapter 3) highlights the fact that as compared to amateur historians and collectors who have been students of military encampment and associated material culture for decades, many professional historical archaeologists are neopyhtes. Many are ignorant of architecture, military accoutrements, and material culture common to military encampments. Moreover, many of the traditional methods used by professionals in identifying historic domestic sites are unreliable when applied to locating military encampments and sites that are not associated with distinct structural features.

Given the above stated facts and assuming the need to establish encampment sites as significant historical resources requiring both interpretation and preservation, we can see that the discussion in Part II (in light of Brandon Bies' experience, as presented in chapter 4) poses an important challenge. The imminent threat of loss to major encampments throughout the Civil War landscape means that preservation and historic interests shared by the professional and amateur communities need to be joined as much as possible and wherever possible in a collaboration in which the two groups inform and educate each other.

Highlighting the successful interaction of professional archaeologists and local relic hunters, Part III provides two examples of documented military encampments of significantly different type. Balicki (chapter 5) documents the Confederate winter cantonment of Fort French, one of a series of encampments established on the Potomac River in the winter of 1861–62. In stark contrast, Stephen and Kim McBride introduce the more permanent U.S. Army Depot of Camp Nelson, Kentucky.

In both cases the importance of researching the available historical record is key to the analysis and interpretation of site evidence; primary records such as letters, diaries, and personal journals often contain insights into architecture, plan, and activities not considered within more formal military documents.

Balicki documents a winter cantonment occupied by 3,500 Confederates between October 1861 and March 1862. For five months, Confederate batteries at Evansport and Shipping Point blockaded the Potomac River, where they engaged Union forces in a prolonged artillery duel. The documented research discusses a well-preserved Civil War landscape that included 697 hut features clustered into four distinct camps or forts, an artillery magazine, a target range, picket posts, an earthwork, paths, and road traces. Balicki notes that while established military doctrine played a role in defining camp layout, the immediate issues of topography, troop preference, and hostile fire were also evident in shaping the camp plan. Detailed mapping of hut features shows that adherence to military protocol varied. Well-ordered camps were laid out and occupied by troops commanded by infantry officers, while camps displaying disorderly patterning were occupied by troops commanded by naval officers. In contrast to camp layout, the design of the soldiers' individual huts was left to the devices of the soldiers themselves and reflected their personal preferences.

In contrast to the five-month occupation of the Confederate forces on the Potomac, the U.S. Army Depot of Camp Nelson, Kentucky, was constructed and occupied for three years, from 1863 to 1866. As the McBrides discuss (chapter 6), the purpose, permanence, and scope of the camp produced a dramatically different plan from more temporary summer or winter camps and included structures of significantly greater permanence. Over the period of its existence, the U.S. Army Depot had a large, diverse, and changing population that included garrison soldiers (both white and black), transient soldiers, civilian employees, and white and black civilian refugees. Providing housing for these people was a constant concern for the commanding officers of the camp and is reflected in camp archaeology and material culture.

The housing challenge was most severe after May–June 1864, when large numbers of African American recruits and their families entered Camp Nelson. These people not only increased the overall population of the camp, but also changed its racial makeup and greatly increased the number of women and children, the latter group posing a challenge to military management.

Solutions to the housing needs at Camp Nelson included tents of all kinds, wooden barracks and dormitories, office-building apartments, former civilian houses, privately run boardinghouses and hotels, wooden cottages, wooden huts or shanties, the U.S. Sanitary Commission's Soldiers' Home, and finally, readapted army buildings of diverse function. The archaeological expression and associated material culture of examples of certain of these structures is presented.

5

"Masterly Inactivity"

The Confederate Cantonment Supporting the 1861–1862
Blockade of the Potomac River, Evansport, Virginia

JOSEPH F. BALICKI

INTRODUCTION

In the fall of 1861, the Northern press lamented that the war in northern Virginia was a case of "masterly inactivity" along the Potomac River, perpetuated by generals prone to inaction (figure 5.1). This was certainly not the case twenty-five miles downstream from Washington, D.C., between October 1861 and March 1862, where Confederate batteries at Evansport and Shipping Point blockaded the river and both sides engaged in a prolonged artillery duel for five months (figure 5.2). The Confederate batteries were commanded jointly by both army and navy officers and were manned and protected by untrained infantry. Associated with the batteries was a large cantonment where about 3,500 troops built winter quarters. John Milner Associates, Inc., of Alexandria, Virginia, conducted archaeological investigations on the cantonment in 2001 through 2003 (Balicki et al. 2002; Balicki et al. 2004). These investigations identified a well-preserved Civil War landscape that included 697 hut features clustered into four camps and with numerous other associated military and transportation features. Military doctrine regulated camp layout, but topography, troop preference, and hostile fire were also influential. Detailed mapping of hut features shows that adherence to military protocol varied. Well-ordered camps were laid out by Confederate infantry officers, while camps displaying disorderly patterning were commanded by naval officers. In contrast to camp layout, the design of individual huts in both camps was left to the devices of the soldiers themselves and reflect their personal preference.

Features associated with the cantonment extend over 193 acres. Cantonment investigations exhibited a very eclectic methodology, as parts of the camp required differing field techniques for their successful assessment (Balicki et al.

Figure 5.1. "'Masterly Inactivity' or Six Months on the Potomac" (*Frank Leslies Illustrated Newspaper* 1862).

2002; Balicki et al. 2004). Sampling for material culture was not emphasized; field strategies instead stressed the importance of the landscape and the need to locate often subtle surface features. Methods used in attaining project goals included a preliminary reconnaissance, conversations with knowledgeable relic hunters, a metal-detector survey, nonsystematic shovel testing, test unit excavations, extensive mapping, and detailed historic research. Using this approach, investigators found that the cantonment was much larger and more complex and contained more features and activity areas than had initially been reported.

CONTEXT

Before the Civil War, the Potomac River was a main supply route to Washington, D.C. Military tacticians quickly realized its strategic value. As early as April 1861, Virginia state troops established batteries above the river at Aquia Landing and began an artillery duel with Federal gunboats (O.R. Series I, Vol. 2:55–59, 780, 820). The Aquia battery, approximately nine miles south

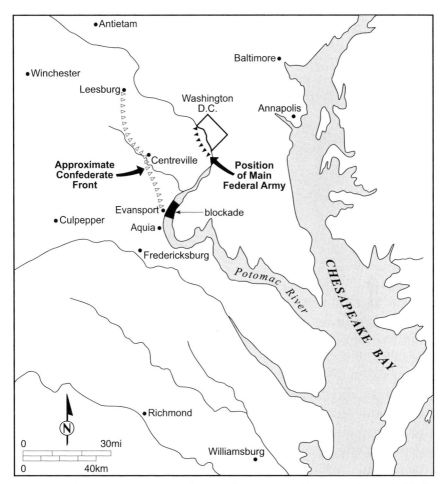

Figure 5.2. The mid-Atlantic region, showing the positions of the armies during the blockade (John Milner Associates).

of Evansport, Virginia, was initially positioned to defend against Federal attacks on the landing and was not used offensively. In June, General Theophilus Holmes, Commander of the Aquia District, recommended that Evansport be selected for the blockade's primary battery sites because the main shipping channel ran close to the Virginia shore. The general stated, "If you can send me two 32–pounders or two 18–inch columbiads, I believe I can stop the navigation of the river" (O.R. Series I, Vol. 2:133–34).

Elsewhere in northern Virginia, events quickly overshadowed the activities along the Potomac. After the First Battle of Manassas on July 22, 1861, Confederate authorities renewed their interest in constructing offensive shore batteries near Evansport. Not until the Confederates consolidated their positions and the Federal army retired to Washington's fortifications did it become feasible for the Confederates to detail enough manpower, equipment, and ordnance to the Potomac shoreline. The main Confederate batteries were at Cockpit Point (Possum Nose), Evansport (the area between Quantico and Chopawamsic creeks), Shipping Point, and for a short time, Freestone Point (figure 5.3). These batteries covered more than a six-mile stretch of the shipping channel of the Potomac (Wills 1975:110).

In September 1861, the Confederates began constructing a series of batteries at Evansport. General Isaac Trimble, with troops under the command of General Holmes, erected the batteries under the direction of Confederate navy commander Frederick Chatard (Scharf 1877:99). The first Evansport battery was completed by 29 September (O.R. Series I, Vol. 5:883). The Confederates held their fire hoping that they would not be discovered until they could surprise the Federals with an overwhelming show of force. However, on 15 October 1861, the United States Navy forced the Confederates to reveal their positions when a brief exchange occurred between the batteries and ships of the Federal Potomac Flotilla (Hanson 1951:48; O.R.N. Series I, Vol. 4:718; Wills 1975:78).

On 17 October 1861, Potomac Flotilla Commander Thomas Craven effectively closed the river to traffic. "Considering the improvement of their gun practice I would respectfully suggest that until the enemy's batteries be silenced or removed that there shall be no more transportation of Government stores upon the river" (O.R.N. Series I, Vol. 4:722). Federal traffic on the Potomac was brought to a standstill, the Confederates controlling approximately fifteen miles of the river (O.R.N. Series I, Vol. 4:736). Although some Federal vessels slipped by the batteries, by 21 October 1861, over forty vessels were holding position on the lower Potomac, waiting to make the passage past the batteries. On 25 October 1861, Captain John Dahlgren, commander of the Washington Navy Yard, informed the secretary of the navy that "the Potomac is now so far obstructed that it is no longer used by the army for transportation of supplies and the sole dependence for that purpose and for the supplies of the inhabitants of this city is limited to railroads alone" (O.R.N. Series I, Vol. 4:735).

Federal troops under General Joseph Hooker established counterbatteries in Maryland opposite the Confederates. From these positions, Federal guns constantly exchanged fire with the Confederate batteries. Both sides' artillery could reach the opposite shore, but with the exception of that from a small

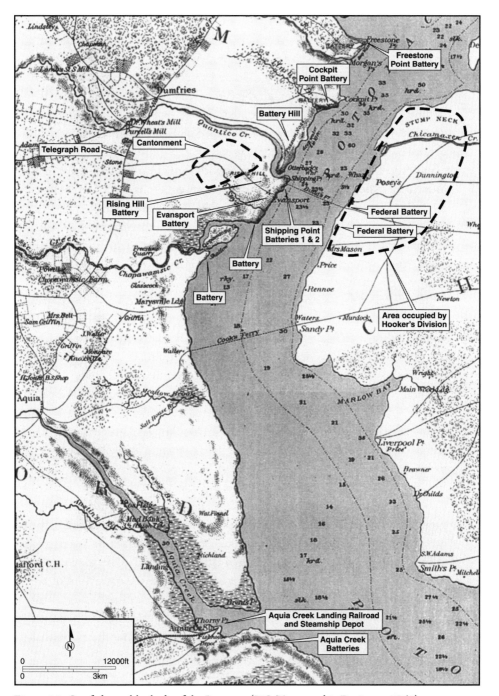

Figure 5.3. Confederate blockade of the Potomac (U.S. Topographic Engineers 1862).

number of rifled guns, the artillery fire was wildly inaccurate. The Federal batteries included several Whitworth rifled artillery pieces. The Federal army tested these guns but never widely adopted Whitworths after the spring of 1862. Later in the war, however, the Confederates found these guns worth the effort it took to run them through the Federal blockade (Thomas 1985). The Whitworth guns fired a solid hexagonal iron bolt approximately 2 miles with great accuracy. Since the distance between the Shipping Point batteries and the Federal batteries at Budd's Creek was approximately 1.8 miles, the Whitworth guns could be fired at the Confederates with some degree of accuracy. It is interesting to note that the Confederate camps were about 2 to 2.5 miles from the Federal batteries, or just out of range of the Whitworth guns.

Although not especially lethal, the Federal counterbattery fire had some success, and as a resort the Confederates worked on their batteries only at night. At one point, the Confederates reported that they had been under fire twenty-eight straight days (Hewett 1994–2001, Vol. 66, Series 78:444–45).

The Federals relied on balloon observations to locate the Confederate batteries and the size of their supporting forces (figure 5.4). Through January and February, constant balloon observation of the Confederate positions was maintained (O.R. Series III, Vol. 124:269). In addition to ascensions done from land, one balloon and its supporting gas apparatus were placed on a barge and floated from location to location, marking the first combined aerial ascension from a navy vessel (O.R. Series III, Vol. 124:265–66).

From the Maryland shore, Federal General Hooker was amused at the Confederate gunners' lack of skill, commenting that boats are "as likely to be struck by lightning as by rebel shot" (O.R. Series I, Vol. 5:638). On another occasion, Hooker concluded that the batteries were not effective: "They do fire wretchedly. Whether it is owing to the projectiles or the guns I am not informed. From what was witnessed today and on previous occasions, I am forced to the conclusion that the rebel batteries in this vicinity should not be a terror to anyone" (O.R. Series I, Vol. 5:649). In a later communiqué, he added, "The rebels will certainly abandon their purpose of claiming the navigation of the Potomac by means of the batteries now in position ere long. They must see that it is labor in vain. Of late a large number of vessels have passed and re-passed at night, and no effort has been made to check them. Thus far their labor has been equally fruitless during the day" (O.R. Series I, Vol. 5:663).

On 7 November 1861, General Samuel French replaced Trimble as commander of the Confederate batteries (O.R. Series I, Vol. 108:372). Despite misgivings, French felt that the blockade was accomplishing its goals. On 14

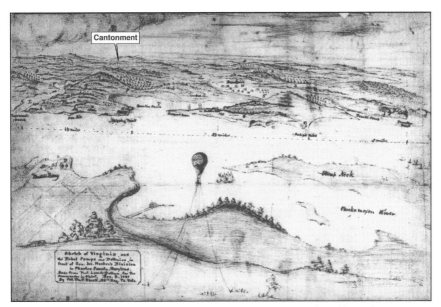

Figure 5.4. "Sketch of Virginia and Rebel Camps and Batteries" (Small 1861).

January 1862, he noted his dissatisfaction with his troops' efforts but added, "As regards the blockade of the river, not a sail has passed for weeks. The river would be lifeless and desolate except for the eight or ten steamers always in sight above and below" (O.R. Series I, Vol. 5:1032–33).

Clearly the blockade had an effect. The Confederate batteries may not have sunk any Federal vessels, but they were such a threat that the Potomac River was closed to most Federal traffic for about five months. The reduction in river traffic to Washington, D.C., caused shortages, but the city was never in grave danger. The sole rail link to the city proved adequate, and although the city's inhabitants and soldiers faced higher prices, they were not in danger of famine. One principal effect of the blockade was to significantly reduce the amount of forage supplied to the city. In the nineteenth century, armies relied on draft animals, principally horses and mules. As the forage supply dwindled, the number of animals available to the army decreased; accordingly, the viability of the army was reduced.

During the five months in which the batteries operated, the Confederates shot more than 5,000 rounds from at least thirty-seven heavy guns and an unknown number of field guns (Wills 1975:66, 110, 112). Notwithstanding shortages of some materials for the Washington area, the blockade's actual successes were the apprehension and embarrassment it caused the Federal leadership, and the use of the blockade as a Confederate propaganda tool. The fact that the Federal government and army could not dislodge Confederate forces approximately twenty-five miles downriver from the Union capital was a source of embarrassment for the Federal leadership. Lord Lyons, the British ambassador at Washington, reportedly sent a dispatch stating, "Washington is the only city in the United States that is really blockaded" (quoted in French 1999:143). At this time in the war, the Federal leadership feared European intervention and saw that the Potomac blockade was a weakness that could provide Europeans a reason to openly support the Confederates.

The 1 March 1862 *New York Tribune* reported:

> There has been no safe communication by water between this city and the capital of the nation during all this time—a period of six months. This is one of the most humiliating of all the national disgraces to which we have been compelled to submit. It has been most damaging to us in the eyes of the world. No one circumstance has been used more to our disadvantage with foreign nations than this. And it has helped the Confederates just in proportion as it has injured us. It has been their haughty boast that they had maintained steady and effectual sway over the great channel of commerce between this city and Washington, through which the immense supplies of our grand army of the Potomac would naturally have passed. (quoted in Scharf 1877:102)

It was not the Federal army, or even the threat of a Federal advance, that compelled the Confederates to give up the blockade; rather, their positions fell victim to Virginia mud. As early as November, upon arriving at Evansport, General French pronounced the local roads awful (O.R. Series I, Vol. 108:378). By February 1861, the worsening conditions of roads between the Confederate front and Richmond led Confederate leaders to order a withdrawal from the entire northern Virginia front to south of the Rappahannock River. Additionally, the Confederates perceived the Federal balloon ascensions as a prelude to an imminent invasion, and they were becoming convinced that they could not adequately respond to the Federal threat.

The withdrawal was a logistical nightmare for the Confederates. Poor weather, combined with a high volume of traffic, turned the roads into quagmires. Also, disease had reduced the number of troops stationed at the front. Compounding the logistics was the need to deal with the massive amount of material the Confederates had moved to their forward positions in northern Virginia.

On the same day (9 March 1862) that the *Monitor* and the *Virginia* (*Merrimac*) dueled at Hampton Rhodes, the Confederate Potomac River blockade ended. Federal landing parties went ashore unopposed and destroyed the batteries, inspected the abandoned camps, and retrieved salvageable ordnance and guns abandoned by the withdrawing Confederates (Donald 1975; Nevins 1962; O.R. Series I, Vol. 5:555–756).

In general terms, the withdrawal was a disaster for the Confederacy. By March 1862, goods were already in short supply for the Southern army. The abandonment of large amounts of needed supplies all along the northern Virginia front created shortages that the South could not afford. At Evansport, General French abandoned most of the heavy guns and ordnance, as well as tons of supplies. Federal landing parties reported that the Confederate camps were well supplied (Cudworth 1866; Nevins 1962). Two days after the withdrawal, Confederate Captain Chatard wrote General French expressing his disappointment: "It is a sad affair, and I suppose you don't require more than absolutely necessary to be said about it" (O.R. Series I, Vol. 108:499).

The Cantonment

Approximately one mile inland from the batteries, just out of range from Federal artillery, the Confederates constructed a large winter cantonment (figure 5.5). Following the Civil War, the cantonment was forgotten and the area became reforested. In the twentieth century, the U.S. Marine Corps acquired the area and used it for training, refuse disposal, and a golf course. These activities destroyed portions of the camps, but a large amount of the cantonment landscape survived and has retained its archaeological integrity. Beginning in the 1950s, the camps were searched by relic hunters. Initially, these activities were allowed and even sanctioned by Marine Corps personnel, but today an environment of preservation prevails, and most illicit collecting has been stopped.

The cantonment is located in a stream valley that runs perpendicular to the Potomac River, as well as in smaller stream valleys that radiate off the main stream (figures 5.3–5.5). Civil War maps label the stream flowing through this valley as the "River Styx"; apparently the occupying soldiers considered this place hell (United States Topographic Engineers 1862). The cantonment contained four large concentrations of soldier domiciles, a magazine, picket posts, a target range, a possible earthwork, and road traces. Initially, the troops lived in tents, but as winter approached, huts were built. Balloon observations from

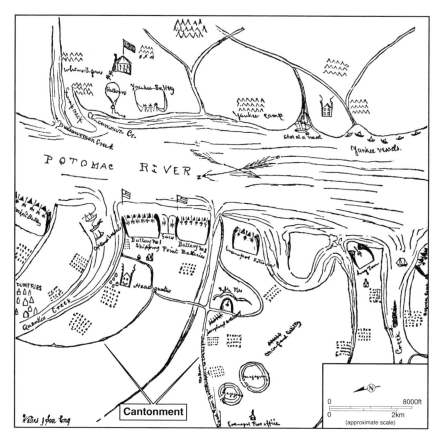

Figure 5.5. "The Rebel batteries on the Lower Potomac" (*New York Herald* 1862).

the Maryland shore and several period sketches noted general camp locations (figures 5.4–5.6).

Terrain differences were certainly considered in developing the cantonment plan. Protection from Federal balloon observation and artillery fire were, however, the most important factors in locating camps. A southern exposure to maximize winter sunlight did not factor into winter quarters positioning. One camp faces west, one faces north, and two are in north-south–running stream valleys. The primary stream valley contained the road to Evansport. Fallow fields flanked this road and were used as a parade ground (Gause 1861).

In the four months during which General French was in charge of the Evansport batteries, he commanded the 47th Virginia, 22nd North Carolina, 2nd Tennessee, 14th Alabama, 35th Georgia, 1st Arkansas, and 2nd Battalion Arkansas Infantry, as well as the Maryland Flying Artillery and a company of

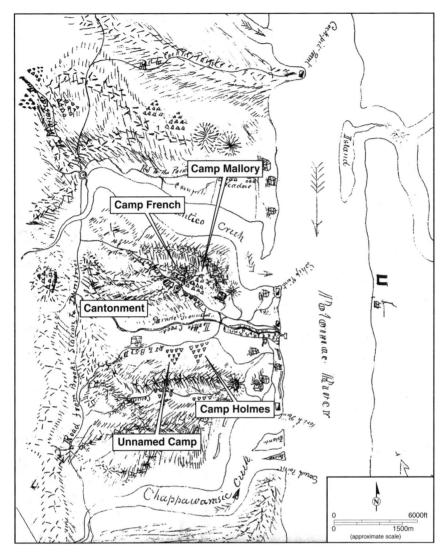

Figure 5.6. Map of the Confederate positions in the vicinity of Evansport, Virginia (Gause 1861).

cavalry. The cantonment area was home to troops from several of these regiments. Troops under direct naval command were also present, but records on the troop affiliations of these men have proven difficult to find.

In letters home, soldiers referred to the cantonment by various names. The portion occupied by the 35th Georgia Infantry Regiment was informally known as "Camp French," after the regional commander. The 22nd North

Carolina Infantry Regiment and 2nd Battalion Arkansas Infantry referred to their locations within the encampment as "Camp Holmes," after Aquia District commander General Theophilus H. Holmes. For a short time, before they established winter quarters (Camp Dave Currin) four miles from Evansport, the 2nd Tennessee Infantry also camped at Camp Holmes. Captain George Washington Parkhill of the Florida Howell Guards referred to his location within the cantonment as "Camp Mallory," a reference to the Confederate secretary of the navy and a fellow Floridian. Now referred to as site 44PW917, the cantonment has been the subject of archaeological investigation (Balicki et al. 2002; Balicki et al 2004).

The location of specific camps within the cantonment was determined through a combination of relic-hunter information and historic-archaeological research (figures 5.6, 5.7). Information provided by relic hunters identified the location of the 35th Georgia's winter quarters. In contrast, notes from a soldier's journal located the camp of the 22nd North Carolina Infantry Regiment (Gause 1861). A description provided in a personal letter from Captain Parkhill identified the camp adjacent to the magazine as being occupied by troops under navy command (Parkhill 1861). The 2nd Battalion Arkansas Infantry, and for a short period the 2nd Tennessee, also had their camps in this area, but specific deployment within the larger cantonment area is not yet clear. The winter quarters of the 47th Virginia Infantry and of the 2nd Tennessee are not in the cantonment but have been identified elsewhere (Balicki et al. 2002; Botwick and McClane 1998).

Several other military units were at the cantonment, but their specific placements within the encampment are not known. These include the Maryland Flying Artillery, the 14th Alabama Infantry Regiment, and the 2nd Battalion Arkansas Infantry (Gerdes 1998; Hewett 1994–2001, Vol. 2, Series 14:309–11, Vol. 127, Series 39:17–18; Hurst 2002; Kelley 1992:6).

During the war, both armies summarized troop strength by completing monthly returns. These reports summarize the number of officers, men, and aggregate, and are usually broken down into infantry, cavalry, and artillery. The term *aggregate* refers to the total troop strength, taking into account both present, absent, and troops on detached service, as well as those fit for duty. Consequently, in September 1861 when General Trimble reported that he had 3,000 men to erect and support the batteries, only 1,885 were actually present for duty (O.R. Series I, Vol. 5:853–54). The remaining men were absent, on leave, assigned other duty, in hospital, or excused from duty for some reason. For the troops in the Evansport vicinity, returns for August, September, Oc-

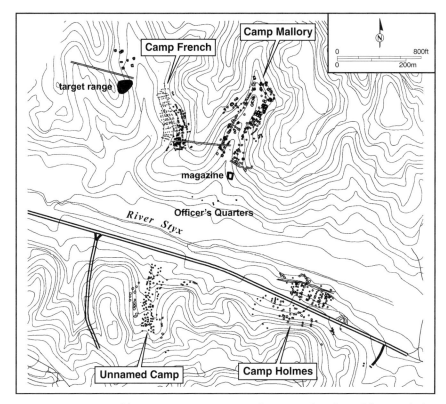

Figure 5.7. Site map of the Evansport cantonment, showing archaeological features (John Milner Associates).

tober, November, and February 1861 have survived (O.R. Series I, Vol. 5:824, 884, 933, 974, 1086). The approximately 3,000 troops reported in the Evansport vicinity for September and October were the total strength. In actuality, the number of officers and men present for duty was about a third less. Absenteeism caused by disease increased after the troops established their winter quarters. Available troops present in October were fewer than those reported for September, and on 30 December 1861, General French reported that he could field only approximately 772 men for duty on the batteries, for picket duty, and for work parties (O.R. Series I, Vol. 5:1012–13).

In two months, the Confederate force had been reduced by 75 percent. In actuality, the force at Evansport was probably somewhat larger, because the men under direct command of naval officers were not accounted for in the Aquia District returns. The small size of the effective force, however, must have contributed to fears of a Federal attack. Also, at the time of the Confederate withdrawal, the depleted force would not have been able to move all the accumulated materials, a fact that must have contributed to the abandonment of some pieces of artillery and large amounts of equipment.

Through the fall and into the winter of 1861–62, contagious diseases (for example, measles) and camp diseases (for example, dysentery) were rampant all along the Confederate front. At Evansport, troops from the Alabama and Georgia regiments were decimated. The 14th Alabama was hard hit: 200 men, approximately 43 percent of the regiment, died of measles, and the regiment was withdrawn to Richmond (Hurst 2002). The 35th Georgia also suffered greatly, losing about 20 percent—approximately 145 men—between September 1861 and spring 1862 (Irvine 1891). The 22nd North Carolina Regiment also suffered a measles epidemic that claimed several dozen soldiers; however, because of their commander's efforts at sanitation and discipline, death from disease was lessened (Wilson 2002:155). In contrast, during this same period, the 47th Virginia, made up of local men, lost only four men to disease (Musselman 1991:12–13).

Duty along the Potomac was harsh. Each regimental company was expected to undertake regular camp duties. These included fatigue (work parties) and policing (camp cleanup) activities; construction and maintenance of batteries and other fortifications; maintenance of roads; and night picket duty along the Potomac River every fifth day (Thomas 1862). Once the epidemics began, fewer and fewer men were available for these duties. The cold winter contributed to the problem. A member of the 5th Alabama stationed at nearby Cockpit Point related that this winter was the coldest that he or any of his fellow soldiers had ever experienced (Fulton 1924:427).

After the Confederate withdrawal, Federal troops crossed from Maryland and inspected the cantonment. The Federals commented on the camps and found that the Confederates were well supplied. Members of the 1st Massachusetts Volunteers were among the initial troops to inspect the camps. They found that

> The deserted camps were found supplied with everything needful for winter-quarters. The houses were built of logs, with floors and roofs of board, some having glazed windows; and one actually had green blinds. Their cooking arrangements were on the most liberal scale; and the utensils good as to quality, and plentiful in quantity; but houses, beds, and everything else, in fact, were filthy to the last degree. If they had been kept neat or clean, and laid out with proper regularity, they would have been very creditable to their late occupants; but they were filled with vile

odors. The houses were infested with vermin, damp, and black with smoke, and most of our men would sooner sleep on the ground than in one of them. The rebels seemed to have lived upon the fat of the land. Beef, pork, flour, bread, salt, and coffee were found among the stores, not to mention whiskey, and a large case of candy. In one instance, a table had just been set for dinner, the meat was already cut, and the cakes by the fire, showing, that from that place the occupants were in too much of a hurry to get away to stop for a lunch. (Cudworth 1866:129–30)

Colonel Charles S. Wainwright, a Federal artillery officer assigned to the Maryland shore batteries, visited Evansport and reported: "The party returned while I was there, each man bringing something in the way of a trophy; pots, pans, axes, shovels, and one even a wheelbarrow. Some too had a rough sort of bowie knife, evidently of home manufacture, but heavy enough no doubt in the eyes of its former owner, to kill a 'damned Yank,' if he could only get at one. The most interesting trophy to me was one of the Whitworth bolts I had myself fired over there" (Nevins 1962:21).

Camp French

The 35th Georgia Infantry Regiment's camp was located on the west-facing slope of a valley, well out of range of Federal artillery and hidden from balloon observation (figures 5.7, 5.8). The 35th Georgia, an infantry regiment consisting of 740 officers and enlisted men, was formed in July of 1861. By fall they had been sent to support the river batteries, arriving at Evansport in November 1861. The 35th fought in seventeen major engagements, and approximately two-thirds of the regiment did not survive the war. At Evansport, the 35th was commanded by Colonel Edward Lloyd Thomas, a veteran infantry officer who received a promotion for gallantry during the Mexican-American War (Fox 2004). The regiment was organized into ten companies of approximately seventy men each. The soldiers of the 35th knew this camp as "Camp French." By the end of January, the men were still in tents because no wood was available for winter quarters (Thomas 1862). As surveyed, the camp contained at least 240 surface features. These features were not randomly distributed and can be separated into two concentrations. Higher on the hill are 98 large depressions and related features representing officers' and company officers' quarters and probably kitchens. Below these features are 142 depressions that were the enlisted men's quarters.

The part of the camp containing soldiers' quarters has been disturbed by golf course construction, but hut depressions are still visible. These depressions contain well-preserved subsurface deposits beneath a disturbed layer measuring one

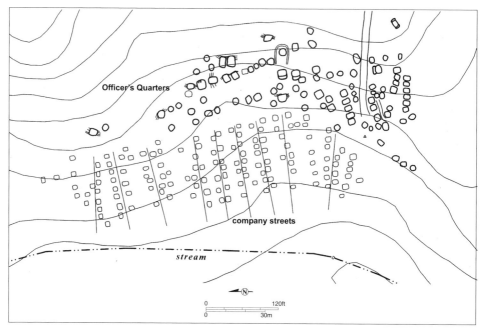

Figure 5.8. Site map, Camp French (John Milner Associates).

to one-and-a-half feet thick. The huts are not arranged randomly but reflect a planned layout. The 142 depressions are arranged in twenty rows running along the hillslope (figure 5.8). This grouping reflects enlisted men's quarters and shows company organization. The rows are singular or grouped in pairs. There are spaces between the rows and groups of rows that reflect company streets. While the 35th's ten companies are reflected in the camp layout, the order of the companies within the camp is not known. For demonstrational purposes, the order is listed from left to right beginning at Company A. In reality, this would not have been the case. The most senior companies, companies that had distinguished themselves, or companies with the best equipment would have occupied streets at the flanks of the camp (Wally Owen, personal communication 2001).

Upslope from the company streets is an area containing 98 hut depressions believed to have been associated with officers' quarters (figure 5.8). Relic hunters have dug into most of these. In general, these huts were larger than those on the company streets. The officers' huts were arranged in rows set perpendicular to the hillslope and the company streets. Various layouts appear to have been used to accommodate the slope of the hill; huts were built partially into the slope or on platforms. Some depressions retain evidence of drainages around them.

Several rows of depressions are on the camp's southeastern side. Whether these features were habitations or other support structures is unclear. In the past, relic hunters found large amounts of ceramic and glass artifacts in these depressions. Based on the amount of artifacts and the odd positioning of these depressions, it is possible that they are cache sites of Confederate supplies. During a mission to destroy the Confederate positions, members of the 1st Massachusetts Volunteers discovered freshly dug graves. Regimental Chaplain Cudworth (1866:132) stated that the apparent graves

> were laid out in streets, carefully labeled, and contained pathetic remonstrances against disturbing the repose of the dead, and violating the sanctity of the tomb, so that suspicions were engendered that the sacred dead might be brought to life again, and made to see a little more service under the sun. Spades and shovels were accordingly brought into requisition; and speedily were exhumed, not the bodies of departed Confederates, but numbers of nice new tents, packages of clothing, mess-chests furnished with all the appliances of modern cookery, trunks of various articles, tools, &c. The grave diggers were complimented for the success of their first sacrilegious experiment, and recommended to try again.

Relic hunters have found a large number of Georgia state insignia within this camp. Archaeological investigations recovered ceramics, glass, faunal remains, and ammunition. Some ceramic sherds have an alkaline glaze that various Southern states, including Georgia, made (Green 1981:202–10). These sherds may be attributed to potteries of South Carolina's Edgefield District or Washington County, Georgia. The Edgefield District was sending supplies to Confederate troops in Virginia (Joe Joseph, personal communication 2004). The presence of this regional ceramic type indicates that 35th Georgia soldiers either brought, or were sent, foodstuffs from the south, probably from Georgia. The sherds also suggest that regional preference and variability may be identified at this site. It may be possible to develop comparative studies focusing not only on differences between Federal and Confederate troops, but also on differences between troops from different states. It would be interesting to see whether regional preferences were retained or changed during the war.

Camp Mallory

Camp Mallory was located in a steep-sided stream valley east of Camp French (figures 5.7, 5.9). While this location is protected from Federal artillery and hidden from view, the reason for the Confederates' locating a camp in this valley is unclear. The area receives no direct sunlight through most of the winter, making it an inhospitable place for winter habitation. Further, the larger cantonment's terrain offered numerous other locations where camps would have been equally or better protected and the living conditions would have been better. Factors of protection and stealth were probably not determining factors in locating the camp.

Camp Mallory was occupied by some of the first troops deployed to Evansport. Letters written from this camp indicate that it was under naval command detailed to erect and man the batteries. The camp is associated with men commanded by naval officers, but Confederate engineers may also have been there. These inexperienced soldiers and their naval officers probably chose the location because it offered relief from the summer heat, and they gave no thought to winter conditions.

Within the camp, 157 hut features were identified, as were a large ammunition magazine and a probable officers' quarter. The probable officers' quarter is located south of the magazine, while the main concentration of winter quarters lies north of it (figure 5.9). The sixty-five-foot by fifty-foot magazine was built into the eastern valley slope, a location offering protection from incoming artillery. An earthen mound forms the foundation, and a drainage ditch surrounds it. This and other magazines were blown up by the Confederates when they pulled out. The force of the explosion destroyed part of the magazine, and a large number of shell fragments are scattered in the vicinity.

The location of the officers' quarters appears in a soldier's notebook (Gause 1861). Relic hunters also concluded, on the basis of material recovered, that this hut depression had been occupied by officers. Samuel Gause (1861) identified the location as the headquarters of Colonel Thomas H. Williamson, a Confederate engineer officer. In the spring of 1861, Williamson erected and commanded batteries at nearby Aquia Creek. His role at Evansport is not clear; no official correspondence mentions his whereabouts in the fall of 1861.

The only known troops occupying Camp Mallory were the Howell Guards, the 1st Florida Infantry Regiment's Company M. The Howell Guards were formed in Tallahassee, Florida, on 20 August 1861, and one week later they were sent to Virginia (Hewett 1994–2001, Vol. 5, Series 17:228–29). Cap-

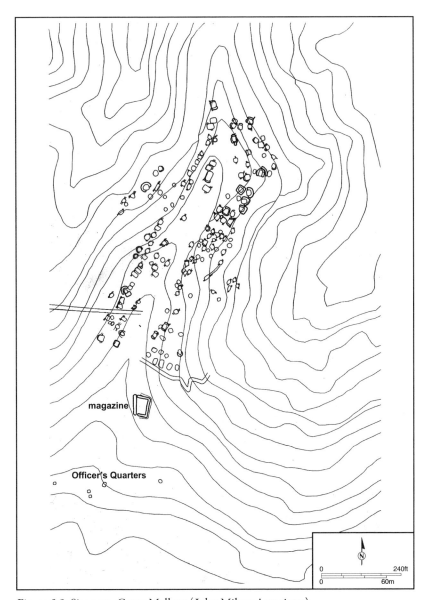

magazine

Officer's Quarters

0   240ft
0   60m

Figure 5.9. Site map, Camp Mallory (John Milner Associates).

tain George Washington Parkhill was the commander of the Howell Guards. He was an inexperienced officer. The Howell Guards helped build and then manned the battery at Shipping Point. Around Christmas 1861, Sergeant Amos G. Whitehead, a member of the Howell Guards, wrote home relating that it was funny that the company enlisted as cavalry, were sent to Virginia as infantry, and were at the time serving as artillery manning a battery of big guns (Eppes 1926:169). On 14 February 1862, a gun exploded and one man was killed; later, two men were "accidentally wounded" by Federal artillery (Hewett 1994–2001, Vol. 5, Series 17:228).

Other units occupying Camp Mallory are not known. They may have been from an Arkansas or Alabama infantry regiment, as the camps of these units are unknown, or the camp may have contained only men under naval command.

The Camp Mallory layout did not follow established protocol for laying out an infantry camp. Here, unlike the 35th Georgia and 22nd North Carolina camps, winter huts were built on steep side slopes, the layout conforming more to local topography than to military organization. The huts parallel each side of the stream, and the street organization evident in other camps is lacking. At some locations, smaller hut features appear to have been clustered around larger hut features, suggesting that companies of enlisted men may have been grouped near their commanding officers or kitchens.

Large variation is evident in the nature of hut features within the camp. Features include earthen platforms, depressions and platforms, depressions with surrounding earthen mounds, and huts partially dug into the slope. Drainages are still recognizable around some hut features.

Camp Holmes

Located on a north-facing slope, the 22nd North Carolina Infantry Regiment camp straddled a historic road leading to Evansport (figures 5.7, 5.10). A modern road bisecting the camp has destroyed an unknown number of hut features. The association of this camp with North Carolina troops is based on information shown in Gause's 1861 notebook and reports from relic hunters who noted the recovery of numerous artifacts bearing North Carolina insignia here.

Originally known as the 12th North Carolina, the 22nd North Carolina Infantry was organized in July 1861 (Hewett 1994–2001, Vol. 48, Series 60:761–63). The 22nd consisted of nearly one thousand men divided into twelve companies (Daves 1991:161). By the fall of 1861, the 22nd North Carolina was stationed at Evansport, erecting and supporting the batteries (Daves 1991:164). The 22nd North Carolina fought in twenty-five large battles in the eastern the-

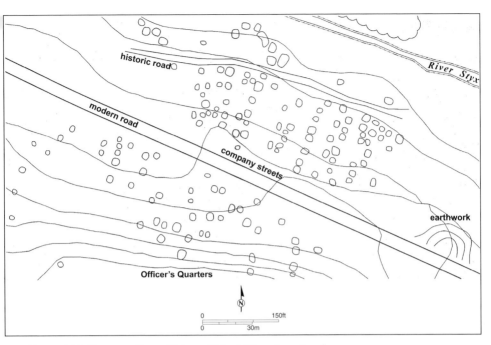

Figure 5.10. Site map, Camp Holmes (John Milner Associates).

ater. At the end of the war, only 110 officers and men surrendered at Appomattox (Rigdon 2003:40–41). Colonel James Johnston Pettigrew, an experienced Mexican-American War infantry officer, commanded the 22nd. Pettigrew was a Confederate hero and beau ideal; at Gettysburg he commanded a division that participated in Pickett's Charge. During the retreat from Gettysburg, Pettigrew was mortally wounded at Falling Waters, Maryland (Wilson 2002).

One hundred and fifty-six hut features were identified in this area (figure 5.10). The camp's north edge bordered Little Creek (colloquially known as the "River Styx"). On the north side of the historic road, adjacent to the stream, are twelve large huts. These huts were clearly separated from the company streets, and it is likely that they were cookhouses or commissary storehouses. Fragments of cast-iron cooking implements from these hut depressions support this interpretation.

South of the historic road are hut features grouped along company streets. The streets are not as evident as at the 35th Georgia camp, but there are still clearly defined spaces between hut features. The huts, for the most part, are grouped into linear patterns. To the south, farther upslope, the huts are positioned to take advantage of natural contours. These huts were probably officers' quarters.

Contemporary accounts of Camp Holmes written by men from both sides have survived. Colonel Pettigrew wrote about the camp and believed that his efforts in camp sanitation and care for the sick kept the measles epidemic (which was raging through other camps) from claiming a larger portion of his troops (Wilson 2002:155). Contemporary accounts indicate that the 22nd North Carolina had fairly good winter quarters, and at Christmastime "the streets of the regimental camp of the Twenty-second were decorated with evergreen branches. A shooting contest was held, and the prize was a pig donated by the colonel. After the contest the colonel was serenaded with Christmas carols, to which he replied with a brief speech" (Wilson 2002:157).

A little over two months after Christmas, Federal visitors to the camp came away with a different impression of the Confederates' living conditions. One Federal officer wrote,

> I went through a number of the camps, including those of the Twelfth and Twenty-Second North Georgia about a mile back from the River. There were but very few tents, most of the men having lived in hovels built in the ravines, which are numerous, with a roof of logs covered with dirt. They were wretched things and awfully dirty. I cannot think that they should have had such wretched huts, for there was a large steam sawmill on the point, and vast piles of lumber and scanting around it. (Nevins 1962:23)

As with most statements issued by opposing groups, the truth lies somewhere in between. By all accounts Pettigrew's troops fared better than the 14th Alabama and 35th Georgia Infantry regiments in winter quarters.

The 22nd North Carolina Infantry Regiment consisted of ten companies, and the spatial relationship of features may reflect this organization. Surviving portions of the camp containing company streets have at least seven streets. Huts from adjacent streets are aligned back to back with no streets between; however, there is one row of huts separated by a company street on either side.

Southwest of the company streets, the camp conforms more to the immediate topography (figures 5.7, 5.10). The huts here may have housed officers, but the number of hut depressions suggests that enlisted men also had huts here. Huts in the vicinity of a twentieth-century Marine Corps dump may have been enlisted men's quarters. These huts may have been arranged in rows, and they appear to be smaller than the huts immediately to the east. The refuse dump probably covers a portion of the camp; consequently, the spatial pattern is not clear. If the huts adjacent to—and, presumably, covered by—the dump were enlisted men's winter quarters, then possibly three companies were housed here.

Upslope from the company streets are huts partially excavated into the hillside. In general, hut depressions in this area are larger than those found elsewhere in the camp. These huts are interpreted as officers' quarters. These huts are in an advantageous position within the camp. At this location, officers would have been able to observe enlisted men, be above the miasmas of Little Creek, and be in a location where they would receive more winter sunlight. (The officers' quarters at the 35th Georgia camp were also positioned upslope from the company streets.)

A notable difference between huts along company streets and huts upslope is the presence or absence of chimneys. Huts along company streets had chimneys, but no evidence of them was found in the upslope huts. Relic hunters report finding cast-iron stoves within some huts located above the company streets. Stoves were a luxury item, and their presence probably reflects officers' quarters.

An earthwork and small hut cluster is just east of Camp Holmes. The earthwork may appear on a map in the 17 March 1862 *New York Herald* (figure 5.5). This map shows a camp at the approximate location of Camp Holmes with a field battery of the Maryland Flying Artillery positioned to the east. It is possible that the small hut cluster southeast of the earthwork was occupied by artillery. The Confederates made efforts to fortify their camps, preparing for the expected Federal movement (O.R. Series I, Vol. 5:959–60).

The hut features at the North Carolina camp were usually square depressions. Many had associated chimney piles. The depth of depressions varied. In some locations along the company streets no depressions were present but cut nails were abundant, suggesting that huts had been built on the ground surface.

Shovel tests, test units, and metal detection recovered sixteen fragments from specialized spider fry pans (figure 5.11). Spider fry pans have tripod legs extending beneath the pan so they can stand alone in a fire. The amount of metal cooking vessel fragments present suggests that the 22nd North Carolina was well supplied and that these items were abandoned when they withdrew. Federal soldiers commented on the cooking items they saw: "Their cooking arrangements were on the most liberal scale; and the utensils good as to quality, and plentiful in quantity" (Cudworth 1866:129–30). Since no spider fry pan fragments were found at the three other camps within the cantonment, these artifacts are likely specific to the 22nd North Carolina. While the 22nd North Carolina's camp may not have possessed specific ceramics, such as that alkaline-

Figure 5.11. Spider fry pan fragments (photo by the author).

glaze stoneware found in the Georgia camp, this type of fry pan seemed common in this camp. Spider fry pans may represent a regional or local cooking style specific to northwestern and north-central North Carolina, the area from which the 22nd was drawn.

Unnamed Camp

The fourth identified camp was located on both sides of a broad stream valley (figures 5.7, 5.12) and cannot be directly associated with any specific military units. In the past, relic hunters report finding artifacts in the camp that bear a variety of insignia including the Confederate States Navy, Georgia, and Arkansas. The recovery of naval insignia lends credence to interpreting this camp as being under navy command.

The camp contains 116 surface features situated in a south-north–sloping drainage (figure 5.12). The huts are not arranged randomly, but determining spatial relationships and patterns was difficult. Part of the difficulty in feature recognition was attributable to disturbance caused by construction of a golf course, changes to drainage patterns, and possibly the Confederate occupation itself. In some places the landscape had been graded, making hut features difficult to see; some were very shallow while others had been filled. At one location, fill was added to create a green. During the Civil War, a stream flowed

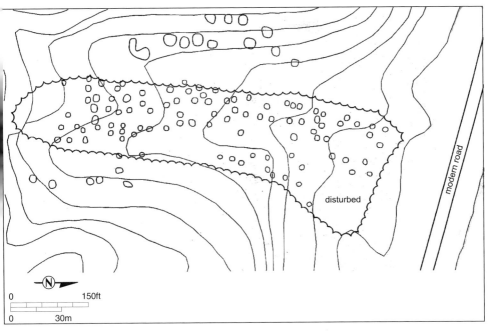

Figure 5.12. Site map, unnamed camp (John Milner Associates).

through the camp. The course of this stream has since been channeled. In addition, a man-made drainage has been constructed on the camp's western side.

The main concentration of identified surface features is on the west side of the channeled stream (figures 5.7, 5.12). Several long hut rows appear to have been laid out north to south, though no clear separation into company streets can be made. The absence of clear spatial patterning may reflect camp organization under the direction of naval officers, troop adaptation to the terrain, and the likelihood that the location was a camp prior to constructing winter quarters. Excavations at the camp encountered intact features that were not oriented with the hut features, suggesting an earlier military occupation.

A man-made stream currently divides the huts on the fairway from a group of eleven huts partially excavated into the side of a steep slope. These eleven hut features are probably officers' quarters because they are larger and are separated from the main hut concentration. Hut features are also present on the east slope of the valley, these being smaller than those to the west. Their position within the camp may reflect maximization of available space rather than adherence to military organization.

Camp Layout

The 1861 *Revised Regulations for the Army of the United* States discussed at length in chapter 2 was the primary guide used by both the Confederate and the Federal armies for camp plan and layout (United States War Department 1980:76–82). Archaeological research at other Civil War camps has demonstrated that armies from both sides followed these regulations when laying out camps, where possible (Botwick and McClane 1998; Robert Jolly, personal communication 2002; Townsend 1989). The 1861 regulations set specific criteria for arranging and spacing regimental camps (see figure 2.5). The enlisted men's quarters were to be laid out in "streets," grouped by company. Each street was flanked by double rows of tents or huts. The width of the streets varied but was to be no less than five paces. On one side of the enlisted men's quarters was a parade ground, where drills and inspections took place. Officers' quarters, company officers' quarters, and buildings for kitchens, sutlers, and police guards were arranged on the other side. The regulations outlined the location and position of each officer's quarters, with the most senior officers in the center of the officers' quarters.

The cantonment at Evansport contained four large camps. Camps French (35th Georgia) and Holmes (22nd North Carolina) were organized according to the 1861 regulations. The company streets are clearly identifiable. At Camp French, the level of preservation is enough to loosely identify ten separate groupings, reflecting the ten companies in the Georgia regiment. The street pattern is not as clear at Camp Holmes. At that camp, later disturbances destroyed or masked some patterning, but at least seven company streets can be interpreted from the hut distribution. While both camps were laid out along company streets, the hut features at Camp Holmes are consistently larger than at Camp French, possibly reflecting differences in their modes of construction.

Camps French and Holmes were both laid out with officers' quarters on higher ground. At these locations, huts lay in rows that conformed to local topography but were placed to overlook company streets. The officers located themselves where they could observe their enlisted men and receive fresh air. This positioning may also have had symbolic meaning, because it reinforced the notion that officers were above the enlisted men.

The locations of kitchens and quartermaster buildings are not clearly evident at either camp, though the large hut features north of the company streets at Camp Holmes are probably cook and quartermaster buildings. At Camp French, these buildings are thought to be between the company streets and the officers' quarters. If this is the case, then Camp French was laid out more with the regulations than was Camp Holmes. Neither camp had an associated parade ground. The cantonment had a central parade ground located elsewhere (Gause 1861). Associated with the Georgia camp was a target range. The location of the sinks or latrines was not discovered.

In contrast to Camps French and Holmes, Camp Mallory and the unnamed camp display feature patterning (figures 5.9, 5.12) but do not conform to the camp layout suggested by the 1861 military regulations (see figure 2.5). Three factors could account for this: environmental constraints, orders, and/or lack of familiarity with the regulations covering infantry encampments. Camp Mallory was occupied by some of the first troops (Howell Guards) assigned to Evansport. These men could have camped anywhere, but they chose a location inhospitable for winter habitation. The larger cantonment area contains numerous locations that offered protection from Federal artillery, were hidden, and provided a southern exposure. Camp French, Camp Holmes, and the unnamed camp were each placed to offer a modicum of exposure to the winter sun. In contrast, at Camp Mallory, the officers do not appear to have considered this factor. Although the position of the camp may have been specifically ordered, this possibility is unlikely, because the Confederate commanders would not have had the intimate knowledge of the Evansport area required to direct units to a specific unnamed stream valley. A more plausible explanation for Camp Mallory's lack of order is that navy officers were in command. These officers would not have been aware of infantry regulations dictating camp layout, and they were probably unfamiliar with environmental factors important to camp positioning. Even though troops detailed to the navy were infantry, all were new recruits with only a few months, at most, of army life and they lacked practical experience.

The units under navy command were composed of elements detailed from several different regiments. As discussed previously, the clustering of huts at Camp Mallory appears to reflect organization by small groups rather than by a single regimental-size group. Hut clustering probably reflects soldiers from one company grouping together and showing little regard for the overall camp layout.

The unnamed camp's location is more climatically hospitable than Camp Mallory. Troops occupying this camp have not been identified. Since this is the only location where naval buttons have been reported, it was likely under naval command. As with Mallory, the unnamed camp was not laid out in conformity to the 1861 regulations. The main hut concentration cannot be grouped into streets. Although the hut features may have been organized into long rows, this pattern is not certain. Within this camp there are no readily identifiable empty spaces between the huts. The absence of detectable patterning might be because the site may initially have been designed as a summer camp, the site being reoccupied during the winter. At this camp, several large hut features are separated from the main concentration, suggesting that they are officers' quarters like those at Camps French and Holmes. However, these huts do not share the same advantages as the ones in those camps in that they do not have a commanding view down company streets. At the unnamed camp, huts downslope would have been hidden from view.

All of the Confederates at Evansport considered protection and stealth when they located their camps. The reach of Federal artillery and the prying eyes of aeronauts were major concerns while livability was secondary. Across the cantonment, adherence to military regulations varied, as evidenced by the archaeological record of individual camp layout. Familiarity with the infantry regulations and the practical field experience of the officers in charge may have contributed to these differences. Infantry officers such as Thomas and Pettigrew were seasoned veterans who participated in the army's traditions and regulations. They were able to transfer these ideas to their men, who were new recruits. In contrast, naval officers, such as Commander Chatard, had no experience organizing infantry camps and were not familiar with army regulations.

HUTS

The cantonment contained 697 identified hut depressions. These features ranged from depressions measuring 9 feet (2.7 meters) in diameter to large combinations of mounds, depressions, and trenches. In some areas, careful inspection of the ground surface revealed subtle depressions where the huts had stood. At other locations, hut depressions were obvious, especially after a snowfall, when the hut features looked like an environmental artist's attempt to polka-dot the landscape (figure 5.13). Some features were flat platforms created by digging into the side of the ridge and building up the downslope area

Figure 5.13. Camp Holmes hut depressions (photo by the author).

with back-dirt (figure 5.14). The platforms were presumably for tents, while the mounds, depressions, or combinations were for huts or tents. The depression depths varied, depending on preservation, slope wash, relic-hunter activity, and original form. The size and square footage of the hut footprints varied. Platforms tended to range around twelve feet by twelve feet (144 square feet) while features with mounds ranged from fourteen feet by fourteen feet (196 square feet) to as big as sixteen feet by sixteen feet (256 square feet). In general, features associated with the 35th Georgia company streets are smaller than the features associated with officers in that camp and hut features at other camps.

No official regulations prescribe what form the soldiers' winter huts were to take. In fact, the design and construction of huts was left to the individual soldiers, and they devised different solutions reflective of their taste and circum-

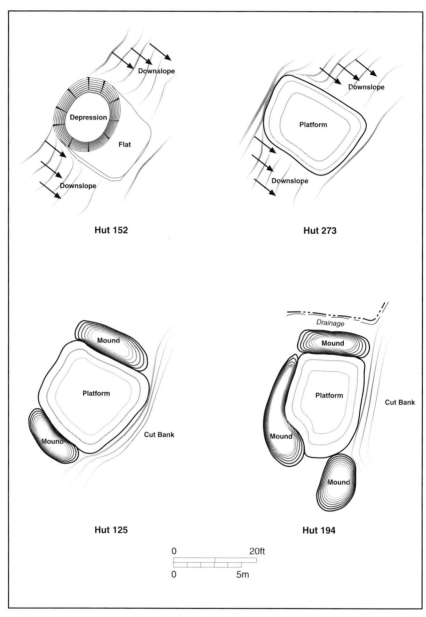

Figure 5.14. Representative sample of aboveground hut features (John Milner Associates).

stance. Consequently, superimposed on the military order of the regulated camp design are expressions of vernacular architecture. Soldiers' memoirs and letters provide some information on hut design. Jonathan Thomas Scharf, a member of the Maryland Flying Artillery, described his "small house" for four men as "eleven feet wide and 12 feet long" (Kelley 1992:8–9). The Federal troops' view of the Confederate winter quarters ranged from Cudworth's (1866:129) observation of log huts with board floors and roofs to "hovels" (Nevins 1962:23). The "hovels" are probably semisubterranean huts built into hillsides.

The variance seen in the size and form is an indication that several different kinds of habitations are present. Shelters built by the troops probably ranged from modified tents to small cabins. During the first winter of the war, some winter huts built by the Confederates were constructed with sawn lumber and had glass windows, slate roofs, and iron stoves. Additionally, some of these first winter quarters were large cabins rather than the small two-person huts common in the later periods of the war.

The larger features are interpreted as the remains of small cabins. The size of these features is larger than the eight- by twelve-foot footprint for huts given by Dean Nelson (1982:84). The difference is attributed to the data set; Nelson (1982) looked at late-war Federal camps. Quarters at the cantonment date to the first winter, a time when the soldiers felt the war would not last long and winter quarters were considered permanent. Later in the war, soldiers' perceptions were different, and they were never sure when they would be ordered to move out.

Platforms scattered throughout the camps may have been bases for tents or huts. Todd Jensen (2000:47, 52–58, 106, 118, and 130) provides information on Federal tent sizes. The Confederates had similar tents. The platforms appear too small for eighteen-foot-diameter Sibley tents, but they may have been bases for wall tents. These tents are fourteen by fourteen and a half feet, ten and a half by eleven and a half feet, and eight and three-quarters by eight and three-quarters feet (Jensen 2000:52).

The smaller depressions on the 35th Georgia's company streets are problematic. At eight by eight feet, the features are roughly a third smaller than other habitations. Grading for a golf course has disturbed the upper one foot to one and a half feet of soil at the 35th Georgia camp. However, this disturbance is not responsible for the hut features' smaller size. Excavations revealed that habitation footprints matched the approximate size of the depressions. On 21 January 1862, Colonel Edward Thomas, commander of the 35th, wrote that his regiment had not built winter quarters but continued to live in tents (Thomas 1862). Apparently, at least the enlisted men continued to live in tents well into the winter. These men attempted to gain more shelter by building semisubterranean habitations roofed by tents. Wedge or A tents were common issue. Jensen (2000:106, 118) indicates that these tents were seven by seven feet, similar to the feature size of those at the 35th Georgia camp.

At the 22nd North Carolina camp, hearth and chimney features were identified. Three possible hearth features were selected for excavation. The configuration of the hearths, vents, and chimney bases exposed by the excavations indicated that the vent for the chimney would have been at the base of the firebox, and this vent would have led underground to a chimney that was detached from the hut (figure 5.15). A draft was created because the firebox was lower than the base of the chimney. A newspaper correspondent writing from the 22nd North Carolina camp described the hearth and chimneys at Camp Holmes in detail:

> To one who had never seen anything like it, the first appearance of our camp would strike him somewhat with wonder, presenting to his view so many diminutive and variously constructed chimneys standing just out of the ground, heterogeneously about in spots, disgorging volumes of black smoke. As the story goes, the snow once fell so deep that the huntsman stepped down a cottager's chimney. It will require very shallow snows to cover up these chimneys; but should one step in them, he would hardly then discover where the fire is. I will explain. Our camp is upon the side of a hill; the men remove the dirt from the upper side of their tents, making the floor level. This gives from two to three feet of dirt wall on the upper side of the tent; in this they cut out a fire-place, and for a chimney cut and cover a trench some six to ten feet to the rear, capping it with a flour barrel, or a few stones set upright, or a little pin of daubed sticks. It is astonishing how well these chimneys draw the smoke, and how small a fire it requires to keep the tent perfectly warm. (Jarrell 2004:17)

No comparative archaeological examples of similar hearths have been identified elsewhere. One period illustration—an 1862 sketch of the 5th Michigan winter camp near Fort Lyon (Alexandria, Virginia) showing a similar hearth, vent, and chimney configuration—was found (Sneden 2001:21). This sketch shows a hut made by stacking logs with a shelter tent acting as a roof. The hut is likely semisubterranean. Extending from the back of the hut is the vent. In this case, the vent appears to be brick and was built on the ground surface. The vent connected to a brick chimney base, on which a barrel was set.

The hearth features at the North Carolina camp appear to be variations of "California" stoves. Describing one such stove, a Federal soldier wrote, "We have in it [hut] a very good California stove—a sheet of iron over a square hole in the ground, with a flue leading to a little chimney of brick and stovepipe outside" (Ward 2002:112).

In 1862, Assistant Surgeon J. Theodore Calhoun was assigned to the 74th New York Volunteers, and in his narrative he described and illustrated a California stove:

> Company B, of the 74th, was composed almost exclusively of Frenchmen, and they economized fuel and at the same time kept their huts properly warmed by an ingenious device somewhat like the camp-stove of the California miners and resembling in shape the ordinary reverberatory furnace. The part containing the fire was made of stone and covered with clay. The chimney was twigs, wattled in, and covered with clay, and the top of the furnace was an old, inverted mess-pan. A piece of sheet iron was used as a

Figure 5.15. Hearth and chimney excavation at Camp Holmes (John Milner Associates).

diaphragm, or damper, to regulate the draft of the furnace, and to econo-
mize fuel. I believe that the most healthful mode of heating tents or huts,
where fuel is plenty, is by an open fire-place and chimney, because of the
ventilation it affords; but an equable heat, by a small amount of fuel, can
be obtained by the *calorifère* as described. (Barnes 1875:91)

The "California" stoves investigated at Camp Holmes probably represent
one of many hearth configurations within the camp and cantonment. Because
there was no design standardization for winter quarters, groups of soldiers designed and built shelters that possibly reflect their ethnicity, socioeconomic
status, prewar occupations, and availability of building materials. The presence
or absence of iron stoves may be an indicator that a hut belonged to an officer;
there is anecdotal relic-hunter evidence for this at Camp Holmes. However,
delineating between officers and soldiers' quarters based on hearth or stoves is
not possible; a better indicator is the location of the hut within the camp.

Conclusion

A camp's military landscape should reflect organization based on principles
ordained by regulation and the collective experiences of the participants, principally the officers. At Evansport, Confederates were predominately concerned
with protection and concealment. The range of Federal artillery and the prying
eyes of aeronauts were factors in camp placement. Camp layout should have
followed regulations dictating design of infantry camps. That regulation layout
was followed only in some camps reflects the command structure. Infantry officers laid out camps following the regulations, while navy officers organized
camps differently. Individual officers can influence camp layout. The expressions of individual soldiers can also be detected within hut design and in fire-
place configuration.

Interpretation of Civil War campsites is difficult archaeology. At Evansport,
we were lucky that hundreds of surface features were present; usually this is
not the case. What is left has been picked over, beginning with the soldiers
themselves and continuing with the aid of sophisticated metal detectors. Investigations at Evansport show that a broad-based approach to field methodology
blended with detailed historical research can shed light on avenues of research
not obtainable though boilerplate cultural resource management Phase I and
II archaeology. The data are there.

Acknowledgments

The Evansport cantonment (44PW917) data used in this chapter are from the 2001 and 2003 archaeological investigations at the Marine Corps Base Quantico (Balicki et al. 2002; Balicki et al. 2004). The Natural Resources and Environmental Affairs Branch (NREAB) at Marine Corps Base Quantico directed John Milner Associates, Inc. (JMA), as a subcontractor of EDAW, Inc., to undertake the investigation. Jeff Gardner of NREAB provided much-appreciated assistance. The following individuals and organizations provided welcomed support: Dr. Charles D. Cheek, Bryan Corle, Kerri Holland, Sarah Ruch, Ron Smith, The Bull Run Civil War Roundtable, Dean Nelson, Eric Mink, Charles Goode, J. Michael Miller, John Fox, Joe Tessandori, Mike O'Donnell, Wally Owen, Duke University Library, and Florida State University Library. My family—Mary Jane, Arielle, Jenna, and Corinne—provided much-appreciated support. Thank you all.

References Cited

Balicki, Joseph, Bryan Corle, and Sarah Goode

2004   Multiple Cultural Resources Investigations at Eight Locations and along Five Tank Trails, Marine Corps Base Quantico, Prince William, Stafford, and Fauquier Counties, Virginia. John Milner Associates, Inc., Alexandria, Va. Report submitted to EDAW, Inc., Alexandria, Va.

Balicki, Joseph, Katherine L. Farnham, Bryan Corle, and Stuart J. Fiedel

2002   Multiple Cultural Resources Investigations, Marine Corps Base Quantico, Prince William and Stafford Counties, Virginia. John Milner Associates, Inc., Alexandria, Va. Report submitted to EDAW, Inc., Alexandria, Va.

Barnes, Joseph K.

1875   *The Medical and Surgical History of the War of Rebellion (1861–1865)*. Prepared, in accordance with acts of Congress, under the direction of Surgeon General Joseph F. Barnes, United States Army. Government Printing Office, Washington, D.C.

Botwick, Brad, and Debra A. McClane

1998   Phase II Historical and Archaeological Investigations of Eight Sites aboard the Marine Corps Base Quantico, Prince William and Stafford Counties, Virginia. Gray and Pape, Richmond, Va. report submitted to United States Army Corps of Engineers, Norfolk, Va.

Cudworth, Warren H.

1866   *History of the First Regiment (Massachusetts Infantry) From the 25th of May, 1861, to the 25th of May, 1864: Including Brief References to the Operations of the Army of the Potomac.* Walker, Fuller, Boston.

Daves, Graham

1991   *History of the Twenty-second Regiment of North Carolina Troops in the late War between the States.* <http://members.aol.com/jweaver301/nc/22ncinf.htm>

Donald, David Herbert (editor)

1975   *Gone for a Soldier: The Civil War Memoirs of Private Alfred Bellard.* Little, Brown, Boston.

Eppes, Susan Bradford

1926   *Through Some Eventful Years.* J. W. Burke, Macon, Ga.

Fox, John J.

2004   *Red Clay to Richmond: Trail of the 35th Georgia Infantry Regiment, CSA.* Angle Valley Press, Winchester, Va.

Frank Leslies Illustrated Newspaper

1862   "Masterly Inactivity," or Six Months on the Potomac. *Frank Leslies Illustrated Newspaper* [New York], 1 February 1862, no. 323, vol. 13:176.

French, Samuel G.

1999   *Two Wars: An Autobiography of Gen. Samuel G. French.* Blue Acorn Press, Huntington, W.Va.

Fulton, W. F.

1924   Picketing the Potomac. *Confederate Veteran* 32(11):427–28.

Gause, Samuel S.

1861   Confederate Engineering Journal of Major Samuel Sidney Gause, 1861–1865. Manuscript on file at the Tennessee State Library and Archives, Nashville.

Gerdes, Edward G.

1998   Arkansas Civil War Page. <http://www.couchgenweb.com/civilwar/2ndbnhis.html>

Green, Georgeanna H.

1981   *American Stonewares: The Art and Craft of Utilitarian Patterns.* Schiffer Publishing, Exton, Penn.

Hanson, Joseph M.

1951   *Bull Run Remembers: The History, Traditions, and Landmarks of the Manassas (Bull Run) Campaigns.* National Capital Publishing, Manassas, Va.

Hewett, Janet B. (editor)

1994–   *Supplement to the Official Records of the Union and Confederate Armies.* Broad-
2001   foot Publishing Company, Wilmington, N.C.

Hurst, M. B.

2002   *History of the Fourteenth Regiment Alabama Volunteers.* Paint Rock River Press, Paint Rock, Ala.

Irvine, W. T.

1891   Old 35th Georgia: A Brief History of the 35th Regiment of Georgia Volunteers from its Organization to its Surrender at Appomattox Court House, April 9, 1865. In *The Sunny South* [Atlanta, Ga.], May 2, 1891.

Jarrell, E. Wallace

2004   *The Randolph Hornets in the Civil War: A History and Roster of Company M, 22nd North Carolina Regiment.* McFarland and Company, Jefferson, N.C.

Jensen, Todd L.

2000   "Gimme Shelter": Union Shelters of the Civil War, A Preliminary Archaeological Typology. M.A. thesis, Department of Anthropology, College of William and Mary in Virginia, Williamsburg.

Kelley, Tom (editor)

1992   *The Personal Memoirs of Jonathan Thomas Scharf of the First Maryland Artillery.* Butternut and Blue, Baltimore, Md.

Musselman, Homer

1991   *47th Virginia Infantry.* H.E. Howard, Lynchburg, Va.

Nelson, Dean E.

1982   "Right Nice Little House(s)": Impermanent Camp Architecture of the American Civil War. In *Perspectives in Vernacular Architecture I.* Edited by Camille Wells, pp. 79–93. University of Missouri Press, Columbia.

Nevins, Allan (editor)

1962   *A Diary of Battle: The Personal Journals of Colonel Charles S. Wainwright (1861–1865).* Harcourt, Brace and World, New York.

New York Herald

1862   The Rebel Batteries on the Lower Potomac. *New York Herald,* March 17, 1862.

Official Records of the Union and Confederate Armies (O.R.).

1997   *The War of the Rebellion: A Compilation of the Official Records of the Union and Confederate Armies.* CD-ROM version, originally published 1880–1901. Guild Press of Indiana, Carmel.

Official Records of the Union and Confederate Navies (O.R.N)

1999   *Official Records of the Union and Confederate Navies in the War of the Rebellion.* CD-ROM version, originally published 1894. H-Bar Enterprises, Oakman, Ala.

Parkhill, George Washington

1861   George Washington Parkhill Papers, Special Collections, Robert Manning Strozier Library, Florida State University, Tallahassee.

Rigdon, John

2003   *Historical Sketch and Roster: The NC 22nd Infantry Regiment.* Eastern Digital Resources, Clearwater, S.C.

Scharf, J. Thomas

1877   *History of the Confederate States Navy from Its Organization to the Surrender of Its Last Vessel.* Fairfax Press, New York.

Small, W. F.

1861   *Sketch of Virginia and the Rebel Camps and Batteries, in Front of Gen. Joe Hooker's Division in Charles County, Maryland.* Made from Prof. Lowe's Balloon, for the Commander in Chief, Dec. 8, 1861. By Col. Wm. F. Small, 26th Reg. Pennsylvania Vols. National Archives and Records Administration, College Park, Md.

Sneden, Robert K.

2001   *Images from the Storm.* Edited by Charles F. Byan Jr., James C. Kelly, and Nelson D. Lankford. Free Press, New York.

Thomas, Dean S.

1985   *Cannons: An Introduction to Civil War Artillery.* Thomas Publications, Gettysburg, Penn.

Thomas, Edward L.

1862   Letter to Honorable J. P. Benjamin, Confederate Secretary of War. Letters received by the Confederate Secretary of War 10430-1862 (21 January 1862). Manuscript on file, National Archives and Records Administration, Washington, D.C.

Townsend, Jan

1989   Louisiana Brigade Winter Camp (Camp Carondelet), National Register of Historic Places Registration Form. Prince William County Planning Office, Prince William, Va.

United States Topographic Engineers

1862   *Map of Northern Eastern Virginia and Vicinity of Washington.* Compiled in Topographical Engineers Office at Division Headquarters of General Irvin McDowell, Arlington, Va. National Archives and Records Administration, College Park, Md.

United States War Department

1980   *Revised Regulations for the Army of the United States, 1861.* National Historical Society, Harrisburg, Pennsylvania. Originally published 1861, United States War Department, Washington, D.C.

Ward, Eric

2002   *Army Life in Virginia: The Civil War Letters of George G. Benedict.* Stackpole Books, Mechanicsburg, Penn.

Wills, Mary A.

1975   *The Confederate Blockade of Washington, D.C., 1861–1862.* McClain Printing Company, Parsons, W.Va.

Wilson, Clyde N.
2002   *Carolina Cavalier: The Life and Mind of James Johnston Pettigrew.* Chronicles
        Press, Rockford, Ill.

6

Civil War Housing Insights
from Camp Nelson, Kentucky

W. STEPHEN McBRIDE AND KIM A. McBRIDE

INTRODUCTION

Over the three years (1863–66) of its existence, the U.S. Army depot at Camp Nelson, Kentucky, had a large, diverse, and changing population that included garrison soldiers (both white and black), transient soldiers, civilian employees, and civilian refugees (both white and black). Providing housing for these people was a constant challenge for the camp's commanding officers.

The housing challenge was most severe after May–June 1864, when large numbers of African American recruits and their families entered Camp Nelson. These people not only increased the overall camp population, but also changed its racial makeup and greatly increased the number of women and children, people the army was not experienced in managing.

Solutions to Camp Nelson's housing needs included tents of all kinds, wooden barracks and dormitories, office-building apartments, former civilian houses, privately run boardinghouses and hotels, wooden cottages, wooden huts or shanties, the U.S. Sanitary Commission Soldiers' Home, and finally, readapted army buildings of diverse function.

BACKGROUND HISTORY

Camp Nelson was a large Union quartermaster and commissary depot, recruitment and training center, and hospital facility that covered more than four thousand acres in southern Jessamine County, Kentucky (figure 6.1). The camp was established June 1863 and stood until June 1866. After spring 1864, it became Kentucky's largest recruitment and training center for African American troops (U.S. Colored Troops, or U.S.C.T.) and also contained a large refugee camp for their wives and children.

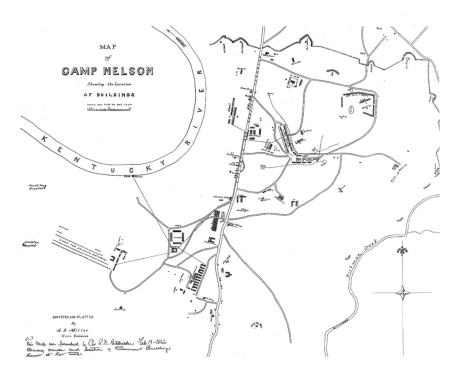

Figure 6.1. Miller (1866) map of Camp Nelson (National Archives, Cartographic Section, College Park, Maryland).

Construction of Camp Nelson began in June 1863 on orders from Major General Ambrose E. Burnside, commander of the newly formed Army of the Ohio. Burnside wanted a large and secure supply depot and encampment for his planned campaign to capture Knoxville, Tennessee. This campaign was to fulfill President Lincoln's promise to free pro-Union areas of east Tennessee from Confederate control. Southern Jessamine County was chosen because of its location on a major turnpike and river. A bridge across the Kentucky River and natural defenses provided by the four-hundred-foot-high limestone palisades on the Kentucky River and Hickman Creek were also factors. As Chief Quartermaster Captain Theron E. Hall (1865) stated, "It is naturally fortified on three sides by the river and creek, the cliffs of which average four hundred feet high and perpendicular. Across the narrow neck from the river [the only exposed part of camp] are fortifications of a most formidable character connected by rifle pits and protected by abatis. Every approach to the camp is commanded by mounted guns and so far as its natural defenses are concerned it is one of the most impregnable points in the country."

Once completed, Camp Nelson consisted of more than three hundred wooden buildings and tents and nine forts spread over four thousand acres on both sides of the Lexington-Danville Turnpike (present U.S. 27) (Hall 1865). There were twenty warehouses for rations, clothing, and equipment, as well as facilities to stable and corral fourteen thousand horses and mules and their feed. Six large workshops were built; there wagons, ambulances, and harnesses were made and repaired, horses shod, and lumber sawed and finished. Two ordnance warehouses and a large powder magazine were also on site. Administrative buildings included the camp headquarters, quartermaster and commissary offices, and the provost marshal's office. Housing and support facilities included two large barracks, tents, mess halls, and a large bakery that produced ten thousand bread rations a day. A waterworks consisting of a steam-driven pump on the river and a 500,000-gallon reservoir were constructed. In addition to the government buildings, there were also private businesses including saloons, hotels, and stores (Hall 1865; Restieaux 1865a; Sears 2002).

Camp Nelson also served as a major Union hospital. This facility consisted of the ten-ward, 700-bed Nelson General Hospital; a measles hospital; a smallpox hospital; the refugee camp hospital; and the prison hospital. The camp also employed between one thousand and two thousand civilian workers. This number included many impressed slaves, carpenters, blacksmiths, teamsters, cooks, and laborers, all of whom were necessary to operate and maintain the facilities, build roads, and haul supplies.

Camp Nelson normally garrisoned one thousand to five thousand soldiers and provided supplies for camps in central and eastern Kentucky and east Tennessee (National Archives 1863–65). The first regiments recruited there were made up of men from eastern Kentucky and east Tennessee. Various regiments from Ohio, Indiana, and Illinois were garrisoned at the camp.

Camp Nelson was also the staging ground and supply depot for three important campaigns: the August–November 1863 Knoxville campaign led by Major General Ambrose E. Burnside; the October 1864 southwestern Virginia campaign led by Major General Stephen G. Burbridge; and Burbridge's wing of Major General George Stoneman's December 1864 Southwestern Virginia Campaign. In addition, the camp provided thousands of horses and mules for the spring–summer 1864 Atlanta Campaign led by Major General William T. Sherman.

The passage of the February 1864 Conscriptive Act allowed the Union to enlist African American troops in Kentucky, but this service was restricted to freedmen and slaves who had their owner's permission. When these restrictions were lifted in April 1864, a flood of slaves began arriving at Camp Nelson. Many risked great danger to reach the camp, attain their freedom, and fight for the freedom of others. By August 1864, two thousand black enrollees were in camp; by the end of the following year, about ten thousand men (40 percent of Kentucky's African American soldiers) had passed through Camp Nelson. Eight United States Colored Troops (U.S.C.T.) regiments were founded there, making it the third largest such center in the United States. These regiments consisted of the 114th, 116th, 119th, and 124th U.S. Colored Infantry regiments, the 5th and 6th U.S. Colored Cavalry regiments, and the 12th and 13th U.S. Colored Heavy Artillery regiments. Parts of five other U.S. Colored regiments were trained or stationed at Camp Nelson, including the 72nd, 117th, 120th, 121st, and 123rd infantry regiments.

At Camp Nelson, many enlistees got their first taste of freedom, although tempered by army life. Sergeant Elijah Marrs of the 12th U.S. Colored Heavy Artillery wrote of his feelings about this change in status: "I can stand this . . . this is better than slavery, though I do march in line at the tap of a drum. I felt freedom in my bones, and when I saw the American eagle with outspread wings, upon the American flag, with the motto E Pluribus Unum, the thought came to me, 'Give me liberty or give me death.' Then all fear banished" (Marrs 1885: 22).

A friend of Sergeant Marrs,' Corporal George Thomas, also of the 12th, stated his strong feelings on escaping slavery: "I enlisted in the 12th U.S. Colored Heavy Artillery in the fall of 1864, and my only sorrow is that I did not enlist sooner. I see, as it were a nation born in a day—men and women—coming forth from slavery's dark dungeons to the noonday sunshine of the greatness of God's gifts—Liberty" (Redkey 1992:189).

After their training, African American troops from Camp Nelson performed a variety of duties. They did garrison duty at Camp Nelson and other Kentucky cities and helped protect the Louisville and Nashville and the Kentucky Central Railroads; critical duty necessary to hold Union territory and protect supply lines.

Camp Nelson's U.S.C.T. were involved in a number of large campaigns and battles: the October 1864 Union attack on Saltville, Virginia (the main saltworks of the Army of Northern Virginia) being noteworthy. The 5th U.S. Colored Cavalry suffered high casualties at the First Battle of Saltville, and Confederate Tennessee soldiers murdered about forty-six of its wounded and captured soldiers after the battle (Davis 1971; Mays 1995). The 5th and 6th U.S. Colored Cavalry regiments were also involved in the December 1864 battles of Marion and Saltville, Virginia, and the 114th and 116th U.S. Colored Infantry regiments were at the sieges of Richmond and Petersburg, respectively.

When African American recruits entered Camp Nelson, their families, who were also seeking freedom and opportunity, often accompanied them. The army had no clear policy as to what to do with these families. Since they were still enslaved, some officers wanted them removed. On a bitterly cold day in November 1864, the new camp commander, Brigadier General Speed S. Fry, ordered over 400 refugees out of camp. This order was eventually countermanded, but not before 102 refugees died of exposure and disease (Sears 1986, 2002).

The political uproar following this incident led to the March 1865 congressional act that freed families of the recruits and established a home for them. This home eventually contained ninety-seven cottages, numerous tents and cabins, a school, barracks, mess halls, a hospital, and a laundry and housed close to four thousand women and children (Fee 1891; Sears 2002). The refugee home was administered jointly by the army (Captain Theron E. Hall, Superintendent) and the American Missionary Association. It provided a safe haven for many refugees but was also known for problems with overcrowding and high mortality (Sears 1986, 2002:ii–iii).

After the Civil War ended (April–May 1865), the military continued to operate Camp Nelson for a time. Until the 13th Amendment ended slavery in December 1865, U.S.C.T. continued to be enlisted at the camp in order to free them. After this, the camp began to be closed down and was finally abandoned by the army in June 1866. Most buildings were sold for their lumber, but the refugee camp buildings and cemeteries remained. The Freedmen's Bureau and the American Missionary Association continued to operate the refugee school while cottages remained as homes for African American families. Many of these families eventually purchased lots and built homes in the former refugee camp, now the community of Hall. In 1866, the Camp Nelson National Cemetery was created from the camp's largest cemetery, and other soldiers were exhumed and moved there.

The remainder of Camp Nelson was returned to its residential and agricultural use. Civilian houses used by the army were reoccupied (generally by the former owners), and the land was reverted to pasture and crops. It remains much the same today. Today, most of the former camp is in farmland, although about five hundred acres are protected and interpreted as Camp Nelson Civil War Heritage Park.

HOUSING: THE ARCHIVAL RECORD

Archival records for Camp Nelson are extraordinary and give details on the function, size, location, and appearance of most of the camp's military buildings. These records include maps, building inventories with dimensions and functions, building elevation drawings, and photographs. Tents and privately owned and operated buildings are also mentioned in archival records, but details such as location and appearance are usually limited, if not completely absent. The records indicate that most army buildings were simple board-and-batten construction, set on piers with glazed windows. Little mention is made of heating sources, but building photographs and elevations indicate that metal stoves rather than fireplaces were usually present.

Building records describing housing for soldiers, civilian employees, and African American refugees indicate a variety of building types, including barracks, a private residence, and cottages. Enlisted men's housing consisted of two 120–by-28–foot one-story barracks and the U.S. Sanitary Commission's Soldiers' Home. The two barracks were located near the fortification line in the northern part of camp and were meant to house the artillery and infantry companies that manned these forts. Each barracks was "filled up with Gun Racks and Sleeping Bunks designed for the accommodation of 170 men" (Hall 1865). A third barracks for soldiers was located at the Nelson U.S. Army General Hospital at the camp's south end. Here, guards for the hospital facilities were housed in a 60-by-24-foot two-story building (Hall 1865).

The U.S. Sanitary Commission's Soldiers' Home was a substantial U-shaped building located just south of the camp's center (figure 6.2). It consisted of a 110-by-20-foot one-story center section used as a dining room and two 80-by-20-foot two-story wings used as apartments. This structure had horizontal weatherboarding and was, therefore, probably of more substantial construction than most Camp Nelson buildings. It also had a serpentine walkway, an ornamental garden, and fountains in front (figure 6.2).

The soldiers' home was built "for the accommodation of soldiers temporarily sojourning in camp en route to join their Regiments at the front" (Hall 1865). It could hold up to 500 men, and throughout 1864 it temporarily lodged 79,883 men (Hall 1865; Newberry 1871:384–85). Records indicate that this building also housed ministers and teachers assigned to the refugee home, east Tennessee white refugees, and later, U.S.C.T. being enlisted or garrisoned at Camp Nelson. Initially, these soldiers were only temporarily housed, but later their stay was much longer (Newberry 1871:380–82, 520–25).

Figure 6.2. U.S. Sanitary Commission Soldiers' Home (1864–65) (National Archives, Still Picture Branch, Washington, D.C.; G. W. Foster and Co., photographers).

Building records indicate that U.S.C.T. were also permanently housed in the ten former hospital wards and associated buildings late in the camp's history (Batchelder 1866). As the main theatre of war moved east following the battle of Nashville, the hospital wards and other hospital buildings were no longer needed. These wards were 120 feet by 25 feet and laid out much like normal barracks, but they had fewer beds (seventy) and more amenities, such as plastered walls, hot and cold running water, and water closets. Other hospital buildings used as military housing were smaller and had previously served a variety of functions.

Officers' housing identified in the building records included the "White House" and the recruiting rendezvous. The White House was a large two-story antebellum residence taken over by the army and used as commissary and quartermaster officers' quarters. This house had three upstairs bedrooms where the chief quartermaster, chief commissary of subsistence, and other officers lived.

The recruiting rendezvous was a U-shaped building located in the southern part of camp. It was originally built as offices and housing for officers. The rendezvous "comprises buildings used by officers engaged in the recruiting service, and also affords accommodation for officers attached to different Regiments while stationed at or being formed in Camp" (Hall 1865). Housing was located in the two 60-by-18-foot two-story wings; offices were located in the 90-by-20-foot one-story central position. Interestingly, a photograph (figure 6.3) of this building is labeled "Barracks for Colored Troops" and therefore suggests that

Figure 6.3. U.S.C.T. barracks (former recruiting rendezvous) (1864–65) (National Archives, Still Picture Branch, Washington, D.C.; G. W. Foster and Co., photographers).

it may have become more permanent soldier barracks after the recruitment of U.S.C.T. This statement is somewhat speculative, but it follows the pattern of the hospital wards noted above.

A cluster of former civilian buildings just north of the fortification line is identified as the engineers' camp or quarters on the Simpson (1864) map and in a photograph (figure 6.4). This cluster consisted of an L-shaped log or frame dwelling house and surrounding log and frame outbuildings. Officers and men of the 23rd Corps Engineers Battalion were housed here.

Both barracks and second-story apartments were noted as housing for civilian employees. Carpenters and laborers who worked at the machine shop were housed in the two-story 93-by-30-foot barracks located near the shop. Blacksmiths, harness makers, and wagon makers employed at the government shops lived in a 140-by-30-foot barracks–mess house combination near their shops. This building had rows of tables and benches on the first floor and seven apartments on the second floor (Restieaux 1865a).

Upstairs sleeping chambers in the camp headquarters and the quartermaster office provided housing for department clerks (Hall 1865). The headquarters consisted of a 40-by-18-foot two-story main frame building with two one-story wings. The quartermaster office was a 121-by-44-foot two-story board-and-batten structure (Restieaux 1865a).

Quarters for medical staff were located at the Nelson General Hospital. Nurses had apartments in eight small 19-by-120-foot or 19-by-204-foot buildings behind the wards. "The Surgeons live in rather an elegant mansion, with highly

Figure 6.4. Engineers' camp (1864–65) (National Archives, Still Picture Branch, Washington, D.C.; G. W. Foster and Co., photographers).

ornamental landscape gardens in front of their quarters, and a fountain playing in the centre" (Davis 1865).

The last group whose housing was mentioned was African American refugees. As noted above, the refugees were families of enlisted U.S. Colored Troops; like their husbands and fathers, they came into Camp Nelson seeking freedom. Following the expulsion of these women and children in November 1864, political pressure was put on the army to readmit them into Camp Nelson and to create housing for them. By early December 1864, construction had begun on the "Home for Colored Refugees" in the southwestern end of camp (figure 6.1). The army's solution was to construct four 25-by-75-foot wards, each of which could house about 120 women and children (Davis 1865). These wards were constructed much like barracks and had a row of beds against the front and back walls (figure 6.5).

While the ward/barrack housing was favored by the army, missionaries to the refugees, particularly the Reverend John G. Fee, argued strongly against them. Fee suggested that the wards would undermine families and, along with the communal mess house, encourage dependency on the army. He wanted refugees to be housed in family-sized cottages and receive training and labor opportunities to become economically independent. He also felt that the crowded wards were very unsanitary (Fee 1865a). Eventually, the army compromised and

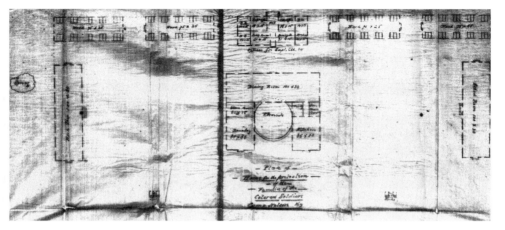

Figure 6.5. Plan of home for the protection of the families of the Colored soldiers, Camp Nelson (1864) (National Archives, Military Records, Record Group 393, Part 4, Entry 734, Box 2. Washington, D.C.).

constructed ninety-seven 32-by-16-foot duplex cottages, along with the four wards (figure 6.6). Each 16-by-16-foot half cottage was occupied by eight to ten people. The wards were later reserved for single women, elderly, and the sick.

The cottages are shown on the right side of figure 6.6. The duplex buildings were eighteen feet apart and described as "box" construction, having cost $306 each to build (Fee 1865b; Hammond 1865). Several descriptions suggest that some had stoves but that some did not. An official list of buildings at the camp describes the floor as "dressed" while most other floors are described as either wooden or dirt (Innis 1865). This suggests a stone floor. Fee complained that the cottages did not have a back door or shed attachment for cooking (Fee 1865c).

Between December 1864 and the fall of 1865, the refugee home population continued to increase until it reached over three thousand (Sears 1986: 38). This was far too many people for the existing cottages and wards, so other structures were added. The army brought in fifty hospital (wall) tents.

Sergeant Marrs, whose duty it was to escort women refugees into Camp Nelson, provides this description of the refugee housing, including these tents: "Down through the streets of the City of Refuge we went, the scene presented being a beautiful one. Every door was open, and in each of them stood some one with a torch in hand to light us on our way. There was no room for us in the neat little cottages, but abundant shelter had been provided in tents for my troop of families, two families being assigned to each tent" (Marrs 1885:60–65).

Figure 6.6. Refugee camp (1864–65) (Photographic Views of Camp Nelson and Vicinity, G. W. Foster and Co., University of Kentucky Special Collections, Lexington).

When these tents were filled, the refugees constructed their own log or frame shanties, at one count at least fifty of each (figure 6.6). Although little documentation exists on them, the shanties appear quite small in an 1865 photograph and probably housed no more than one or two families each. The following description has survived: "Slabs nailed in the form of a pen, about eight feet square, with a rude fire place on one side, one bench and a pail, comprised the whole furniture. On a few loose boards, which served for a floor, lay a pile of rags, which served for a bed, a loose board answered for a door, and open cracks and corners supplied the place of windows! And whom do you think I found there? Two women and six children, two of them quite young" (Scofield 1866).

Tents and shanties existed in other parts of Camp Nelson, but documentation on them is limited. Many tents are illustrated in the 1865 camp photographs and the 1864 Simpson map but are not identified by function. Shanties are identified on the 1866 Miller map (figure 6.1). The occupants of these shanties are not noted on the map, but by late 1865 and 1866 the most likely occupants were white east Tennessee refugees.

Tents were the most common camp housing for soldiers, particularly those just passing through. The type of tents utilized is rarely mentioned in archival records, but wedge and shelter tents were the most likely type for enlisted men doing garrison duty, and shelter tents were probably utilized by soldiers passing through.

Regimental or company tent encampments are mentioned in few official records. Detachments of the 5th and 6th Colored Cavalry regiments encamped in shelter tents above the recruiting rendezvous and above the Camp Nelson House, respectively, in December 1864 (Saunders 1864). The 13th Kentucky Cavalry was encamped at the west end of the northern line of fortifications in December 1864; the 26th Kentucky Infantry was encamped south of the camp's sawmill (Court Martial Records 1864; Saunders 1864).

Sergeant Marrs (1885) noted an encampment of the 12th U.S. Colored Heavy Artillery: "We went by way of Lexington, and arrived at Camp Nelson, without the loss of a man. The barracks being crowded, we were assigned to tents, mine being pitched beside the bull-pen." The location of the bull-pen is unknown, but most corrals were on the camp's eastern side. No other regimental or battalion encampment locations have been found, although dozens of regiments encamped at Camp Nelson between 1863 and 1866.

Interestingly, Abram McLellan of the 1st Ohio Heavy Artillery was assigned to winterize Camp Nelson's tents in November 1863. According to McLellan (1863), "I have been busy for a week building chimneys and fixing up for winter. . . . I made a tabl for the captain to day and a door to our tent. I built a chimney for capt last week all are hard on stick chimneys we have our tent fixed up pretty well we have raised it up three feet of[f] the ground with slabs stood up end wise and dirt throwed up all around with a good fire-place the chimney is not high enough. I will build it up higher tomorrow."

Archival records indicate that hospital tents were used to house officers. These were not always acceptable, however, as Lieutenant Colonel George A. Hanaford of the 124th U.S. Colored Infantry noted:

> I again beg leave to submit the subject heretofor presented too frequently perhaps, of the neccesity [*sic*] of providing suitable quarters for this Regiment. They are now occupying old rotten, and condemned hospital tents which the high wind of the past few weeks have torn almost in shreds and the canvass is so very rotten that the guy ropes will not hold. . . . The duties of the officers are such that they cannot perform them in Shelter tents and it seems to me that it would [be] economical to the Government if quarters for officers and Barracks for the men were erected at this post. (Hanaford 1865)

Another type of housing identified in archival records was private hotels or boardinghouses within or near Camp Nelson. Official army records mention

Mrs. Connor's as well as unnamed hotels within camp. Documents also mention the Owens House and the Camp Nelson House but do not state their exact function.

Captain Daniel James Larned, General Burnside's assistant adjutant, stated that Burnside and his staff lived at Mrs. Hanly's at Camp Nelson (Larned 1863). This house was northwest of Camp Nelson. It is likely, because of the cost and military regulations, that officers and supervisory civilian employees were the primary occupants of these hotels or boardinghouses.

Housing for white east Tennessee and African American refugees was probably the most irregular in camp. When African American refugees first entered Camp Nelson in May 1864, there was no "Home for Colored Refugees." Where these refugees initially lived is not completely clear because of poor documentation, but they were apparently scattered in different places over the camp in tents and homemade shanties. Testimony from U.S.C.T. after the expulsion of refugees in November 22–25, 1864, indicates that some refugee women lived in tents and shanties with their soldier husbands. On November 28, 1864, Private Joseph Miller of the 12th U.S. Colored Infantry stated, "On my presenting myself as a recruit I was told by the Lieut. in command to take my family into a tent within the limits of Camp. My wife and family occupied this tent by the express permission of the aforementioned Officer. . . . About eight O'clock Wednesday morning November 25th a mounted guard come to my tent and ordered my wife and children out of Camp" (Miller 1864). A *New York Tribune* reporter wrote on November 28, 1864, about the expulsion of the refugees: "Armed soldiers attack humble huts inhabited by poor negroes—helpless women and sick children—order the inmates on pain of instant death, and complete their valorous achievements by demolishing dilapidated dwellings." Private John Higgins of the 124th U.S. Colored Infantry also mentions living in a small hut: "In company with another man I built a small hut wher[e] I resided with my family. We were never notified to move until the Nov. 25th, 1864, the guard came with a wagon into which they ordered my family" (Higgins 1864).

The Reverend Abisha Scofield, a missionary to the refugees, gave the only estimate on the number of huts:

> The families of the colored soldiers who were in Camp lived in cabins and huts erected by the colored soldiers or at the expense of the women. During my labors among them I have witnessed about fifty of these huts and cabins erected, and the material of which they were constructed was unserviceable to the Government. I have had extensive dealing with these

people and from my observation I believe that they supported themselves by washing cooking and etc. . . . On Tuesday the 22nd of November last the huts and cabins in which the families of the colored soldiers lived were torn down and the inhabitants were placed on Government wagons and driven outside the lines. (Scofield 1865)

Taken as a whole, archival records suggest that African American refugees were initially housed unofficially and irregularly across Camp Nelson, sometimes with their husbands and sometimes separately. White refugees appear to have been housed exclusively in shanties or huts their entire stay at Camp Nelson. Thomas Butler of the U.S. Sanitary Commission noted that by February 1865, "Good buildings were erected for the negroes, while the white refugees remained in old log huts and miserable dilapidated places" (Newberry 1871:533–35). Some of these are illustrated at the east side of camp on the Miller (1866) map (figure 6.1).

Housing: Archaeological Evidence

Archaeological excavations at Camp Nelson give additional insights into the variety of housing available. They also provide strong evidence for changing building functions as Camp Nelson became a major U.S.C.T. training camp and African American refugee center. In the discussion below, four sites will be utilized to illustrate housing variability and evolution at Camp Nelson. These sites include the Owens House (15Js97), the employee mess houses and encampment area (15Js96), the warehouse/bakery encampment area (15Js164), and the Home for Colored Refugees (15Js163). The first two sites were excavated as part of the U.S. 27 realignment project (McBride et al. 2003), while the last two were the focus of ongoing excavation at Camp Nelson Civil War Heritage Park.

The Owens House (15Js97)

The Owens House was located just west of the Lexington-Danville Turnpike (U.S. 27) in the camp's north section, north of the employees' mess house complex. The 1864 Simpson map shows three buildings, and the 1866 Miller map shows eleven buildings in this area. The 1866 Miller map identifies only two of the eleven structures, the Owens House and the post office. Additional archival research suggests that the other buildings were likely private establishments such as sutler shops and a photographic studio. Sutler shops were especially important sources of food and drink and sundry supplies, as well as being social centers, on a military site (Lord 1969; Spear 1970). The post office was run by

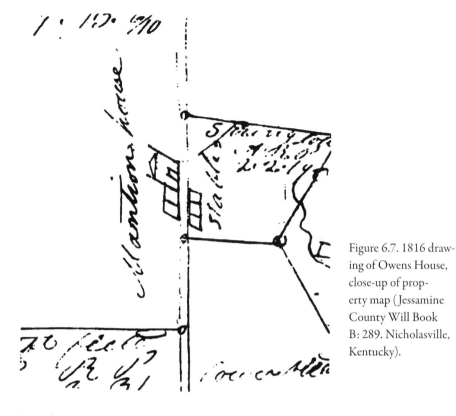

Figure 6.7. 1816 drawing of Owens House, close-up of property map (Jessamine County Will Book B: 289. Nicholasville, Kentucky).

the Adams Express Company, a private company under contract to the army. Thus, the entire area seems to have been under private operation (McBride et al. 2000, 2003).

It is possible that the Owens House was one of two identified structures on the 1866 Simpson map because it was a more substantial, permanent structure. Archival research determined that this house was built before 1805 and was a private residence until the 1850s, when it was rented to David Owens, a tavern keeper. Owens was licensed to keep a tavern in 1852 (Jessamine County Order Book M:20). A sketch of the house made in 1816 shows it as a two-story building with a one-story addition (figure 6.7).

Nineteenth-century taverns provided food and drink and other social functions, as did the sutlers' stores, but were more complex, also providing lodging and being more similar to hotels. Taverns typically provided accommodations for four or more persons to qualify for licensing (Wagner and McCorvie 1992; Yoder 1969). A tavern often had dining, bar, and sitting rooms downstairs and sleeping rooms upstairs (Coleman 1935:65; McBride and Fenton 1996).

At least four archival records from Camp Nelson include references to the Owens House. Two brief mentions of the Owens House are in relation to sutler stores or hucksters peddling vegetables in the area. The third reference also mentions sutler stores but provides some information on the grounds behind the house, confirming that it was not run by the army: "Notify proprietors of the Owens House and the sutler on the west side of the pike and in the vicinity of the Owens House that they must police the grounds in the rear of their buildings. The filth will be removed and covered in earth, so as not to endanger the health of the camp" (Clark 1864a). The final reference verifies that the structure was two stories high, as in the 1816 sketch, and suggests that officers spent some time there. In this case, a lieutenant was ordered to "get the government pack saddle in the room over the Owens' House kitchen" (Clark 1864b).

Archaeological excavations at the Owens House revealed four limestone chimney pads and a cellar foundation surrounded by numerous antebellum and Civil War refuse-filled features (figure 6.8). The placement of the main north and south chimney pads suggests that the structure's main, front portion was forty feet wide (north-south). Some partial side walls helped establish that this main portion was twenty feet deep (east-west). A stone-lined cellar pit was found extending perpendicular, to the west, from the back, or west, wall of the structure (figure 6.8). This cellar was sixteen feet north-south by twenty feet east-west and was located under the back ell. Another chimney pad was found at the back, or west, end of this cellar (figure 6.8), suggesting that it defined the size of the ell. The most likely interpretation is that this back ell was the kitchen.

A fourth chimney pad was found about twenty-six feet to the south of the main house (figure 6.8). No clear connection was found between this chimney pad and the main house. The most likely interpretation is that this feature represents a separate dependency.

Civil War features include seven rectangular privies, two root cellars, and five refuse pits or middens, all suggestive of a fairly intensive occupation. These features, along with extensive domestic artifacts, confirm that eating and drinking took place at the Owens House during the Civil War. But artifacts from the Owens House also include personal items such as sixteen prescription medicine/chemical bottles. These artifacts suggest that a greater variety of activities took place, such as might be expected with overnight lodging.

If the Owens House provided lodging, who might have been its occupants during the Camp Nelson period? Artifacts from the Owens House provide some clues. Although military artifacts were relatively few in number, they suggest that some of the clientele were officers. Two out of four eagle buttons found

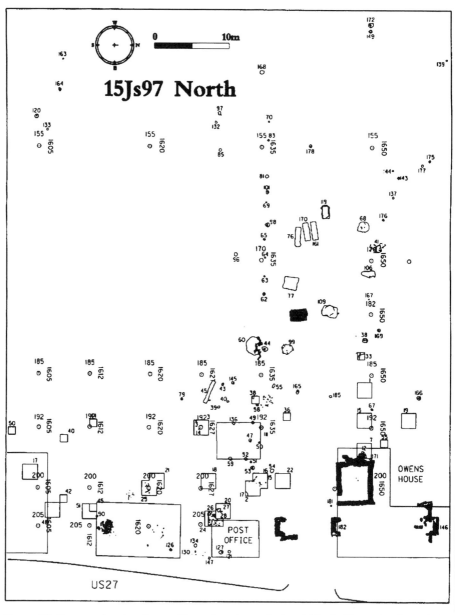

Figure 6.8. Site map showing Owens House foundation (15Js97) (drafted by Richard Wright).

at the Owens House were officers' buttons, and two hat insignia were both from officers' uniforms. Especially telling is the presence of a gold-plated brass sword scabbard guide. These artifacts are in contrast to the military artifacts recovered from the sutler store area south of the Owens House, which are almost exclusively buttons and other artifacts indicative of enlisted men (McBride et al. 2000, 2003).

The presence of a higher-class clientele, including officers, at the Owens House and a lower-class clientele, including enlisted men, at the sutler stores area is also suggested by detailed analysis of the ceramics and bottle glass at these two adjacent areas. Ceramic storage and serving vessels were found in a higher proportion at the Owens House. Serving vessels were more expensive than standard table wares and may indicate more formal dining behavior. A higher proportion of flatware (in contrast to bowls) and standardized decorative sets were recovered from the Owens House, again suggesting more formal dining patterns. These patterns, as well as a higher ceramic index value (Miller 1991) for the Owens House assemblage, suggest a higher socioeconomic clientele at the Owens House. Similarly, the table glass assemblage at the Owens House differed from the south site assemblage, with a much lower proportion of beer bottles recovered.

More direct evidence of dining patterns can be found in the faunal assemblages. The Owens House faunal remains reveal a higher variety of meats, including more sheep and rabbit, and even within the standards of pork and beef, a greater diversity of cuts, when compared to the south site's faunal remains. The greater frequency of sliced meat cuts and cut marks on femurs at the Owens House is suggestive of more meat having been served on platters and cut at the table. The much lower proportion of tin cans at the Owens House also suggests more elaborate food preparation and dining patterns there (McBride et al. 2000).

Taken together, the archaeological evidence from the Owens House site helps explain a topic that is not well documented in the military archival records—housing options for officers. While archival records mention quartermaster and commissary officers lodging in the White House, a private residence that Camp Nelson had taken over, it is unlikely this structure provided enough housing for most of these officers. To date, no archival record of the headquarters or ordnance officers' housing has been located. No records have been found that shed light on the housing of officers who commanded the garrison. Many of these officers may have lived in tents near their men. But they, and other officers, may have also preferred lodging in a private establishment such as the Owens House if they could afford it.

Employee Mess Houses/Encampment (South Half 15Js96)

The employee mess houses/encampment site was located just west of the Lexington-Danville Turnpike (U.S. 27) in the north-central section of the camp headquarters. According to the 1866 Miller map, it contained four employee mess houses and one unidentified building (figure 6.1). The mess houses were 40-by-18-foot two-story buildings where employees from the machine shop were fed (Hall 1865; Restieaux 1865a). The unidentified building (#82 on map; figure 6.9) was a 44-by-22-foot one-story building that was probably a mess house, according to the building lists (Hall 1865; Restieaux 1865a).

Archaeological survey and excavations located two Civil War–era artifact concentrations (Blocks 2 and 4) at the mess houses and one concentration (Block 5) near the area of Building #82 (figure 6.10). A limestone chimney pad was found in the area of Building #82. A drip line was found running parallel to the long axis of what must have been a mess house in the Block 4 area (figure 6.10).

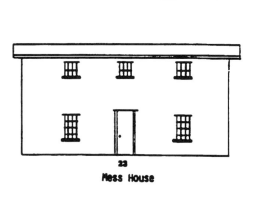

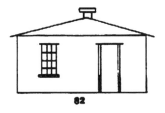

Figure 6.9. Elevation drawing of 15Js96 mess house and Building #82 (National Archives, Military Records, Record Group 92, Entry 225, Box 720, Washington, D.C.).

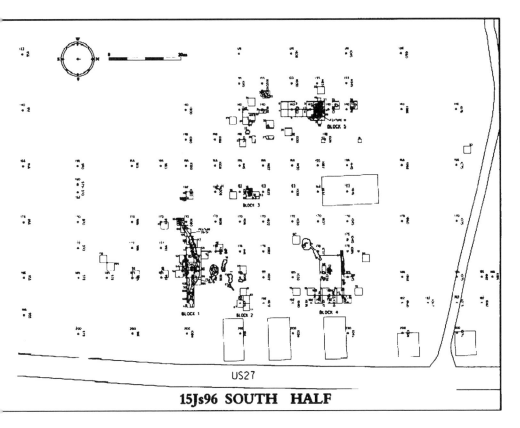

Figure 6.10. Site map showing ditches and mess houses (15Js96) (drafted by Richard Wright).

Surprisingly, the archaeological investigations also located a dense concentration of military and other nineteenth-century artifacts and features south of the area of the mess houses (Block 1) (figure 6.10). No buildings or tents were illustrated in this area (Miller 1866; Simpson 1864). However, the density of military artifacts—including sixteen U.S. Army eagle buttons, eight military accoutrements, and ten Civil War ammunition items—suggests that it may have been an encampment. Parallel and perpendicular ditch features were also found.

The ditch features consisted of one 72-foot-long main ditch (Feature 35/51) and two shorter, 21- to 15-foot ditches (Features 33/39 and 50) roughly parallel to the large one. The shorter ditches were probably once connected and likely continued west beyond the excavation limits. Both had short perpendicular ditch arms as well, which were 6.6 to 7.5 feet apart.

During the Civil War, drainage ditches were often dug between tents in encampments to keep them dry (Billings 1993; Wiley 1952). Feature 35/51 and Features 33/39 and 50 are about six to ten feet apart in the center and may represent the two sides of a "street" separating tents or huts. The four short arms extending out from Features 33/39 and 50 are almost certainly the remains of ditches around wedge tents or shelter tents. These types of tents were seven by seven feet and five and one half by five and one half feet, respectively (Jensen 2000).

Military artifacts from the ditch area included thirteen general service (enlisted men's) eagle buttons and three eagle I (officer) buttons, indicating the presence of both enlisted men and officers in this area. The enlisted men's items predominate and include, besides the general service buttons, an oval U.S. waist belt plate, one eagle hat pin, one shoulder scale, one bayonet scabbard finial, and two knapsack hooks. Another probable military artifact type present in the area of the ditches was tin cups/plates. Whole vessels or fragments representing four tin cups, two tin plates, and two tin bowls/pots were recovered.

The refined ceramics, animal bone, and botanical remains also suggest predominately lower-status occupants such as enlisted men. The refined ceramic vessel assemblage consisted of a large majority (71 percent) of plain or minimally decorated (sponged) whiteware vessels as compared to the more expensive ironstone (29 percent) vessels. No porcelain was recovered in the area of the ditches, for which a rather low Miller Ceramic Index value of 1.36 was calculated (Miller 1991).

Recovered faunal and floral remains also support an enlisted men's occupation of the ditch area. Flotation samples from the ditch features are the only ones from Camp Nelson that produced a large quantity of legumes, particularly beans but also cowpeas and lentils (Rossen 2003). Beans were certainly a staple among Civil War enlisted men (Billings 1993; Wiley 1952).

Faunal remains from the ditches are dominated slightly by beef, which is greatly at variance with the pork-dominated meat assemblages common to Kentucky civilian sites. Of the identified beef cuts, the largest type by far were ribs (48.4 percent), followed by hind shanks (11.9 percent) (McBride et al. 2003)—all medium- to low-quality cuts that are fairly easy to prepare.

Pork remains were, surprisingly, dominated by hams (50.9 percent) and hocks (18.9 percent) (Coughlin and Patterson 2003). The high proportion of hams was unexpected because these are relatively high quality cuts. Since most were thinly cut, they may have been selected because of ease of preparation, particularly over an open fire.

The large assemblage of cut nails (*N*=5,369) and window glass (*N*=671) from the ditch features suggest that the structures here were not simply canvas tents but tents with wooden floors and perhaps wooden walls, as Abram McLellan described above. They may also have included wooden huts. Improving tents by adding wooden floors and walls and even glazed windows was common in permanent camps such as Camp Nelson (Nelson 1987). In fact, Camp Nelson photographs show tents with wooden bases and even wooden front walls with doors.

A closer analysis of the complete nails indicated, not surprisingly, that six-penny and eight-penny nails were very common. These nails are generally associated with siding, light framing, and flooring and would be expected in the improved tents (Young and Carr 1989–90). What was surprising, however, was that four-penny nails were the most common size. These nails are usually associated with shingle or shake roofs and suggest structures more substantial than improved tents. A complicating factor with these smaller nails is that they could also come from army supply and ammunition boxes (Faulkner 1993:88; Legg and Smith 1989:124). The large numbers of metal packing straps in the ditch feature support this alternative explanation for at least some four-penny nails. Another possibility is that soldiers did not follow carpenters' norms and used whatever nails they could find.

A pit or cellar (Feature 99) was discovered just north of the ditches. This feature was nine by six feet and eighteen inches deep. It may have been a cellar under a building or an excavated tent floor. The latter was a common adaptation in winter tents (Bentz and Kim 1993). If this pit had been under a tent, it was a larger wall tent, rather than a wedge or shelter tent.

The position of this feature between the ditches and the most southern mess house (Block 2) complicates the task of associating it with one area or the other, but it did contain two U.S. Army eagle buttons and one U.S. waist belt plate, indicating a military association. All buttons were general service enlisted men's buttons. The large number of nails (*N*=850), 65 percent of all the artifacts, and window glass (*N*=142) from this feature suggests that a building or winterized tent may have been over this pit. As in the area of the ditches, refined ceramics were primarily plain whiteware, again suggesting lower-status occupants such as enlisted men.

Artifacts from Feature 99 and the ditch features, as well as the ditch configu-

rations, suggest this area was a soldiers' encampment. But who were these soldiers and why was this encampment placed close to civilian mess houses, when
the mixing of military and civilian accommodations was usually discouraged
if not prohibited by the army? Certain artifacts found in the ditch area and at
the mess house may offer an answer to these questions.

Excavations at the mess houses and at Building #82 (Block 5) produced
many foodways and architectural artifacts but also numerous military artifacts,
suggesting that these structures had a military occupation. Military artifacts
from the southern (Block 2) and northern (Block 4) mess houses include seven
general service eagle buttons, one eagle I button, one eagle staff button, one
U.S. waist belt plate, one backpack hook, one canteen, two .58-caliber muzzle-
loaded bullets, one carbine cartridge, and four musket barrel bands. The Building #82 area (Block 5) produced five general service eagle buttons, one U.S.
waist belt plate, one cavalry picket pin, one cavalry carbine sling buckle, six
carbine or repeater cartridges or bullets, six .58 caliber bullets, and two percussion caps. The picket pin, sling buckle, and ammunition suggest the presence
of cavalrymen in Block 5. Whether these soldiers used the structures as mess
houses or as barracks is unclear, but they certainly used the buildings fairly
intensively.

When did soldiers utilize these structures? Although we have no direct
documentation on the changing use of these particular buildings, documents
such as employee records and building lists do document a reduction in civilian employees and changing use of some buildings in the second half of the
camp's existence (Hall 1863–64; Restieaux 1865b). Documents record the use
of U.S.C.T. as laborers in a number of camp areas and buildings, including the
nearby machine shop. In August 1865, Chief Quartermaster Captain E. B. W.
Restieaux (1865c) stated, "In addition to the above number of employees there
are detailed from the 124th U.S.C.I. one hundred and fifty nine men for various duties in the [Quartermaster] Department."

The U.S.C.T. used as laborers included not only the "invalid" 123rd and
124th regiments, but also men from the regular U.S.C.T. regiments. Some men
could have easily utilized the mess houses and encampment area around the
ditches.

Another line of evidence that may suggest the presence of U.S.C.T. in this
site area is the discovery of women's and children's artifacts in the ditches, mess
houses, and Building #82. These artifacts include three faceted blue and black
glass beads, one round white glass bead, one gold broach clasp, and one rubber
hair comb (barrette). Ten colored glass or brass buttons have been positively

identified as women's dress buttons (Shelly Foote, personal communication 1998). Children's artifacts include two porcelain doll fragments.

Who were these women and children? One strong possibility is that they were family members of African American soldiers. Although other white and black women were employed in camp and although officers' wives sometimes visited, wives of the U.S.C.T. were by far the most numerous women in camp and the only ones documented as cohabiting with their husbands in camp. Children of the U.S.C.T. were the only documented children. Military records document officers' complaints about the U.S.C.T. cohabiting with their families even after the "Home for Colored Refugees" was constructed (Frazee 1865; Hanaford 1865). This cohabitation was widespread and condoned before the November 1864 expulsion of women and children (see above).

Although the premise is difficult to prove conclusively, the presence of U.S.C.T. and their families in the area of the ditches and mess houses has the best fit with archaeological and documentary evidence. A military presence in what was originally civilian mess housing underlines the fluid nature of Camp Nelson as it evolved to meet changing needs.

The Bakery/Warehouse Encampment (15Js164)

Recent archaeological survey at the Camp Nelson Civil War Heritage Park discovered another campsite between the documented locations of the commissary and quartermaster warehouses and the bakery. This encampment is not illustrated on any Civil War–era Camp Nelson maps. An extensive search in Camp Nelson archival records led to the discovery of two orders mentioning an encampment near the warehouses. These orders both date to June 17, 1864:

> Lieut.
>
> Information has reached these Headquarters that a bevy of women and children are quartered near the Commissary Warehouses, the women (colored) are engaged in lewd business annoying everything and every body in the vicinity. You are directed to place the whole kit beyond the lines five (5) miles, with a parting injunction to not return on pain of being imprisoned. (Hanaford 1864a)
>
> Captain: The Col. Commanding authorizes you to raze the shanties near the commissary warehouses now occupied by negroes. Orders have been issued to the Provost Marshall to place the occupants beyond the lines. (Hanaford 1864b)

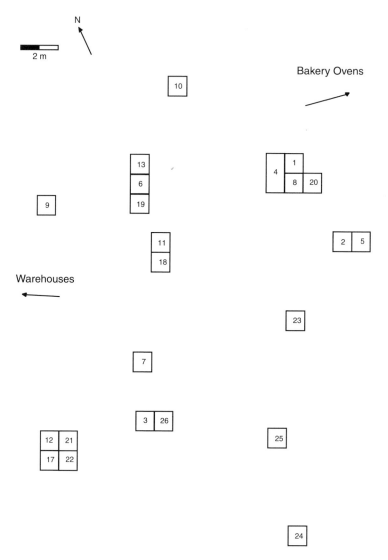

Figure 6.11. Site map of bakery/encampment area (15Js164) (drafted by J. David McBride).

Could these refugee shanties be our encampment site?

Survey and test units produced an interesting artifact assemblage that gives insights into the occupants of this roughly 34-by-22-meter area (figure 6.11). Recovered military artifacts—including nine general service U.S. Army eagle buttons, one .54-caliber Minié bullet, and an iron shoe heel plate—certainly indicate the presence of soldiers. The eagle buttons suggest that they were en-

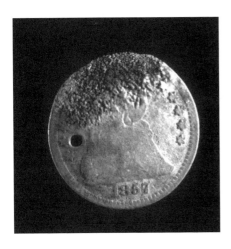

Figure 6.12. Pierced half-dime from bakery/encampment area (15Js164) (photograph by J. David McBride).

listed men, and the low quality of refined ceramics, predominantly plain whiteware, tends to support this.

Other personal and clothing artifacts suggest that this occupation, like that at 15Js96, was complex. Recovery of three black beads, one white bead, two blue-glass-and-metal dress buttons, and a porcelain doll head strongly suggests the presence of women and possibly children. Could these artifacts be associated with African American women and children?

One artifact supporting an African American occupation is a pierced silver 1857 half-dime (figure 6.12). Pierced coins, particularly silver ones, have been found on a number of African American sites and are thought to have been worn as magical charms protecting the wearer from evil spirits (Singleton 1991; Wilkie 1995; Young 1996, 1997). As a former Kentucky slave stated in a 1930s WPA interview: "Every one of my children wears a silver dime on a string around their leg to keep off the witches spell" (Rawick 1977:35, cited in Young 1997).

Interestingly, one unpierced silver half-dime was also found. While this could simply be lost money, the fact that few silver coins have been found at Camp Nelson makes one wonder. Wilkie notes reports of coins being worn in shoes for protection and used to detect conjurers (1995:144).

Unfortunately, no structural features have been found at this site, but it has produced a large assemblage of cut nails, a moderate quantity of window glass, a door lock plate, and a hinge, suggesting structures of some kind. The distribution of nails across the site suggests the existence of at least three structures, or structure demolition areas, and possibly more. Three one-by-one-meter units

(Units 1, 21, 25) with the most cut nails produced an astonishing 2,452, 856, and 540 nails, respectively. Two units also had extensive evidence of burning in the form of ash, burned nails, and burned ceramics and glass. This could be evidence of the shanty destruction mentioned in the June 1864 orders or shanty destruction that occurred later in November 1864. U.S.C.T. soldier John Higgins' testimony following the November expulsion recorded a guard telling Higgins' wife that "if you do not get out we will burn the house over your heads" (Higgins 1864). This statement is the only one that clearly mentions the burning of the structures.

In sum, archaeological and archival evidence suggests that this encampment was occupied by soldiers as well as women and children and that these people were most probably African Americans. They most likely lived in wooden huts or shanties although substantially altered tents could have been used as well. Whether or not this site is the so-called lewd women's occupation mentioned in the June 1864 order is uncertain, but the presence of so many military and some female artifacts supports a multigender occupation.

The Home for Colored Refugees

Archaeology at the Home for Colored Refugees focused upon locating the original refugee cottage area. One hundred and ninety nine shovel test pits were excavated in 1995 and a hundred more in 2002, typically on a five-to-ten-meter grid. Unfortunately, none of the ninety-seven cottages or larger institutional buildings from the Home for Colored Refugees survived, although a rural community with some ties to the refugee camp's history was located on the site. Additional archival research, supplementing official military records with deeds, census records, and other public records, as well as oral history, provided clues. Census records showed that the size of the community, which Fee named Ariel but later was called Hall or Camp Nelson, remained fairly stable. About forty households occupied the community from the late 1860s into the early twentieth century. Out-migration began when Prohibition ended employment in a nearby distillery, and it accelerated greatly after World War II. Today the community is about half of its original size, only a few residents have ties back to the refugee camp, and not all are African American.

The 1866 Miller map (figure 6.1) shows the refugee camp, though a period sketch map gives more detail on the buildings located there (figure 6.13). Comparison of modern street layouts with the Home for Colored Refugees map suggests that the main thoroughfare of the modern community shifted slightly south of the original cottages over time and has been somewhat realigned. This

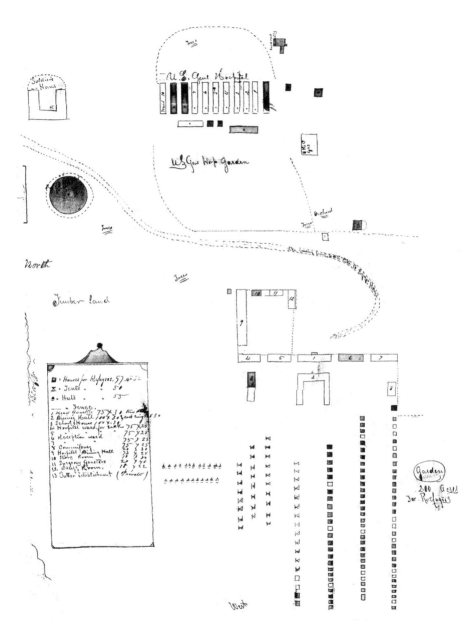

Figure 6.13. Period sketch map of refugee camp layout (circa 1865) (National Archives, Military Records, Record Group 105, Entry 3379, Box 1, Washington, D.C.).

shift put most contemporary houses on flatter ground that was in the 1864–65 camp layout set aside for two hundred acres of gardens (figure 6.13). This is fortunate, for the former rows of refugee cottages are today located in pasture, tobacco fields, or garden areas, with few modern houses. Two small streets in this northern part of the contemporary community retained the southeast-to-northwest orientation of the original refugee cottage rows and helped pinpoint the survey area.

The refugee camp also contained larger institutional wards at the cottage rows' east end (figures 6.1, 6.13). This area contains houses today but has retained some of its institutional nature, having been the former location of the Ariel Academy/Camp Nelson Academy, founded by missionary John Fee in 1868. It is the contemporary site of the early twentieth-century Presbyterian church and parsonage, still standing today.

The archaeological survey of the refugee camp focused on the church and its parsonage (today part of Camp Nelson Civil War Heritage Park) and on private lands in pasture or agricultural fields, within the surmised location of the cottage rows. Not surprisingly, the land around the church (and former site of the 1868–1904 school) contained a moderate density of both nineteenth- and twentieth-century materials. These were primarily nails, window glass, brick and limestone fragments, and other architectural indicators but also included considerable bottle glass. Buildings from the Ariel Academy were known to stand here until at least the 1930s.

Shovel testing in the hypothesized cottage row areas was especially successful. Over half of the shovel test pits here contained artifacts. The most common artifacts found were plain whiteware and container glass, but window glass and nails were also found. Windows are shown in the Civil War–era photograph of the cottages. Of the sixty-eight nails recovered, fifty-six are machine cut, nine are wire, and three are unidentified. Personal artifacts found were a doll foot, a black glass button, a metal button, and a marble. A file and a hinge were also recovered. These artifacts are quite similar to what would be expected from a short-term mid-nineteenth-century occupation. Since little other documented occupation is suggested by archival and oral history research, the likelihood that these materials represent refugee cottages is strong. Especially promising was the recovery of a Civil War eagle button.

No structural features were found, but this is not surprising since the cottages were simple "box" structures without substantial foundations or chimney pads. Small limestone pieces were observed. Whether they represent remains from the "dressed" cottage floors will have to await further investigation. Most of the area has been plowed, so a high degree of preservation of such ephemeral floors is not expected. However, the front yard fences seen in the cottage photograph should leave subsurface post molds that could be recovered by block excavation.

CONCLUSION

Camp Nelson was a large and complex facility where functions grew even more diverse over time. Archaeological and archival investigations of housing within the camp highlight this occupational complexity and some changes that occurred at the camp. Research at the Owens House (15Js97) produced evidence of high-status residents, including officers, living at this privately operated tavern within Camp Nelson.

Two excavated sites—the mess houses/encampment (15Js96) and the warehouse/bakery (15Js164)—produced architectural evidence of soldiers, women, and children living in the same encampment. Both sites likely represent examples of African American soldiers and their families camping together, although only the latter site has clear African American material culture.

The distribution of military artifacts at the mess houses/encampment site also suggests that these originally civilian employee mess houses had been taken over, or at least heavily utilized, by soldiers. This site likely documents the transformation of Camp Nelson into a major African American troop and refugee center with a reduction in quartermaster functions and civilian employees.

The final site examined, the "Home for Colored Refugees," produced evidence of the neat rows of cottages constructed for the refugees after their November 1864 expulsion from camp. Construction of these cottages represented the culmination of the army's constantly changing policy on refugees. By building a home, and particularly by adding cottages to the barracks, the army agreed not only to shelter the refugees from their owners, but also to assist the American Missionary Association in preparing them for a life as free people.

The size, location, functional complexity, and cost of Camp Nelson were constant sore points for the army high command. Inspectors and generals were often critical of Camp Nelson and its solutions to various problems, including housing. In March 1864, none other than Lieutenant General Ulysses S. Grant stated, "I have had an inspection made of Camp Nelson and Mount Sterling. It shows a wasteful extravagance there. . . . It seems to me that Camp Nelson should be broken up entirely and the public property issued where it will be of service" (Grant 1864).

Others, such as the camp's chief quartermasters, missionary leaders, and African American troops and refugees, had a much different and more positive view of Camp Nelson, especially after December 1864, when refugee policy changed. Although Camp Nelson certainly made an impact on the war as a supply depot, its position as an African American emancipation center for soldiers and their families is what struck an emotional chord then and now. Archaeology provided tangible evidence of these people's camp and lifeways. Although it certainly had its ups and downs, Camp Nelson's ultimate success and legacy was perhaps best articulated by an African American soldier, when he stated, "See how much better off we are now than we was four years ago. It used to be five hundred miles to get to Canada from Lexington, but now its only eighteen miles! Camp Nelson is now our Canada" (Simpson 1865).

References Cited

Batchelder, Col. R. E.
1866   List of Public Buildings at Camp Nelson, February 1866. National Archives, Military Records, Record Group 92, Entry 225, Box 720. Washington, D.C.
Bentz, Charles, and Yong W. Kim (editors)
1993   *The Sevierville Hill Site: A Civil War Union Encampment of the Southern Heights of Knoxville, Tennessee.* Report of Investigations No. 1. University of Tennessee Transportation Center, Knoxville.
Billings, John D.
1993   *Hardtack and Coffee.* University of Nebraska Press, Lincoln.
Clark, Col. Andrew H.
1864a   Letter to Major, May 23. National Archives, Military Records, Record Group 383, Part 4, Entry 902, p. 8. Washington, D.C.
1864b   Letter to Lieut., May 31. National Archives, Military Records, Record Group 383, Part 4, Entry 902, p. 58. Washington, D.C.
Coleman, J. Winston
1935   *Stage-coach Days in the Bluegrass.* Standard Press, Louisville, Ky.
Coughlin, Sean, and Judy A. Patterson
2003   Appendix D: Faunal Remains from Camp Nelson. In *From Supply Depot to Emancipation Center: The Archaeology of Camp Nelson.* Edited by Stephen McBride et al., pp. D1–D74. Wilbur Smith Associates, Lexington, Ky.
Court Martial Records
1864   Court Martial of Lt. Michael A. Hogar, Feb. 2, 1864. National Archives, Military Records, Record Group 153, LL 2260, Folder 1. Washington, D.C.

Davis, Maj. Murray

1865   Inspection Report of Camp Nelson, Kentucky, May 13, 1865. National Archives, Military Records, Record Group 159, Entry 15, Box 7, Folder 6, File D-17. Washington, D.C.

Davis, William C.

1971   The Saltville Massacre. *Civil War Times Illustrated*, February, pages 4–11, 44–48.

Faulkner, Charles H.

1993   Artifacts. In *The Sevierville Hill Site: A Civil War Union Encampment of the Southern Heights of Knoxville, Tennessee*. Edited by Charles Bentz and Yong W. Kim, pp. 81–110. Report of Investigations No. 1. University of Tennessee Transportation Center, Knoxville.

Fee, John G.

1865a   Letter to Brother Whipple, Feb. 25, 1865. American Missionary Association Archives, Tulane University, New Orleans, LA, Roll 44097–101.

1865b   Letter to Brother Whipple, June 9, 1865. American Missionary Association Archives, Tulane University, New Orleans, LA, Roll 44145–7.

1865c   Letter to Brother Whipple, June 27, 1865. American Missionary Association Archives, Tulane University, New Orleans, LA, Roll 44149.

1891   *Autobiography of John G. Fee*. National Christian Association, Chicago.

Frazee, Maj. J. W.

1865   Letter to Samuel English, Apr. 4, 1864. National Archives, Military Records, Record Group 393, Part 2, Entry 1661. Washington, D.C.

Grant, Ulysses S.

1864   Letter to Schofield, Mar. 17, 1864. In *The War of the Rebellion: A Compilation of the Official Records of the Union and Confederate Armies*, Series 1, Volume 32, part 3, pages 83–84. Published 1880–1901, U.S. Government Printing Office, Washington, D.C.

Hall, Theron E.

1863–64 List of Persons and Articles Employed at Camp Nelson, Kentucky, June 1863–Oct. 1864. National Archives, Military Records, Record Group 92, Entry 238. Washington, D.C.

1865   Report to M. C. Meigs, May 30, 1865. National Archives, Military Records, Record Group 92, Entry 225, Box 720. Washington, D.C.

Hammond, Lafayette

1865   Letter to Capt. Harlan, June 10, 1865. National Archives, Military Records, Reports of Inspections, Record Group 393, Part 1, Entry 2217. Washington, D.C.

Hanaford, Lt. Col. George A.

1864a   Letter to Lt. Jno McQueen, June 17, 1864. National Archives, Military Records, Record Group 393, Press Copies, vol. 107, p. 234. Washington, D.C.

1864b   Letter to Capt. J. H. Johnson, June 17, 1864. National Archives, Military Records, Record Group 393, Press Copies, vol. 107, p. 253. Washington, D.C.

1865   Letter to Lieut. G. E. Goodyear, Mar. 17, 1865. National Archives Military Records, Record Group 92, Entry 225, Box 720. Washington, D.C.

Higgins, John

1864   Affidavit of John Higgins, Nov. 28, 1864. National Archives, Military Records, Record Group 92, Entry 225, Box 720. Washington, D.C.

Innis, Charles A.

1865   Letter to Maj. Gen. M. Meigs, Nov. 21, 1865. National Archives, Military Records, Record Group 92, Entry 225, Box 720. Washington, D.C.

Jensen, Todd L.

2000   Civil War Archaeology at Fort Pocahontas: Life between the Trenches. *Quarterly Bulletin of the Virginia Archaeological Society* 55:126–34.

Jessamine County Court Records

1852   Order Book M:20. Jessamine County Courthouse, Nicholasville, Ky.

Larned, Daniel R.

1863   D. R. Larned journal, August 10–11, 1863. D. R. Larned Papers. Library of Congress, Washington, D.C.

Legg, James B., and Steven D. Smith

1989   *"The Best Ever Occupied . . .": Archaeological Investigations of Civil War Encampment on Folly Island, S.C.* Research Manuscript Series 209. South Carolina Institute of Archaeology and Anthropology, University of South Carolina, Columbia.

Lord, Francis

1969   *Civil War Sutlers and Their Wares.* Thomas Yoseloff, New York.

Marrs, Elijah P.

1885   *Life and History of the Reverend Elijah P. Marrs, First Pastor of Beargrass Baptist Church, and Author.* Bradley and Gilbert, Louisville, Ky.

Mays, Thomas D.

1995   *The Saltville Massacre.* Ryan Place Publishers, Fort Worth, Tex.

McBride, W. Stephen, Susan C. Andrews, J. Howard Beverly, and Tracey A. Sandefur, with contributions by Sean P. Coughlin, Judy A. Patterson, Melody Pope, Jack Rossen, and Sarah C. Sherwood

2003   *From Supply Depot to Emancipation Center: The Archaeology of Camp Nelson.* Wilbur Smith Associates, Lexington, Ky.

McBride, W. Stephen, Susan C. Andrews, and Sean P. Coughlin

2000   "For the Convenience and Comforts of the Soldiers and Employees at the Depot": Archaeology of the Owens' House/Post Office Complex, Camp Nelson, Kentucky. In *Archaeological Perspectives on the American Civil War.* Edited by Clarence R. Geier and Stephen R. Potter, pp. 99–124. University Press of Florida, Gainesville.

McBride, W. Stephen, and James P. Fenton
1996   *Phase II Testing of 15Mc137 at the Ky 81 Bridge over the Green River at Calhoun-Rumsey, McLean County, Kentucky.* Wilbur Smith Associates, Lexington, Ky.

McLellan, Abram
1863   Letter, Nov. 24, 1863, Abram McLellan to Mage McLellan. Abram McLellan Papers. Ohio Historical Society, Columbus.

Miller, A. B.
1866   Map of Camp Nelson Showing the Locations of Buildings. Cartographic Section, National Archives, Washington, D.C.

Miller, George L.
1991   A Revised Set of CC Index Values for Classification and Economic Scaling of English Ceramics from 1778 to 1880. *Historical Archaeology* 25(1):1–25.

Miller, Joseph
1864   Affidavit of Joseph Miller, Nov. 28, 1864. National Archives, Military Records, RG 92, Entry 225, Box 720. Washington, D.C.

National Archives
1863–65 Return of Posts, Camp Nelson, Kentucky. Military Records Group M:617, Microfilm Roll 1527. Washington, D.C.

Nelson, Dean E.
1987   "Right Nice Little Houses: Impermanent Camp Architecture of the American Civil War." In *Perspectives in Vernacular Architecture.* Edited by Camille Wells, pp. 79–83. University of Missouri Press, Columbia.

New York Herald, correspondent
1864   "Cruel Treatment of the Wives and Children of U.S. Colored Soldiers," Nov. 28, 1864.

Newberry, John S.
1871   *The U.S. Sanitary Commission in the Valley of the Mississippi during the War of the Rebellion.* Fairbanks, Benedict, and Co., Cleveland, Ohio.

Redkey, Edwin S.
1992   *A Grand Army of Black Men: Letters from African American Soldiers in the Union Army, 1861–1865.* Cambridge University Press, Cambridge.

Restieaux, Capt. E. B. W.
1865a   Letter to Brig. Gen. Robert Allen, Mar. 20, 1865. National Archives, Military Records, Record Group 92, Entry 225, Box 720. Washington, D.C.
1865b   List of Persons and Articles Employed at Camp Nelson, Ky., Jan.–Dec. 1865. National Archives, Military Records, Record Group 92, Entry 238. Washington, D.C.
1865c   List of Employees, August 31, 1865. National Archives, Military Records, Record Group 92, Entry 225, Box 720. Washington, D.C.

Rossen, Jack
2003   Appendix E: The Antebellum and Civil War Archaeobotany of Camp Nelson,

Kentucky. In *From Supply Depot to Emancipation Center: The Archaeology of Camp Nelson*. Edited by Stephen McBride et al., pp. E1–E42. Wilbur Smith Associates, Lexington, Ky.

Saunders, Capt. M. C.

1864   Inspection of Camp Nelson, Dec. 15, 1864. National Archives, Military Records, Record Group 393, Part 1, Entry 2217. Washington, D.C.

Scofield, Abisha

1865   Affidavit of Abisha Scofield, Dec. 16, 1865. National Archives, Military Records, Record Group 92, Entry 225, Box 720. Washington, D.C.

1866   Laboring at Camp Nelson, February 1866. *American Missionary* 10(4):85–86.

Sears, Richard

2002   *Camp Nelson, Kentucky: A Civil War History*. University Press of Kentucky, Lexington.

1986   *A Practical Recognition of the Brotherhood of Man: John G Fee and the Camp Nelson Experience*. Berea College, Berea, Ky.

2002   *Camp Nelson, Kentucky: A Civil War History*. University Press of Kentucky, Lexington.

Simpson, Lt. Col. James H.

1864   Camp Nelson and Its Defenses, Jessamine County, Kentucky. Cartographic Section, National Archives, Washington, D.C.

Simpson, Joseph

1865   Letter to James H. Tuke and Frederick Seebchom, July 1, 1865. Friends Central Committee for the Relief of Emancipated Negroes, London.

Singleton, Theresa

1991   "The Archaeology of Slave Life." In *Before Freedom Came: African American Life in the Antebellum South*. Edited by Edward D. C. Campbell and Kym S. Rice, pp. 176–191. University Press of Virginia, Charlottesville.

Spear, Donald P.

1970   The Sutler in the Union Army. *Civil War History* 16(2):121–38.

Wagner, Mark J., and Mary R. McCorvie

1992   The Archaeology of the Old Landmark. Center for American Archaeology, Kampsville, Ill. Report submitted to Illinois Department of Transportation, Springfield.

Weaver, Lt. Col. T. R.

1865   Letters Sent, 119th U.S. Colored Infantry, June 4, 1865. National Archives, Military Records, Record Group 94, Entry 326. Washington, D.C.

Wiley, Bell Irvin

1952   *The Life of Billy Yank*. Louisiana State University Press, Baton Rouge.

Wilkie, Laurie A.

1995   Magic and Empowerment on the Plantation: An Archaeological Consideration of African-American World View. *Southeastern Archaeology* 14(2):136–148.

Yoder, Paton

1969   *Taverns and Travelers: Inns of the Early Midwest.* Indiana University Press, Bloomington.

Young, Amy

1996   Archaeological Evidence of African-Style Ritual and Healing Practices in the Upland South. *Tennessee Anthropologist* 21: 139–155.

1997   Risk Management Strategies Among African-American Slaves at Locust Grove Plantation. *International Journal of Historical Archaeology* 1(1):5–37.

Young, Amy L., and Phillip J. Carr

1989–   Building Middle Range Research for Historical Archaeology with Nails. *Ohio*
1990   *Valley Historical Archaeology* 7/8:1–8.

Part IV

Encampment Architecture and Material Culture

DAVID G. ORR, CLARENCE R. GEIER, AND MATTHEW B. REEVES

The study of material culture has been broadly defined by historical archaeologists. It includes not only the smallest fragments of archaeological artifacts but also buildings, cities, and landscapes; indeed, everything made by human hands. All these surviving materials are exploited to test our theories, and all must endure our scrutiny. Some archaeologists (Deetz 1967:83–96) would include fields of study whose techniques and approaches are compatible with the great range present in archaeological subjects. From another perspective, folklorist Henry Glassie considers material culture to be an "odd term," for he would argue that culture is mostly immaterial, being chiefly expressed as patterns in mind: inward, invisible, and shifting. Yet he admits that it is a useful term, an "ungainly conjunction of the concrete and the abstract" (Glassie 1999:41). Glassie's definition sets up an excellent way to begin thinking about the study of material forms as they are expressed on the landscape. Proceeding from this, we reach the definition that most archaeologists accept and that James Deetz has aptly expressed: "that sector of our physical environment that we modify through culturally determined behavior" (1996:35). Thus material culture has become a term expressed in artifacts, those objects made by humans and whose formal range is both vast and diverse. The study of material culture can then be our most important research activity for discussing social change. Art historians have long appreciated this as well: "The history of things is about material presences which are far more tangible than the ghostly evocations of civil history" (Kubler 1962:58).

The emerging studies of Civil War encampments benefit from theoretical bulwarks already established by the archaeological discipline. Given this background, however, the study of military encampments also presents unique challenges, especially in regard to their ephemeral nature, that create a need to draw inspiration from yet even more disciplines. Among the genres of material culture analysis that we stand to benefit from, architecture emerges as one of the most profitable approaches, since buildings are complex and even monumental. Yet a "humbler" subfield of architecture, vernacular architecture, has taken shape in our most recent past, produced by the holistic research of anthropologists, sociologists, geographers, folklorists, and social historians. Emerging from this energetic interchange of ideas is a fresh way of looking at buildings and their contexts that can best be described as an "archaeological approach" (Lanier and Herman 1996:4–7). Accepting this philosophy, the authors in our book give us an "archaeological approach" to a tightly related group of architectural forms whose physical presence can best be "read" by archaeological analysis and excavation.

In 1980, the importance of an interdisciplinary approach was recognized when the Vernacular Architectural Forum was founded. At the second annual convention of this group, held in 1981 at Sturbridge, Massachusetts, two of the papers in this section (chapter 7 by Dean Nelson and chapter 10 by David Orr) were presented. The important and long-obscure properties of ephemeral, or impermanent, architecture—mostly transitory and designed for immediate occupation—were covered by these papers (Wells 1982:5–6). Additionally, and more to the point of this volume, the research potential of American Civil War military encampment architecture was first introduced. Dean Nelson's seminal study is here updated by over two decades of field research as some rarely seen and equally ephemeral images of the Civil War's "Right Nice Little Houses" are assembled for examination. Most of these are previously unpublished and give us a rich harvest of images to use in comparison with archaeological sites discussed by the majority of our authors. Nelson interprets camp structures as significant vernacular architectural data and explains them in the light of Civil War encampments.

David Orr's work at City Point presents a complete picture of Ulysses S. Grant's headquarters cabin, the only surviving ephemeral structure from the Civil War, as he details its original use, its unique peregrinations, and its archaeological discovery. Its symbolic use dramatically changed as our national memory of the Civil War evolved over time.

Matthew Reeves and Clarence Geier provide an emerging portrait of a camp of the Army of Northern Virginia (General A. P. Hill's Corps) dating to the winter of 1863–64. Occupied by Samuel McGowan's South Carolina Brigade, this site is one of eleven known campsites on the property of James Madison's Montpelier in Orange County, Virginia. Here the overall camp layout has been revealed by examination of over a hundred hut sites positioned on ten company streets. The site is enriched by ancillary features (fire pits and so forth) whose presence adds to the interpretation of the behavior of these encamped troops. The excavation of four hut sites in this camp revealed significant differences in material culture and architectural elements. The authors interpret these differences as potentially reflecting the hierarchical military structure.

Correspondingly, Garrett Fesler, Matthew Laird, and Hank Lutton at Yorktown produced a rich assemblage of material culture as well. They archaeologically examined a Confederate camp dating from the Peninsula Campaign of 1861–62. One very special hut was abandoned and then used as a trash dump when its occupants sought more comfortable accommodations as the weather warmed in the spring. The array of objects recovered give us valuable lessons in social status, foodways, alcohol consumption, and the role of "personal" items in an imposed and regimented military system. The authors argue that artifact types that relate to more idiosyncratic personal behavior possess the potential to enrich our understanding of how soldiers reacted to severe social and economic stress.

As the study of military encampments develops in the future, we will be able to better understand the experiences of soldiers in war. As regrettable as it is endemic, war exists as a critical human institution for archaeological explorations. The material culture approach adopted by historical archaeologists and a special subset of cultural historians can give all of us new data on this most significant subject.

References Cited

Deetz, James
1967   *Invitation to Archaeology.* Natural History Press, New York.
1996   *In Small Things Forgotten: An Archaeology of Early American Life.* Expanded and revised edition. Anchor Books, New York.
Glassie, Henry
1999   *Material Culture.* University of Indiana Press. Bloomington and Indianapolis.
Kubler, George
1962   *The Shape of Time: Remarks on the History of Things.* Yale University Press, New Haven, Conn.
Lanier, Gabrielle M., and Bernard L. Herman
1996   *Everyday Architecture of the Mid-Atlantic: Looking at Buildings and Landscapes.* Johns Hopkins University Press, Baltimore, Md.
Wells, Camille, ed.
1982   *Perspectives in Vernacular Architecture.* Vernacular Architecture Forum, Annapolis, Md.

7

"Right Nice Little House[s]"

Winter Camp Architecture of the American Civil War

DEAN E. NELSON

In the course of four agonizing Civil War years, over three million Americans from both sides of Mason's and Dixon's Line left family, home, and work to answer sectionalism's urgent call to arms. Raising mass armies during the Civil War generated an unprecedented demand for temporary housing, the greatest ever to occur in the United States prior to the First World War a half century later, when even larger armies were formed. Organizational responsibilities for the procurement, erection, and maintenance of military buildings were jointly shared by Union and Confederate quartermaster departments and engineer corps. As was their wont, both military establishments published regulations and manuals, regulating all aspects of soldierly regimen, from musketry and proper officer conduct to the minutiae of filling out government forms. It is curious then, that they failed to develop and promulgate plans and specifications for housing soldiers in the field. As a result, soldiers had little option but to rely on individual and collective ingenuities in providing shelter as a winter brought the seasonal halt to active campaigning. Most winter camp construction began by early November, but some regiments did not start work until late January or early February. Borrowing freely from familiar vernacular building practices, they developed several general forms of temporary winter housing, varying widely in detail, with remarkable sheltering qualities well adapted to the particular circumstances confronting impermanent camps.

Official regulations prescribed for all service branches the manner in which camps were to be laid out, reflecting the army's insistence on uniformity, order, and hierarchy. A plot of relatively flat land, serving as the regimental drill and parade ground, provided camp orientation. Ten parallel company streets, lined with tents or huts, led off the parade ground. At the opposite end was a line of company kitchen sheds, one per company. Behind the kitchens were separate rows of quarters for noncommissioned officers, company grade officers, and then the staff officers. Trash pits and latrines, known as "sinks," lay outside a camp perimeter (Babcock 1922:27–28; Billings 1887:45). Encampments near Washington, better constructed and frequently occupied throughout the war, often featured huge evergreen archways defining entrances to company streets as a mark of martial esprit-de-corps to curious civilians who flocked to see what soldiering was all about. Such garnishments, however, lost favor in camps closer to actual war.

In theory, this was the plan of encampment for a regiment. Vagaries of topography often precluded arranging military housing in this ideal form. Much of the southern countryside occupied by wintering armies was interrupted by gullies and ridges that determined the actual camp configuration. Lieutenant Millet S. Thompson, 13th New Hampshire Volunteers, noted the irregular nature of his regiment's camp at Falmouth, Virginia, in the winter of 1862–63: "The ends of the company . . . streets, are widest down near the brook, the narrower where they rise upon the slope, though on the whole quite irregular, and thrown upon the curve of the slope something like the ribs of a huge fan . . . there can be on this campground neither order or regularity" (Thompson 1888:89, 94). According to another Army of the Potomac historian of soldier life, winter cantonments were generally established with a "go-as-you please arrangement" (Billings 1887:45).

Union soldiers were each issued standard field equipment that included a woolen blanket, a rubberized or painted muslin blanket or poncho, and a canvas shelter half. It was general practice for soldiers to pair off and share sleeping equipment, in effect doubling their potential for warmth. If the weather was mild, the men did not bother to set up shelter tents each night. Instead, they first laid one rubber blanket and tent half on the ground to ward off dampness. Next, the pair would lie on the ground cloths, covering themselves with their two woolen blankets and topping all with the second rubber blanket and remaining tent half. Layers of wool, rubber, and tenting held body heat fairly well. If rain threatened, they buttoned together the shelter halves and stretched the canvas over tent poles fashioned from saplings. On occasion, infantrymen affixed their bayonets to their muskets and stuck these impromptu tent poles vertically into the ground if there was no anticipation of a night alarm. One veteran recalled, "A guy rope . . . was stretched between the trigger-guards of the muskets . . . the tent was pitched in a twinkling" (Billings 1887:53). Tent pins secured the two-man-tent corners to the ground.

Private Richard Cullen, an eighteen-year-old marble cutter from Assabet, Massachusetts, in the 32nd Massachusetts Volunteers included a detailed sketch of his portable quarters made of cotton drilling in a letter to a loved one at home, requesting of his correspondent: "Tell me what you think of this house to live in" (Cullen 1862). Under the best of circumstances, the shelter tent, also called a "dog" tent, afforded only minimal protection to its inhabitants. It measured a mere five feet long and was hardly a bastion against the rain, sleet, or snow. A Massachusetts artilleryman wrote after the war: "Just why it is called the shelter tent I cannot say unless on the principle stated by the Reverend George Ellis for calling the pond on Boston Common a frog pond, namely because there are no frogs there"(Billings 1887:28). Some soldiers preferred a solitary sleeping arrangement. With the caption: "Here is a picture of the little house that I live in" (Walkeley 1863), a Connecticut soldier illustrated for his son a one-man, open-ended stall of trimmed saplings that were lashed between pairs of thin posts set vertically into the ground. His single shelter half was tied over sapling rafter pairs to form a tent cloth gable roof for his abode.

A more advanced form of military tent, the "wedge" tent or wall tent, offered several advantages over the shelter tent. It was larger, one-piece, and had closed ends. Soldiers further adapted the wedge tent for use as winter quarters by pitching it on a low platform of boards that formed a floor and removed the occupants from direct contact with the earth. In addition, the interior walls of the tent were often sheathed with lumber to impart greater rigidity and increased resistance to chilling winds and rain. A Delaware officer described the process, writing in December 1863, from his camp near Alexandria, Virginia:

> I first only put a board floor in my tent and after trying that for a time, concluded to stockade, which is done in the following way. On the inside of a wall tent we put up four sides of boarding 3½ feet height and in the front we board up to the peak and put in a door and in the door a 4 light window, swung on hinges so as to be able to ventilate as much as we wish. This gives us four walls and one gable of tent and board and the double of roof canvas which makes it as warm as heart could wish. (Lammott 1863)

An alternative method consisted of raising the tent on a low wall of boards conforming to the length and width of the tent. In essence, the tent became the roof of a rudimentary structure. This widespread practice "doubled the interior space of a tent; tripled the comfort of the inhabitants" (Benedict 1895:60). The soldiers welcomed this additional room. As recorded by a Vermont infantryman: "How we enjoyed a residence in which we could stretch our arms at length above out heads, and sit around the sides without doubling together like so many jackknives" (44).

From journal entries and photographic evidence it appears that the stockaded wedge tent was in greatest vogue in the winter encampments circling Washington, D.C. The reinforced wedge tent presented a more uniform appearance than roughly finished log huts. Federal camps in the vicinity of Washington had greater access to the larger tents, as they were nearer to major army supply depots.

Lumber was also easier to come by in that area. The troops prized boards for hut construction, as their use saved much labor. Once lumber was transported to the camp site, it was a simple matter to saw boards to length and nail them in place to line the walls of the tent, with little of the back breaking labor associated with building log huts. The Federal army established sawmills in the field to cut timber for use by the military engineers in repairing railroads, building bridges and constructing structures of all sorts necessary to the progress and welfare of the army. But these field sawmills could not begin to satisfy the demand for lumber when troops built their little wooden cities. One Vermont regiment secured lumber from a private mill in Washington at a cost of 25 dollars per thousand board feet. However, the Vermonters received orders to move to another location deeper into Virginia, "where there was not a sawmill or lumberyard this side of Washington or Richmond so far as we know . . . the pangs with which we left our wooden walls and floors were indescribable" (Benedict 1895:44). The colonel of the regiment offered a ray of hope, promising his men they could salvage their hut lumber and transport it for use at the new campsite if wagons could be procured. A Pennsylvania man wrote: "Lumber in Virginia is out of the question. A very patriotic Union Man . . . refused to sell me a couple of fence boards six inches wide for $1.50" (Norton 1903:48).

One regiment prepared building materials for their winter quarters near Halltown, Virginia, in the winter of 1864–65. Corporal James H. Sawyer of Company B recorded,

> About a mile from camp was the ruins of an old saw mill. . . . The machinists of the regiment soon had it in running order. Each mess went into the woods, cut down a suitable tree, and employed the regimental teams to haul them to the mill and saw them into boards. . . . in due time our load of green oak boards and a few pieces of scantling was delivered to the spot that was to be the site of our winter residence. Our house was 10 feet long, 6 wide and about four feet high from the ground to the eaves. It was high enough to stand up in the middle and to set down in around the eaves. The roof was covered with the shelter tents of the occupants.

... when they were all buttoned together and thrown over the rafters it made a pretty good roof. . . . We made two bunks in the end opposite the door; the lower about 18 inches from the ground and the other as high up as it could be put. . . . A little sheet iron stove, some boxes for rations, some stools to sit on and a shelf along one side to eat on, completed our list of furnishings. Altogether it made quite a comfortable shanty. . . . I made a sketch of the camp during the winter and had it engraved in New York. I made a little money from the operation and many of those engravings hang in homes in Connecticut to this day. (Sawyer 1880s:224, 225) (figures 7.1, 7.2, 7.3)

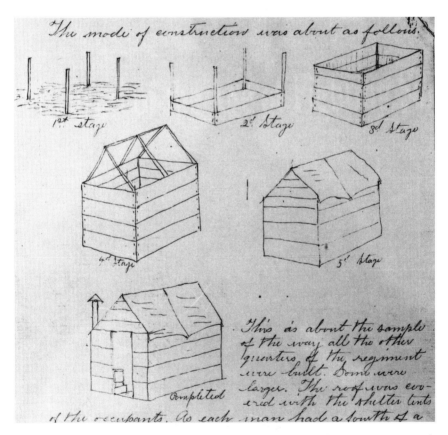

Figure 7.1. Board hut construction sequence, sketched by Corporal James H. Sawyer, 18th Connecticut Volunteers (1880s: Museum of Connecticut History, Hartford).

Figure 7.2. Hut interior, bunk end, sketched by Corporal James H. Sawyer (Museum of Connecticut History, Hartford).

Figure 7.3. Hut, sketched by Corporal James H. Sawyer (Courtesy Museum of Connecticut History, Hartford).

Figure 7.4. Stockaded Sibley tents (1863) (NWNS-111–B-236, National Archives, College Park, Md.).

Another common military-issue tent was the "bell" tent, used by the English army as early as 1810 and by a few American militia units in the 1840s. During the Civil War it was known as the Sibley tent, after West Point graduate Henry Sibley's patented improvements and his special sheet-iron stove (figure 7.4). Conical in shape and about sixteen feet in diameter, the tent was a canvas version of the Indian tepee of western frontier fame. With a bit of crowding, it could house almost twenty soldiers. Like the wedge tent, it was too bulky for extensive use in the field, and it was therefore confined to rear areas or encampments near supply depots. Sibley tents were frequently stockaded by being raised on halved logs set vertically, probably in a backfilled circular trench conforming to the diameter of the tent skirt. A central vertical pole, set on an army-issue adjustable-legged iron tripod, supported the tent. One proud Federal infantry officer recounted his unit's stockaded Sibleys in a letter to his mother: "Our camp is beginning to look beautiful. The men have sodded all around their tents and planted flowers which are thriving finely, the avenues between the tents are rolled hard and smooth and cleanly swept every morning and woe betide the unfortunate man who throws anything on them. The tents are all stockaded and all the stockades white washed and our camp the admiration of all who see it" (Lammott 1864).

The average Union Civil War regiment, comprised of five hundred to eight hundred men, invariably included a cross section of the occupational spectrum. A typical muster roll listed men with the skills of a carpenter, bricklayer, mason, housewright, and lumberjack. Most men were capable of learning the basics of hut building if given a little guidance. A Union cavalryman wrote of the flurry of activity arising from winter cantonment construction: "Nearly everyman has suddenly become a mason or carpenter, and the hammer, the axe and the trowel are being plied with the utmost vigor, if not with the highest skill. Many of us, however, are astonished at the ingenuity that is displayed with this department" (Glazier 1874:116).

At times, a lack of tools hindered camp building. A soldier might carry a small camp hatchet for securing firewood, but that was about the only tool immediately at hand for him to use in any ambitious architectural endeavor. Some spades and axes carried in regimental baggage wagons were available, but when construction of winter quarters began, tools were in high demand and relatively short supply. A Federal cavalryman, about to build winter quarters near Winchester, Virginia, bemoaned the fact that there would be no chance to borrow an axe or hatchet, as everyone would be using his own. Resigned to his plight, he wrote philosophically, "so much the better, as it would throw us on our own resources and we would have to hustle to get tools of our own" (Gouse 1908:349).

By far, the most common form of Union, soldier-built winter housing was the single-room log hut of horizontally laid, end-notched log walls with a single doorway set into the gable end or the side wall (figure 7.5). More rarely, logs were set vertically into the ground, a technique that involved more work, requiring excavation of a foundation trench and more shorter, cut-off logs (figure 7.6). An exterior chimney protruded from a wall opposite the door. The wall ranged from three to seven feet to the eaves. The ends of logs were either roughly chopped or sometimes sawn, if hut builders could use large wood saws. To weatherproof gaps between the logs (at least until the next heavy rain), soldiers worked thick mud into the joints.

The size of the hut varied according to the number of soldiers it was intended to house. Basic hut dimensions for four men were about eight feet by twelve feet. The hut size might be dictated by the availability of building materials. When shelter halves were the only handy means of covering a hut, walls were made no longer than could be covered by the buttoned-together halves. Ac-

Figure 7.5. *Home Sweet Home* by Civil War artist Edwin Forbes (1876:plate 24, Connecticut State Archives, Connecticut State Library, Hartford).

Figure 7.6. Officers' quarters, Army of the Potomac, Brandy Station, Virginia (March 1864) (PG 85, Brady Collection #113, Connecticut State Archives, Connecticut State Library, Hartford).

cess to roofing shingles or tent flies made it possible to fabricate larger cabins. While most winter huts featured a gable roof, some had a shed roof of boards or closely spaced trimmed saplings, perhaps also bolstered or covered by canvas. Shed-roofed structures usually featured a doorway set into the taller of the two long walls. Most huts had earth floors, perhaps covered by straw or small pine branches.

Where a supply of timber was strained, soldiers dug rectangular holes in the ground to a depth of two or three feet to reduce the number of wall logs required for head room under the tent roof. Troops banked dirt from the excavations against wall exteriors to insulate and waterproof. A contemporary reported that these semisubterranean dwellings leaked terribly and pools of water made life miserable (Thompson 1888:99). In some areas, nature provided rough surface stone as another building material used for a low, dry-masonry wall several feet high and topped off by log superstructures. Many of these foundations survive as camp ruins on the heights dominating Harpers Ferry, West Virginia, at the confluence of the Shenandoah and Potomac rivers.

Roof frames were typically trimmed sapling ridge pieces and rafters nailed to the top walling logs and then covered with shelter halves. The lashed or nailed cloth roofs offered little protection in the severest weather, and it became the practice in one Federal camp to "sprinkle them with water at evening. The water freezes and makes the cloth windproof. A little touch of the Esquimaux ice made hut" (Valentine 1896:23, 24). Rarely were commercial shingles available. Some huts used logs to fill in the end walls up to the gables, while others used boards set vertically or horizontally. Some huts had only shelter halves or gum blankets to fill in the gables. When boards could be had, they were used for roofs by being run from plate to ridge. Additional boards formed battens for the interstices. Often roof boards were lapped horizontally, running from gable to gable (figure 7.7.) In many cases, tent cloths were put over the boards anyway to help keep the elements away from the inevitable cracks and spaces. In the South, with its great pine trees, soldiers copied the clever local technique to manufacture roofing materials. One soldier described this cladding type as follows: "A rough sort of board about five feet long, half an inch [thick] and six or eight inches wide, split off from yellow pine logs, peeled off with the grain like bark round and round the log, and then piled up to be pressed into shape and dry. A capitol roofing material" (Thompson 1888:209, 210).

Yankee soldiers often obtained building materials from abandoned houses. One Pennsylvania lieutenant, writing to his sister, related that "Generals and 'two rows of buttons' [officers from the rank of major upward] generally are

Figure 7.7. Building winter quarters at City Point, Virginia (winter 1864–65) (NWDNS-111–B-140, National Archives at College Park Archives II, College Park, Md.).

demolishing the residences of the F. F. V.'s [First Families of Virginia] and working them in with logs into cozy quarters" (Norton 1903:240).

Doors might be little more than an extra shelter half or gum blanket draped over an entrance, but some soldiers were fortunate enough to erect board doors with a glass window. Most enlisted men's huts were without windows. More commonly, officer's huts might feature a multipaned window either fixed or hinged into a wall.

Makeshift fireplaces and chimneys set into the walls of huts provided warmth and dryness (figure 7.8), as described in great detail by a Massachusetts soldier:

The chimney was built outside after the Southern fashion. It stood sometimes at the end and sometimes at the middle of one side of the stockade. It started from a fireplace which was fashioned with more or less skill, according to the taste or mechanical genius of the workman, or the tools and material, or both. In my own company there were two masons who had opportunities whenever a winter camp was pitched to practice their trade far more than they were inclined to do. The fireplaces were built of brick, of stone or of wood. . . . When built of wood the chimneys were lined with a very thick coating of mud. They were generally continued above the fireplace with split wood built cob fashion. . . . Very frequently pork barrels were secured to serve this purpose, being put one above the other and now and then a lively hurrah would run through the camp when one of these was discovered on fire. It is hardly necessary to remark that not all of these chimneys were monuments of success. . . . Too often the draft was down instead of up and the inside of some of the stockades resembled smokehouses. (Billings 1887:30, 31)

Small cast-iron and sheet-iron stoves produced during this period were relatively inexpensive. Soldiers obtained them from various sources or cobbled a "make-do" from camp scrap metal for heating their quarters, as did a member of the 1st Connecticut Light Battery: "One comrade took an old camp kettle, cut a hole in the bottom for a smoke pipe, which he made by rudely fastening together some condensed milk cans, with the bottoms cut out, and so he had a stove complete" (Beecher 1901:286). With a proper supply of wood, cheap bought-stoves or soldier-made expedients could throw out a prodigious amount of heat and make the huts very comfortable. A Delaware officer commented on a factory cast-iron stove installed in his two-room hut: "A large and lustrous ten

Figure 7.8. 18th Pennsylvania Cavalry in winter quarters near Brandy Station, Virginia (March 1864) (detail, from PG 85, Brady Collection #7625, Connecticut State Archives, Connecticut State Library, Hartford).

plate stove will render the air of the reception room or front parlor, balmy with its generous radiations from semi ignited green pine. . . .(Lammott 1861).

A primitive, yet capable, heating system known as a California stove consisted of an iron plate set over a small hole containing a modest fire located within a hut or a tent. A shallow underground air hole leading to the exterior of the hut served as a flue. George F. Meech, 21st Connecticut Volunteers, described the construction of such a stove as well as its effectiveness at heating his tent at Falmouth, Virginia, the winter of 1862–63: "we have dug down about a foot and a half all but a place about 2 feet square which we dug a place in the middle of it about 1 foot wide and run it out under the tent 2 feet from it and then took and built a chimney of wood cob fashion and plastered it with mud. Then on the inside we covered the top with a large frying pan flattened out that we found so we build our fire under that and can soon have it so hot you can't stay in that tent" (Meech 1863).

In building winter quarters, the uncertainty of a stay produced mixed enthusiasm for any labor. Naturally, it was in the soldier's best interests to construct a quality hut and make it as comfortable as possible, but orders to camp were soon revoked, so the men were hesitant to expend much effort until satisfied that they would remain to enjoy the fruits of their labor. An officer of a Massachusetts infantry regiment recalled, "The fear of such constant movements perpetually haunted us. This was the army bugaboo. We lived in constant expectation of orders to move. . . . I had already built two houses and now went to work on a third" (Tyler 1912:130).

Where troops with a few tools and a limitless labor supply were confronted with an immediate need for good shelter in an environment with abundant standing timber, the log hut provided an expedient means of resisting the debilitating effects of the southern winter. A volunteer in the 27th Connecticut opposite Fredericksburg in the winter of 1862–63 wrote that

the men vigorously applied themselves to the work of building huts. . . . In the hundred and thirty log houses of our little regimental village was embraced an amount of comfort wholly inconceivable by those who know nothing of the numerous contrivances a soldier's ingenuity can suggest to supply the place of ordinary conveniences. . . . with no little satisfaction we surveyed our rough architecture, pork-barrel chimneys, and cracker box doors, feeling that though the winds might blow, and the rainy season pour down its flood, we were prepared to endure it patiently. (Sheldon 1866:35–37)

The cabin, hut, or house of round or square logs became a typical American dwelling quite common in many rural areas (New England excepted) in the mid-nineteenth century (Kniffen and Glassie 1966:40–66; Shurtleff 1939:4). Many Civil War regiments were undoubtedly familiar with small log dwellings and outbuildings; some lived in such houses back home. One soldier from Maryland wrote home telling of a camp near the Weldon Road, Virginia, in November 1864, "I wish you could see some of the log houses here. They are put up as well as those at home and some a great deal neater" (Lord 1960:238). Private Wesley Jackson, 5th Maryland Veteran Volunteers, mentioned his unit's winter quarters near Point of Rocks, Virginia: "we have a rite pretty camping place since we got it fixed up and we got a right nice little house fixed up here and live right with what little we get" (Jackson 1864). A soldier of the 29th Massachusetts commented, "No duty which the soldier is required to perform is so pleasant as that of erecting a house to live in" (Osborne 1877:234). Another from the 33rd Massachusetts summed up hut building with, "Such is the house that jack built. It will do for a corporal, if not for a king" (Boies 1880:90). These statements capture generally favorable sentiments expressed by soldiers about the houses they built. Such comments permit an approach to the outlook and experiences of the Civil War soldier and their "right nice little house[s]" on their own terms and in the immediate context of their extraordinary circumstances.

Standing apart from the typical rough-finished huts of the combat rank and file were the masterful buildings that Federal engineer regiments erected under the direction of officers who were engineering professionals, commanding enlisted artisans, builders, and other skilled construction tradesmen. They experimented with a popular mid-nineteenth-century rusticated Gothic style in building their officers' quarters and barracks. Poplar Grove Church, outside of Petersburg, Virginia, was an amazing structure of vertical logs with a multistoried square-and-octagonal spire faced with unbarked logs in various geometric patterns. Contemporaries were so impressed by the Poplar Grove Church that there were enthusiastic, though fruitless, proposals to move it to New York City's Central Park at the conclusion of the war (Gardner 1866:plate 4).

Documentary problems inherent in the photographic evidence of impermanent Civil War camp architecture make it difficult to sketch even broad generalities about regional vernacular influences in hut design and construction. Period images are notorious for their vague and haphazard captioning. With credible state and unit identity for a camp photograph, it would be possible, through regimental histories and service records, to determine the general area of a state from which a unit came. There is seldom any way to know whether the soldiers pictured were the actual hut builders, given the frequency at which troops were moved about, leaving huts for others to occupy and, in turn, moving into quarters built by others.

Close examination of period photographs reveals a broad range of construction techniques employed in the winter camp architecture of the American Civil War (Gardner 1866; Horan 1966; Miller 1911). Although most of these building practices were common in most parts of mid-nineteenth-century America, they are rarely encountered today. Indeed, with the remarkable exception of Ulysses S. Grant's headquarters cabin built at City Point, Virginia (chapter 10), no other Civil War huts are known to have survived. The study of Civil War camp architecture, with its richness of photographic and documentary evidence, is significant for its kinship with related topics such as frontier housing, slave housing, hunting and mining camps (Randolph 1978), and other forms of less well documented impermanent nineteenth-century vernacular architecture.

References Cited

Babcock, Willoughby M., Jr.

1922   *Selections from the Letters and Diaries of Brevet Brigadier General Willoughby Babcock of the Seventy-Fifth New York Volunteers.* War of the Rebellion Series, Bulletin 2. University of the State of New York, Buffalo.

Beecher, Herbert W.

1901   *History of the First Light Battery Connecticut Volunteers, 1861–1865.* A. T. DeLa Mare, New York.

Benedict, George Grenville

1895   *Army Life in Virginia: Letters from the 12th Regiment Vermont Volunteers.* Free Press Association, Burlington, Vt.

Billings, John D.

1887   *Hardtack and Coffee.* George M. Smith and Company, Boston.

Boies, Andrew J.

1880   *Record of the Thirty-Third Massachusetts Volunteer Infantry from Aug. 1862 to Aug. 1865.* Sentinel, Fitchburg, Mass.

Bowen, James L.

1884   *History of the Thirty-Seventh Regiment Mass. Volunteers, in the Civil War of 1861–1865.* Clark W. Bryan and Company, Holyoke, Mass.

Cullen, Richard S.

1863   Incomplete letter with tent sketch to unknown correspondent. Private collection.

Forbes, Edwin

1876 *Life Studies of the Great Army: A Historical Work of Art, in Copper-Plate Etching, Containing Forty Plates, Illustrating the Life of the Union Army during the Late Rebellion.* E. Forbes, New York.

Gardner, Alexander

1866 *Photographic Sketch Book of the Civil War.* Washington, D.C. Reprinted 1959 by Dover Publications, New York.

Glazier, Willard

1874 *Three Years in the Federal Cavalry.* R. H. Ferguson and Company, New York.

Gouse, Issac

1908 *Four Years with Five Armies: Army of the Frontier, Army of the Potomac, Army of the Missouri, Army of the Ohio, Army of the Shenandoah.* Neale, New York.

Hartford Daily Courant

1864 From the 16th Regiment. *Hartford Daily Courant* [Hartford, Conn.], 28(34):2.

Horan, James D.

1966 *Timothy O'Sullivan: America's Forgotten Photographer.* Bonanza Books, New York.

Jackson, Wesley

1864 Letter to Frank Jackson, 4 September. Collection of Susan Emory, Milford, Del.

Kniffen, Fred, and Henry Glassie

1966 Building in Wood in the Eastern United States: A Time-Place Perspective. *Geographic Review* 56:40–65.

Lammott, Charles E.

1861 Letter to Mother, 27 December. Lammott Civil War Papers, Delaware Division of Historical and Cultural Affairs, Dover.

1863 Letter to Father, 26 December. Lammott Civil War Papers, Delaware Division of Historical and Cultural Affairs, Dover.

1864 Letter to Mother, 25 April. Lammott Civil War Papers, Delaware Division of Historical and Cultural Affairs, Dover.

Lord, Francis A.

1960 *They Fought for the Union.* Bonanza Books, New York.

Meech, George F.

1863 Letter to Parents, 1 January. George F. Meech Civil War Letters, Connecticut State Archives, Connecticut State Library, Hartford.

Miller, Francis Trevelyan (editor)

1911 *The Photographic History of the Civil War.* Review of Reviews, New York.

Norton, Oliver Wilcox

1903 *Army Letters, 1861–1865.* O. L. Deming, Chicago.

Osborne, William H.
1877   *The History of the Twenty-Ninth Regiment of Massachusetts Volunteer Infantry in the Late War of the Rebellion.* Albert J. Wright, Boston.

Randolph, Wayne
1978   Wilderness Architecture: A Trappers Cabin Survey. In *14th Annual Traditional Craft Days.* Madison County Historical Society, Oneida, N.Y.

Sawyer, James H.
1880s   Civil War journal. Reprographic copy, Connecticut Civil War Unit Files, Museum of Connecticut History, Hartford.

Sheldon, Winthrop D.
1866   *The "Twenty-Seventh": A Regimental History.* Morris and Benham, New Haven, Conn.

Shurtleff, Harold R.
1939   *The Log Cabin Myth: A Study of the Early Dwellings of the English Colonists in North America.* Howard University Press, Cambridge, Mass.

Thompson, Millett S.
1888   *Thirteenth Regiment of New Hampshire Volunteer Infantry in the War of the Rebellion, 1861–1865.* Houghton, Mifflin, Boston.

Tyler, William S. (editor)
1912   *Recollections of the Civil War.* G. P. Putnam's Sons, New York.

Valentine, Herbert E.
1896   *Story of Co. F., 23d Massachusetts Volunteers in the War for the Union.* W. B. Clarke and Company, Boston.

Walkeley, Stephen, Jr.
1863   Letter to Eddie Walkeley. Private collection.

8

Under the Forest Floor

Excavations at a Confederate Winter Encampment, Orange, Virginia

MATTHEW B. REEVES AND CLARENCE R. GEIER

Situated in Orange County, Virginia, on the lands of Montpelier (plantation home of James and Dolly Madison), are a series of encampments occupied by the Confederacy during the winter of 1863 and 1864 (figure 8.1). Preliminary surveys and historical research indicate that three brigades—nearly 4,600 men—were camped on the Montpelier property now owned by the National Trust for Historic Preservation and operated by the Montpelier Foundation. In the spring of 2002, the Montpelier Archaeology Department began surveys on the northern portion of the property where local relic hunters had noted the presence of a number of Confederate winter encampments. These surveys revealed several camps, one of which was surveyed and was determined to be well preserved, containing over five acres of hut sites. With this discovery in hand, Montpelier hosted two field schools (one with James Madison University and one with the State University of New York at Potsdam) that conducted additional field survey, the mapping of one section of the encampment, and the excavation of four hut locations. This paper presents the initial findings of this fieldwork. Observations are made concerning camp layout and differences in the architectural plan of the four excavated huts and their associated material goods.

HISTORICAL CONTEXT

For Robert E. Lee and his Army of Northern Virginia, 1863 had been a period of contrasting emotion. Following decisive Confederate victories at Fredericksburg in December of 1862 and at Chancellorsville in May of 1863, July produced a decisive defeat on the fields of Gettysburg. In early December 1863, following months of anticlimactic activity after Gettysburg, the Union army ceased active operations and established winter quarters in the vicinity of Brandy Station, Virginia, north of the Rapidan River. Some twenty-six miles

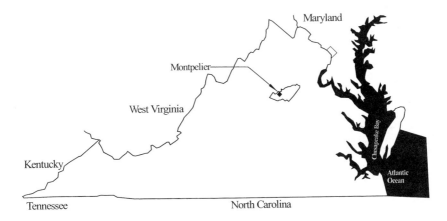

Figure 8.1. Location of Montpelier and camps (photo by the author).

southwest of Brandy Station and south of the Rapidan, near the town of Orange, Lee's army made similar preparations. By this time, both armies had suffered staggering casualties, the figures reaching into the hundreds of thousands. Yet in the winter of 1863–64, despite these losses, both sides maintained the will to fight. No end of the war was in sight.

As the Army of Northern Virginia endured the harsh winter, the Union army received a new overall commander. While General George G. Meade retained direct control of the Army of the Potomac, General Ulysses S. Grant was made commander of all Union armies, east and west. Despite this position, Grant kept himself apart from the political enterprises of Washington and established his headquarters with Meade's army in the field. After a winter that was alternately good and bad, cold and mild, and in general wet, the aggressive new Union commander prepared his army for a spring offensive. On Tuesday, May 3, 1864, shortly after midnight and under a shield of darkness, his troops crossed the Rapidan at Ely's and Germanna fords in an effort to advance through the terrible landscape known as the "Wilderness" before being detected and countered by Lee's army. Despite these efforts, Lee's army responded at surprise, and on May 5, 1864, Lee and Grant came head to head at the Battle of the Wilderness; the first of a devastating series of engagements that would bring Grant to the doors of Richmond.

Given this background, the winter encampments at Montpelier were established as part of an overall deployment whereby Lee used the high banks of the

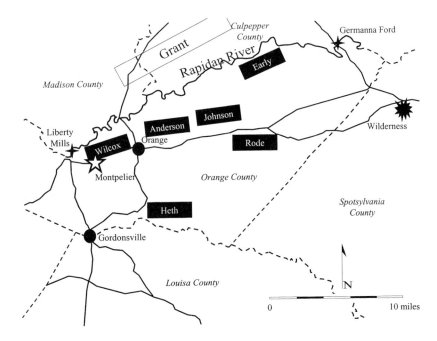

Figure 8.2. Map showing locale of Montpelier and the Confederate Division Camps in Orange County, Virigia (photo by the author)

Rapidan River as a defensive shield to keep the Union army stalled during the winter of 1863 and 1864. The Montpelier camps were the westernmost portion of a twenty-mile shield that stretched from the area of Liberty Mills, just west of Montpelier (figure 8.2) through Orange and toward Germanna Ford—the point where Grant would initiate his spring offensive.

As part of Lee's Army of Northern Virginia, General Cadmus M. Wilcox's Division occupied the area of Montpelier with Brigadier General Samuel McGowan's Brigade of South Carolinians occupying the lands north of the Plank Road leading to the Wilderness. The camps discussed in this paper are located in this locale. Historic records, combined with artifacts recovered from the camp, suggest that this complex was occupied by one of the three regiments commanded by McGowan between January 27 and May 4, 1864. The brigade affiliation of this camp was initially determined through discussions with local relic hunters who recovered South Carolina palmetto buttons in this area during the 1970s and early 1980s. Association with McGowan's Brigade was easily determined, as his were the only South Carolina troops encamped in the area.

Prior to February 1864, McGowan's Brigade had been encamped one-half mile farther east. By late January his men had been forced to move to the Montpelier site locale because of a depletion of their firewood supply (Caldwell 1992:168). Brigade history relates that during their occupation of the camp, soldiers spent time foraging for firewood and supplies, conducting patrols along the Rapidan River, and preparing and repairing a ten-mile stretch of the Plank Road leading from Liberty Mills to Orange (Caldwell 1992:168). The latter two activities were closely tied to Lee's desire to be able to respond quickly, and in strength, to any Union attempt to move south across the Rapidan River. Lee's relentless efforts to secure intelligence on Union movements allowed him to rapidly deploy against Grant's troops at the onset of the spring offensive, forcing Grant to fight in the "wilderness." Paramount to this effort were the repairs that Lee's troops made to the local road networks. Paving of local roads not only alleviated the boredom of camp life and kept the troops active, but also ensured that local transportation routes were well maintained, guaranteeing a quick deployment of troops and supplies.

The value of these efforts was made clear in May 1864, when Lee consolidated his forces and moved them quickly to the front when Grant's army crossed the Rapidan some thirty miles east of McGowan's camp. Grant's advance caused a rapid chain reaction down the Confederate line. Within half an hour of receiving marching orders, the Montpelier camps were abandoned. The hurried manner in which McGowan's camp was abandoned was recalled by a staff officer:

> On the 4th of May, 1864, about eleven o'clock in the morning, we received orders to cook rations immediately and prepare for the march. We at once set to work, but before the bread could be baked the command was given to fall in. A universal stir ensued. In pursuance of a previous order, the officers' tents were torn down and cut up for distribution among the men. Knapsacks were packed, blankets rolled up, half-cooked dough or raw meat thrust into haversacks, the accumulated plunder of nine months thrown into streets, accouterments girded on, arms taken, and in a half an hour we were on the march. It was a beautiful calm day. (Caldwell 1992:173)

From this account, it is clear that little time was spent breaking down cabins or sorting through accumulated possessions. Once the camp was abandoned by McGowan's troops, there is little doubt that local citizens scavenged the camp. The rapid withdrawal left an array of materials including hut timbers that could serve as fencing, boards, and hardware. The remaining supplies would eventually be picked through by local community members to augment their depleted resources caused by over eight months of occupation by Lee's army. One local resident, Buck Smith, recalled that, by the 1930s, there was no evidence remaining of the log walls of the camp structures (Buck Smith, personal communication 2003). This observation, combined with archaeological evidence, suggests that the log walls were removed soon after abandonment, likely for reuse.

One group that deserves a special note in this reclamation process is the newly freed African Americans, who are recorded as having reused abandoned hut sites for homes following the war (Hurst 1989:32; Lyman 1866). Recent archaeological findings at an adjacent freedman's farm built by George Gilmore, a former slave of James Madison's, provided evidence that this family may have briefly occupied a camp hut. Materials salvaged from McGowan's camp may have been used in the cabin the Gilmores built in 1873 (Reeves 2003).

Since the abandonment of the hut sites, historical accounts (confirmed by archaeological testing) indicate that the encampment area has never been plowed. Hut surface remains and associated features, mainly in the form of depressions and mounds, remain evident.

In addition to providing clues about camp abandonment, Lieutenant J. F. J. Caldwell's account also provides information on how quickly units were organized and moved out of camp. Part of the speed of deployment came from the manner in which the camps were laid out and organized. Recognized protocols of camp layout used by both Union and Confederate infantry called for huts to be organized by company along parallel set streets that accessed either a defended front or a primary road (see chapter 2). A five-hundred-man regiment, such as the three that were part of McGowan's Brigade, would have been organized into ten or eleven companies. If, then, the encampment guidelines were followed, the regimental camp would include ten or eleven rows of huts, every two of which would open onto a common street, with each row containing around ten huts each housing four to five men.

The logic of this camp plan was such that when the order was given to prepare to march, the soldiers, at their huts with haversacks and accouterments strapped on, would be in marching order. This encampment plan, organized by regiment, was suggested by the survey results of the McGowan encampment.

SURVEY OF MCGOWAN'S CAMP

In the spring of 2002, one of the regimental camps occupied by McGowan's Brigade was surveyed. Features within the camp were identified through surface reconnaissance, and individual features were mapped using a laser transit. In all,

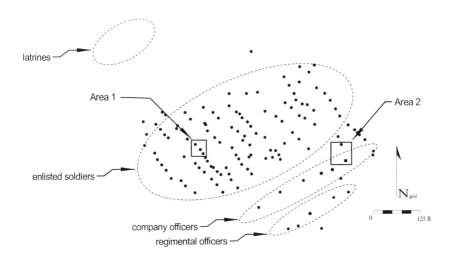

Figure 8.3. Layout of McGowan Camp showing two excavation areas (photo by the author).

some 125 depressions (most of which were interpreted as borrow pits associated with individual hut sites), hearth features, and trench latrines were recorded. As the site had not been plowed, surface features were readily discernable. Factors negatively impacting the camp remains include extensive scavenging by local residents, probably starting immediately after the troops withdrew, for timbers and other resources. Stumps reveal evidence of twentieth-century timbering activities and, prior to acquisition by the National Trust for Historic Preservation in 1983, relic hunting.

Survey data reveal that the South Carolina troops carefully located the encampment on moderately sloping terrain that allowed drainage and provided access to water (figure 8.3). The defined camp covers five acres and is placed at the end of a southwestward-trending ridge bounded on the southwest by a spring-fed stream that drains into the Rapidan River. This camp is separated from neighboring camps on the north by shallow ravines that may have allowed intermediary woodlots to be carefully rationed between individual regiments (Caldwell 1992:168).

Survey of the McGowan camp, the southernmost of the five camps located, showed hut sites to be arrayed along ten streets set parallel to each other, consistent with guidelines used by both the Union and the Confederate armies (see chapter 2). Streets and their bounding hut rows ran from the ridge crest

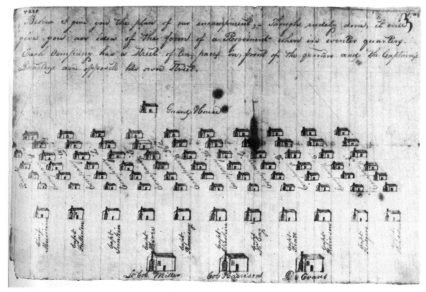

Figure 8.4. South Carolina camp (sketch, 1862) (Farr Family papers, South Caroliniana Library, University of South Carolina. Photo by the author)).

downslope to the northwest for approximately 180 feet. Using a regular 16-foot interval between hearths, as identified during site surveys, 10 to 12 hut sites would have been located on each street, with an estimated total of 120 huts in the larger camp. The 125 depressions documented in the field and interpreted as borrow/trash pits closely mirror this predicted hut number. Again, with reference to established military guidelines (see chapter 2), these rows of huts would have housed enlisted men organized by company (figure 8.4) (United States War Department 1861:77).

Army guidelines called for the huts of company officers to be placed at the top of each street with regimental officers' huts above them. The McGowan camp plan suggested the implementation of these guidelines with four possible officer's huts being constructed beyond and above the rows of company huts (figure 8.3). Between these four, isolated hut sites and the rows of company huts are a series of additional hut structures that are set apart spatially from the company rows. These could be company officer huts, a possibility supported by excavation results discussed below.

Hut Architecture

In the summer of 2002, a sample of four hut features was excavated. In preparation for this excavation, documentary accounts from members of McGowan's Brigade were reviewed to obtain information on the type of hut architecture and material culture that might be found. These accounts recall that supplies were scarce, as they were for most of Lee's Brigades. Foodstuffs issued to the troops were limited to cornmeal and bacon (Benson 1962:55). Beyond these items, available "household" supplies included what could be scavenged or acquired locally, a practice that placed a serious drain on the local domestic economy, and clothing shipped from South Carolina ladies' relief societies (Caldwell 1992:168).

A soldier in McGowan's Brigade provided a detailed description of his new quarters, erected after the brigade relocated to the project area in January 27, 1864: "The size of the house when finished was about 12 feet square, being entirely built of logs, chinked with clay. The chimney was built of split wood, chinked with clay the same as the house, but having a thick coat of clay inside to prevent taking fire. The protection, however, was but partial, so that there was hardly a day in the winter but somebody's chimney was on fire in the camp" (Benson 1962:55).

A reconstructed hut at the White Oak Museum northeast of Fredericksburg, Virginia, is similar to this description (figure 8.5). Further, the 2002 archaeological excavations carried out in the McGowan camp exposed hut features with characteristics that match this description—namely, soldiers' having constructed log huts built at-grade with stick-and-mud chimneys. One of the most defining features of the hut architecture was that the rural locale of the Montpelier area ensured that soldiers were forced to rely upon natural resources. This meant that huts were constructed using readily available rocks, trees, and clay combined with issue tents and tarps. Limited (or nonexistent) was the opportunity to obtain bricks, milled timbers, or other finished materials for construction.

A goal of the excavation project was to gather information on the nature and diversity of hut architecture and material items present in a camp. To accomplish this, two areas containing hut features were selected for intensive testing. Area 2 (figure 8.3) is located in the easternmost portion of the camp, close to the ridge crest. In contrast, Area 1 (figure 8.3) is located in the western area of the camp, downslope in the company streets.

The first step in testing these areas was to clear the site of brush and leaf litter to expose surface features. What immediately became apparent was that each de-

Figure 8.5a. Reconstruction of hut site, White Oak Museum, Falmouth, Virginia (photo by the author).

Figure 8.5b. Hearth of hut site, White Oak Museum, Falmouth, Virginia, (photo by the author).

pression was associated with a very slight mound with rocks protruding from the ground surface on one side. Subsequent excavation revealed these mounds to be the remains of hut structures while the associated depressions were borrow/trash pits associated with each hut. In both of the study areas, two neighboring hut sites were excavated to permit assessment of the structural remains and determination of the distance between their hearth features. While the four excavated huts varied in their superficial expression, all had three characteristics in common: an at-grade hearth, evidence for stick-and-mud chimneys, and adjoining borrow pits that were used as a source of the chimney daub and subsequently for refuse disposal. Despite these similarities, noticeable differences in hut structure and associated material culture were found. These differences allowed one hut to be interpreted as a possible officers' quarter, while the others were most likely occupied by enlisted men.

AREA 1

The hut remains associated with Area 1 (figure 8.6) contain the most commonly found camp features. This row of approximately ten huts consists of a series of tightly spaced depressions and pronounced mounds of rock.

The excavation of two rock mound features (Features 94 and 95) identified them as the remains of crudely formed fireboxes and chimney bases attributed to two different huts. The topmost stratum encountered in these features consisted of a concentration of loose rubble set in a clay matrix containing large amounts of burnt clay. This initial deposit was probably formed from the clay daub of the collapsed stick-and-mud chimney and stone firebox base. Once the overburden of clay daub and loose rocks was archaeologically removed, the fireboxes for the hut sites were very evident (figure 8.7).

Feature 95 is a particularly well-preserved firebox consisting of rock bonded together by burnt clay mortar that had been scorched by hearth fires. This burnt clay and rock feature was roughly U-shaped, with the interior containing a dense deposit of ash. Excavation of the ash revealed a very well-defined firebox with a distinct area of bright red clay at the base. This burned clay lens is subsoil scorched by the hut fires. Ash within this firebox contained numerous small, burnt, machine-cut nails and chunks of burned clay. The nails are possibly the remains of boxes, such as hardtack boxes, that may have been used by the soldiers as kindling. The burnt clay is likely from the clay flue lining that periodically flaked into the hearth.

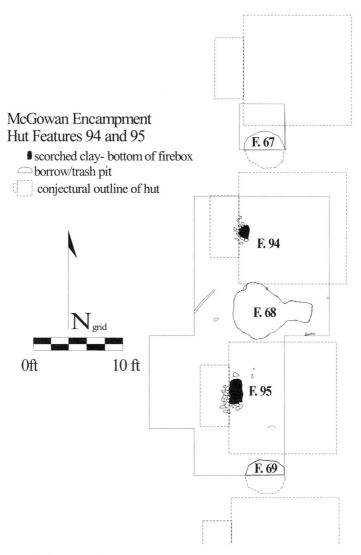

Figure 8.6. Plan view of excavations in Area 1 (photo by the author).

The position of the hearth relative to the street suggests that the remainder of the hut lay to the east. Given the layout of most hut features, this would mean that the entrance was on the east side. No evidence for walls was encountered—either in the form of postholes or as raised mounds of clay from the disintegrated logs and clay chinking. Instead, the area surrounding the hearth contained a lens that appeared as clay fill overlying subsoil. Field observations resulted in this layer's being interpreted as the residue of clay chinking from the

Figure 8.7. Photograph of excavations in Area 1, view to the south (photo by the author).

structure's log walls. The lack of evidence for in situ decay of the huts' walls possibly reflects the immediate postabandonment scavenging of the logs by locals and the resultant dispersal of the clay daub.

North of Feature 95, an additional stone mound, Feature 94, was excavated. As with Feature 95, a rubble deposit of stone and clay was archaeologically removed that was interpreted as a collapsed chimney. Unlike Feature 95, a discernable firebox was not recovered; only the presence of scorched clay suggested the firebox location. Surrounding the scorched clay were several large stones, interpreted as possible displaced firebox remnants.

One interesting set of features east of the firebox in Feature 95 was a series of rodent holes. These rodent burrows were located immediately in front of the hearth and were absent where the chimney base stood. In addition, these rodent holes were located below the rubble stratum of collapsed hearth material and clay daub. The stratigraphic location of these rodent holes suggests that they were potentially contemporaneous with occupation and might have existed below planks placed in front of the firebox as a hearth. The rodents might have been drawn to the area by the combination of heat from the hearth and scattered food remains.

Between Features 94 and 95 is a large depression, Feature 68 (figure 8.6). A possible explanation for this feature, and similar features located throughout the camp, is that it began life as a borrow pit. Such pits were excavated by soldiers to obtain clay daub for chinking and chimney construction. Often soldiers had only smaller trees available for hut construction. These small timbers would have needed a large amount of chinking (wood and other debris shoved between timbers) and then daubing (clay used to seal the smaller cracks) to keep the weather out.

In addition to serving as a clay source for the huts, during occupation these open pits would have been used for drainage and waste disposal. In terms of drainage, none of the characteristic drain trenches found at many Civil War encampments were identified at McGowan's camp (see Jensen 2000). The intermediary borrow pits may have served as sumps drawing both groundwater and storm water away from the huts. In addition, these pits would have served as convenient hearth dumps. Artifacts recovered from the pits are similar to those found within the hearth, consisting of dense concentrations of small burnt nails and scorched clay, materials potentially swept from the hearth and deposited in the pit.

In addition to hearth sweepings, Feature 68 also contained a shattered alkaline-glazed jug (figure 8.8). Excavation of the mound north of this pit (Feature

Figure 8.8. Reconstruction of alkaline-glazed jug from Area 1 (photo by the author).

94) uncovered the top and handle to this same vessel. This cross-mend suggests that hut occupants (Feature 94) disposed of their garbage upslope, in Feature 68. In addition to the large jug, a portion of a clay tobacco pipe was recovered along with a dozen percussion caps—possibly the result of pranksters dropping them down the chimney to surprise hut inhabitants. The materials recovered from this pit suggest that what had originated as a borrow pit subsequently served as a convenient trash receptacle and demarcated boundaries between huts.

The hut layout and pit features in this portion of the camp are particularly revealing concerning cramped living conditions. The distance between Feature 94 and Feature 95 is sixteen feet, similar to spacing found between other mound features in this row of huts. As the trash pits are four feet in diameter, this spacing leaves approximately twelve feet for the hut—which is the dimension reported by members of McGowan's Brigade (Benson 1962:55). Given this spacing, this section of the camp would have been tightly packed with very little space existing between huts and trash pits.

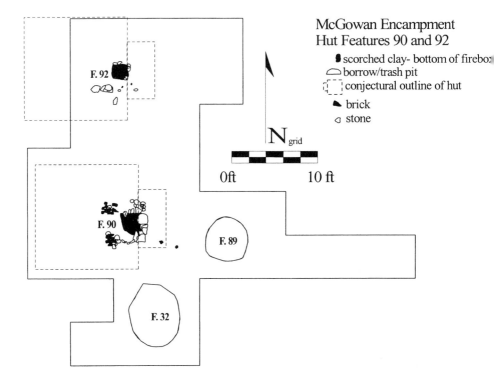

Figure 8.9. Plan view of excavations in Area 2 (photo by the author).

AREA 2

The second series of hut sites excavated is in the camp's eastern portion, on the ridge crest (figure 8.3). Area 2 includes two mound features (Features 90 and 92), interpreted as hut remains with associated depressions. Feature 92 is the most similar to the huts just discussed. Feature 90 is much larger and more distinctive (figure 8.9).

Feature 92 is located north and downslope of Feature 90. Removal of the rubble overburden revealed a poorly formed firebox surrounding scorched clay. In fact, if not for the scorched clay area, archaeologists would have been hard-pressed to identify this feature as a hut site (figure 8.10). The hearth appears to have opened west into the structure, given the position of the firebox in relation to the scorched clay. Whether the firebox for Feature 92 was largely clay with very little stone or postabandonment processes resulted in the removal of

Figure 8.10. Photograph of excavations in Area 2, view to the north.

stone and disturbance of the firebox is unclear. Whatever the case, the firebox structure was very similar to that seen in the two huts in Area 1.

Hut feature 90 lies immediately south of hut feature 92. The mound associated with the feature is the more prominent of the two huts. Removal of leaf litter revealed a concentration of rock and brick, possibly related to a chimney fall. Once accumulated topsoil was cleared, a very distinct pattern of stone was revealed, consisting of a single layer of loosely laid but closely placed rock rubble forming a clearly defined square that measured twelve feet by twelve feet. The twelve-foot-square dimension is identical to those described by historical descriptions. While this was initially thought to be a stone hut platform, excavation revealed the rock rubble to be set within the camp's abandonment layer—a layer of clay containing charred clay inclusions that lay directly upon a grey loam (interpreted as the living surface). Within this context it is possible that the square pattern was produced postabandonment by the standing chimney's collapsing into the still-standing walls of the structure. In this scenario, the resultant scatter of stones from the chimney fall would be confined to the interior walls, thus forming a twelve-foot square. Either way, the remains from this hut provide the only direct evidence recovered for the size and shape of the camp structures.

Following removal of the rock rubble and clay layer, a laid brick hearth was uncovered, along with a firebox that was defined by several large stones. The brick hearth is located west of the firebox and consists of two brick pads. The firebox is marked by several large stones and a patch of scorched clay (figure 8.10). Inside the firebox, excavation revealed ash deposits interbedded with burnt clay patches. The interbedded, scorched clay layers are potentially the result of the firebox collapsing (as evidenced by the presence of rock and clay debris against the inside wall of the firebox) and being rebuilt during occupation.

The size of the firebox and hearth and amount of architectural debris recovered from Feature 90 are suggestive of a more substantial structure as compared to Features 92, 94, and 95. The firebox and hearth dimensions of Feature 90 are close to three times the size of the other hearth features excavated (figures 8.6, 8.9). In addition, the amount of stone rubble recovered is twice that of the other features and represents either a more substantial firebox or a stone chimney base below a stick-and-mud flue (figure 8.11). The number of nails in Feature 90 is also significantly greater than in other features. The factors of hearth size, weight of stone, and nail numbers indicate that the amount of resources, both labor and raw materials, invested in the construction of hut feature 90 was substantially more than with the other huts examined at the McGowan site.

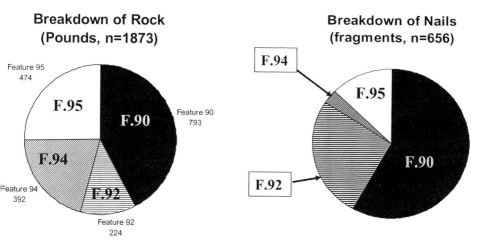

Figure 8.11. Architectural materials recovered from hut sites (images by the author).

Two pit depressions were excavated around Feature 90 (figure 8.9). The larger of the two pits, Feature 32, was quite deep and contained a continuous layer of burned wood across the bottom that was overlain with deposits of ash, burnt clay, burnt bone, and small burnt nails. Unlike Features 94 and 95, these pits do not appear to demarcate structural boundaries, as no pit exists between Feature 92 and Feature 90.

The quantity of rock and number of nails recovered from Feature 92 was much less than that from Feature 90—suggesting an overall simpler structure built with far fewer resources. The much smaller firebox of Feature 92 and the lack of a brick hearth further highlight the disparity between the two huts. Despite this, the two hearths line up with each other and are open to the west—suggesting that these were huts whose doors faced west. Unlike Features 94 and 95, however, the spacing between these two huts is much greater. With a space of twenty feet between hearths and a lack of pit features between the two structures, there appears to be more open space surrounding Feature 90. However, as one moves downslope of Feature 92, the spacing of depressions and mounds is more reminiscent of that found in Area 1.

Given the position of Feature 90 at the ridge top, along with the differences already noted in architectural form, this hut stands out as being different from the other three hut sites excavated. A similar difference is observed when the material assemblage from this hut is compared to that found in the other three.

Material Assemblages from Hut Sites

Aside from architectural debris, the most commonly encountered artifacts at the hut sites were fragments of ceramic and glass vessels, clothing-related artifacts, and animal bone. Interestingly, military items such as haversack hooks, ammunition, and military buttons were rather rare finds. In all excavations, only one bullet, two military buttons, and two haversack hooks were recovered. The scarcity of these items may reflect any, or all, of three factors: (1) the limited availability of military equipage of Confederate soldiers at this time (Caldwell 1992), (2) camp cleaning, and (3) recurrent relic hunting at the site prior to 1984. Most military items were recovered from hut yards, none being recovered from the borrow/trash pits. As relic hunting prior to 1984 was largely confined to surface hunting in areas surrounding the huts, there is a good chance that many of the military items were recovered by relic hunters. It should be noted, however, that in the areas excavated, no evidence of shovel pits—either in the yards or in the features—from relic collecting were identified.

While the impact of relic collecting could affect the composition of the military assemblage, Confederate troops had significant difficulty obtaining supplies during this time of the war. Some evidence for the scarcity of standard-issue military items is seen in the fact that soldiers in McGowan's Brigade cast their own lead palmetto buttons in camp. Local relic hunters have recovered lead spew attached to miscast buttons, obviously an attempt by McGowan's troops to replace missing uniform buttons (Mike Clatterbuck, personal communication 2002).

Among the four huts excavated, eight of fourteen buttons recovered were glass undergarment buttons. Their distribution between hut sites was far from proportionate, however. Feature 90 yielded the largest number of buttons (ten), with the remainder being evenly distributed between Features 92, 94, and 95. Feature 90 was the only hut where military-style buttons—one eagle shield and one South Carolina palmetto—were recovered. The discrepancy in the number of buttons present at Feature 90 suggests that this hut's inhabitants may have had more access to clothing and supplies.

A quantitative comparison of ceramic and glass vessels recovered from the various hut sites reveals the same discrepancy between Feature 90 and the other hut sites. The soldiers inhabiting the small Feature 94 and 95 huts had the fewest goods. The combined vessel assemblage recovered from these structures consists of sherds from an alkaline-glaze stoneware jug and crock, probably of Carolina manufacture, and two glass bottles. In addition, a stoneware tobacco pipe, a portion of a carved Gardner bullet, a cow vertebra, the phalanges of a young pig, and ten percussion caps were recovered. While the trash pit associated with Feature 92 was not excavated, glass and ceramic vessels recovered from the hut area consist of an ironstone plate, an Albany-slipped vessel, and three glass bottles.

In contrast, the assemblage from Feature 90 consists of elements from ten tableware vessels, including fragments of a flow-blue plate, an agateware bowl, three ironstone plates, a sponged bowl, two leaded-glass tumblers, and two pressed-glass dishes. In terms of storage vessels, pieces of eight glass bottles were recovered from Feature 90, along with four stoneware storage vessels. The presence of three inkwells and an ink bottle in Feature 90 suggests that hut occupants were literate and needed to conduct correspondence, such as an officer writing reports. In contrast, fragments from only one inkwell were recovered from the other three hut sites.

The number of artifacts recovered from Feature 90 provides hints into this hut's inhabitants' lives beyond their evident greater access to material goods. First, the range of diversity of items is such that these goods would not be carried in a soldier's haversack. More likely, these items would be carried by baggage wagons. While other items, such as the alkaline-glazed jugs and crocks, would also be carried by baggage train, such items would likely be from general military allocations provided to all soldiers. The more specialized ceramics and glasswares found with Feature 90 are more likely personal accoutrements packaged for a specific individual—likely an officer. More specifically, the occupant of Feature 90 was potentially a company officer positioned at the head of a company street.

Interestingly, these differences did not appear in the faunal assemblage. While Feature 90 contained the largest amount of faunal material, Features 94 and 95 held strong at 20 percent and 35 percent respectively of the total amount of bone recovered, compared to Feature 90's 45 percent. Most of the bones in the assemblage are highly fragmented. The only identifiable bone consists of vertebrae from a young pig and a cow.

Conclusion

Archaeological research at the McGowan brigade encampment provided important insights into the plan and appearance of a Confederate winter encampment occupied when the tide of victory began to turn against Lee's troops. Analyses of what have been interpreted as one officer's and three enlisted men's huts illustrate the crowded and sparse living conditions in which Confederate soldiers spent their winter months during 1863–64. One common denominator that appears throughout the huts excavated is the ephemeral nature of architectural features and the sparseness of artifacts. The lack of material goods recovered is very apparent when one contrasts the finds from this camp with those made by relic hunters in contemporary Union camps across the Rapidan River. In these locations, hundreds of bottles, ceramic vessels, and military equipage and paraphernalia have been excavated (John Kendrick, personal communication 2002).

While the smaller quantity of goods at the McGowan encampment is evident, excavations revealed material disparities between hut sites indicative of the hierarchical chain of command in the camps. While these differences are not surprising given the rigorous hierarchy built into any military organization, what is exciting is how this hierarchy manifests itself in the material record. In particular, the variables most affected, as seen in many other structured societies, are location, resources available for shelter construction, and access to goods. What needs further exploration through excavation of additional hut sites is whether this pattern repeats itself throughout this camp and the other regimental camps of different states that shared the winter at Montpelier and the subtleties these differences may take. It is through such contrasts that we can begin to reconstruct an understanding of the web of human interaction that is woven into complex organizational structures and can begin to develop a more personal history of individuals who placed their lives on the line during this pivotal period of American history.

References Cited

Benson, Susan Williams

1962   *Berry Benson's Civil War Book.* University of Georgia Press, Athens.

Caldwell, J.F.J.

1992   *The History of a Brigade of South Carolinians, First Known as "Gregg's" Brigade and Subsequently as "McGowan's Brigade."* Originally published 1866. Morningside Press, Dayton, Ohio.

Hurst, Patricia

1989   *The War between the States, 1862–1865: Rapidan River Area of Clark Mountain, Orange County, Virginia.* Patricia J. Hurst, Rapidan, Va.

Jensen, Todd L.

2000   "Gimme Shelter": Union Shelters of the Civil War, A Preliminary Archaeological Typology. M.A. thesis, Department of Anthropology, College of William and Mary in Virginia, Williamsburg.

Lehman, O. J., 33rd North Carolina

1922   "Additional Sketch to August 23, 1921, Camp Life." Manuscript on file, North Carolina Archives, Raleigh.

Lyman, Theodore

1866   Postwar letters, April 12, 1866, and April 14, 1866. Lyman Family Papers, Massachusetts Historic Society, Boston.

Power, J. Tracy

1998   *Lee's Miserables: Life in the Army of Northern Virginia from Wilderness to Appomattox.* University of North Carolina Press, Chapel Hill.

Reeves, Matthew B.

2003   Historical, Archaeological, and Architectural Research at the Gilmore Cabin. Report on file, Montpelier Foundation, Orange, Va.

United States War Department

1861   *Regulations for the Army of the United States, 1861.* Harper and Brothers, New York.

9

"Beautiful Confusion"

The Archaeology of Civil War Camp Life in an Urban Context

GARRETT R. FESLER, MATTHEW R. LAIRD, AND HANK D. LUTTON

We had no chance to examine the works as we marched through [Yorktown]
without halting. Blankets, clothing, knapsacks, and in fact everything pertaining
to the make up of a soldier was strewn about in beautiful confusion.
Private Alfred Bellard, 5th New Jersey Infantry

"Cities are messy places," Eric Sandweiss cautions, and "rarely present us with neat historical pictures that we can comprehend at a glance (Sandweiss 1996:319). Though Yorktown, Virginia, was hardly a metropolis on the eve of the Civil War, this sleepy York River county seat would soon find itself overwhelmed by thousands of temporary inhabitants who would leave a lasting physical imprint on its landscape. Not since the late eighteenth century had the town held such importance as a port and urban center. First appropriated by Confederate forces that expanded and enlarged Lord Cornwallis's Revolutionary War defenses, Yorktown endured a month-long siege during the Peninsula Campaign, then two more years as a Federal garrison before it was finally relinquished to its war-weary residents.

Given Yorktown's complex and compressed Civil War history, interpreting the archaeological evidence of its wartime occupation poses many of the same challenges faced in any urban setting once inhabited by transient and underdocumented populations. A case in point is the 1989 discovery and subsequent excavation of a semisubterranean "dug-out" winter hut identified by the James River Institute for Archaeology, Inc. (JRIA), on one of Yorktown's central blocks. Situated in the midst of a confined urban setting successively occupied by Confederate and Union forces, this temporary domestic feature defied straightforward categorization. Was it constructed during the initial Confederate occupation in the winter of 1861–62 or later, while the town was in Federal hands? How long was it occupied? When was it backfilled, and by whom? These fundamental questions shaped this feature's analysis; for without a solid historical context, the interpretive value of the rich material culture yielded by excavation would be significantly diminished. Simply put, this hut and its contents could potentially "mean" something entirely different if associated with Yorktown's earlier Southern defenders or with Northern soldiers who later occupied the town.

This chapter details the attempt to deal with the unique interpretive problems posed by excavating this single dugout winter hut. Beginning with a historical overview of the town and its Civil War occupation, the study continues with a detailed discussion of the feature's archaeological excavation and a preliminary analysis of its architectural characteristics and material culture evidence. Finally, in lieu of a definitive statement concerning the feature's association and significance, the conclusion seeks to summarize and evaluate the interpretive possibilities that emerged from the study of available documentary and physical evidence.

An Embattled Town: Yorktown, Virginia, 1781–1864

A bustling and prosperous port in the eighteenth century, Yorktown's fortunes were dramatically reversed in the fall of 1781 when British and Franco-American armies descended on the town in the climactic battle of the Revolutionary War. The resulting siege proved equally devastating to the town's inhabitants and built landscape. The fighting, coming as it did on the heels of a long, slow decline of Tidewater Virginia's tobacco trade, severely shook Yorktown's economic foundation. "Yorktown is going fast to decay," observed architect Benjamin Henry Latrobe after a 1790s visit. "It has an excellent harbor, safe from every wind but the east. But of what use is a harbor without a trade?" (Hatch 1973:73). After the war, the booming ports of Baltimore and Norfolk steadily siphoned off Yorktown's commerce, leaving many townspeople "destitute of employment." Then, on March 4, 1814, a devastating fire destroyed much of the town. When he visited Yorktown in 1848, historian Benson J. Lossing noted the persistent effects of the conflagration: "from that blow," he recorded, "the village never seems to have recovered" (Richter 1998:21, 27).

In spite of its difficulties, Yorktown continued to function as the seat for York County. The Marquis de Lafayette paid a visit on his triumphal 1824 American tour, and he participated in activities commemorating the forty-fourth anniversary of the victory over Cornwallis. In the late 1830s, York County resident Richard Randolph unsuccessfully attempted to promote the riverside town as a summer resort, with "an extensive Hotel and bathery establishment, for the accommodation of the Publick, during the summer" (Hatch 1973:83). In the antebellum years, Robert Anderson of nearby Williamsburg became Yorktown's largest landholder, purchasing most of the town's lots between 1817 and his death in 1858. Lot 16, on which the hut feature was located, was one of Anderson's holdings. An 1860 county valuation of Yorktown's lots attributes Lot 16 to Anderson's estate, yet indicates no taxable buildings on the property. By the beginning of the Civil War, Lot 16—like many of the town's other lots—lay vacant, a visible reminder of Yorktown's long, slow decline (Hatch 1973:193–94; Richter 1998:28–29; York County Circuit Court, Land Book, 1860).

For the second time in eighty years, war overwhelmed the small town on the York. Within months of the onset of the Civil War, the Hampton Roads area was engulfed in armed conflict. Fort Monroe, at the easternmost tip of the James-York Peninsula, was an important Federal stronghold that lay within the heart of Confederate territory. Union military planners were convinced that by using Fort Monroe as a launching point they could move up the James-York Peninsula to Richmond, capture the Confederate capital, and bring the war to a timely end. The deepwater port of Yorktown would play a critical role, serving as a staging area for the final amphibious movement up the York River to West Point, a railhead port within striking distance of Richmond.

Recognizing the threat of a Federal assault, Confederate military authorities in Richmond realized that a series of strong defensive lines would be necessary to defend the Peninsula. In May 1861, Colonel Benjamin S. Ewell, then serving as president of the College of William and Mary, was given temporary command of Confederate land forces on the Peninsula and responsibility for defending the area between the James and York Rivers. Ewell planned defensive lines east of Williamsburg, comprised of infantry outposts and artillery redoubts between the two rivers. The most advanced was anchored at Yorktown, with an associated artillery position across the river at Gloucester Point (figure 9.1). The line then ran south from Yorktown across the Peninsula to Mulberry Island on the James River. After a visit to Williamsburg, Confederate commander General Robert E. Lee approved Ewell's plan, and construction soon commenced. Ewell was soon replaced by his friend, Major General John Bankhead Magruder, widely known as "Prince John." After some debate over the proposed alignment of the fortifications, construction of the Peninsula defenses was in full swing by the summer of 1861. Slaves provided the bulk of the labor, but maintaining consistent progress on fortifications was often difficult, given the extent of military construction projects then under way throughout

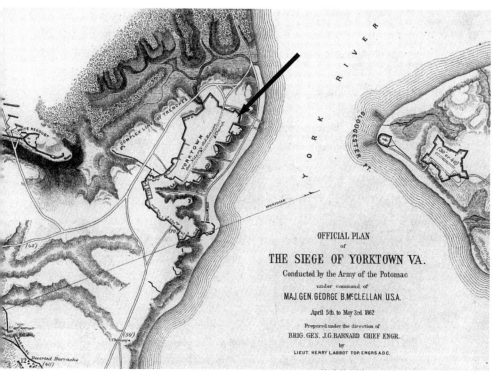

Figure 9.1. Detail from "Official Plan of the Siege of Yorktown, Va., Conducted by the Army of the Potomac under command of Maj. Gen. George B. McClellan, U.S.A., April 5th to May 3rd 1862. Prepared under the direction of Brig. Gen. J. G. Barnard, Chief Engr., by Lieut. Henry L. Abbot, Top. Engrs. A.D.C. Chas. G. Krebs, Engr. Lith. by J. F. Gedney, Washn." (G3884.Y6s5 1862.A2CW673, Library of Congress Geography and Map Division, Washington, D.C.).

the Peninsula and local slave owners' resistance to their slaves being "impressed" for construction details (Hastings and Hastings 1997:39–45).

Yorktown's defenses were recognized as critical to protecting against the anticipated Federal movement by sea and land against Richmond. Confederate engineers supervised the construction of massive earthworks surrounding the town, many of them overlying earlier British defenses. Three bastions facing south and southeast, the direction of expected approach, had parapets fifteen feet thick, with ditches eight to ten feet deep. Additional parapets were located to the west, and fifty-six heavy guns were mounted along the works (Hatch 1974:143).

On October 3, 1861, Magruder issued General Order No. 89, reorganizing the Army of the Peninsula: "To Yorktown are assigned: First, the Eighth and Thirteenth Alabama Regiments, Colonel Winston commanding the post; second, the water batteries at that post, which will be served by Peyton's and Bouton's companies, the detachment of Captain Macon's company, De Gournay's Zouaves, and such other men as may have been detailed to report to Captain De Gournay" (OR, Series 1, vol. 4, p. 669).

Magruder proceeded to make arrangements for the men's winter accommodations. "The troops will be hutted for the winter," he ordered, "under the direction of the commanding officers of regiments and detachments, the work to be performed by details from each command" (OR, Series 1, vol. 4, p. 670). In January 1862, the First Division under Brigadier G. J. Rains was posted to "Yorktown, vicinity, and Ship Point" (OR, Series 1, vol. 9, p. 37).

As spring approached, and with it the anticipated Union onslaught, Magruder well understood the historic significance of a second Yorktown siege. "To the army of the Peninsula," he wrote,

> The long war of the Revolution culminated at length in victorious triumph on these very plains of Yorktown. These frowning battlements on the heights of York are turned in this second war of liberty against the enemies of our country. You breathe the air and tread the soil consecrated by the presence and heroism of our patriotic sires. Shall we, their sons, imitate their example, or basely bow the neck to the yoke of the oppressor? I know your answer. (OR, Series 1, vol. 9, pp. 53–54)

By March 1862, the Army of the Potomac under Major General George B. McClellan had begun massing at Fort Monroe in preparation for a planned assault on Richmond. The Confederates responded by reorganized the defending forces, merging the Army of the Peninsula and the Army of Northern Virginia, with Magruder commanding its right wing. At this time, General D. H. Hill had two divisions totaling about 12,600 men on the left of the advanced Peninsula line near Yorktown (Hastings and Hastings 1997:27).

With McClellan in command, the Army of the Potomac began advancing up the Peninsula on April 4, 1862. McClellan's plan called for an amphibious assault below Yorktown to turn the Confederate line, while a simultaneous thrust up the Peninsula would encircle the town and cut it off from Richmond. At this point, he believed that the Confederates would likely recognize the futility of their position and withdraw. If not, an assault on Yorktown was destined to be a rapid success. But McClellan's optimism soon waned when President Lincoln refused to commit Major General Irvin McDowell's 1st Corps, and he began receiving vastly inflated reports of Confederate troop strength. In fact, Confederate reinforcements had been arriving at Yorktown, and by April 7, Magruder had 34,400 men. Although Lincoln himself urged McClellan to move quickly toward his ultimate objective, the general became convinced that a sustained assault on Yorktown was required before the way to Richmond could be cleared. McClellan considered himself an expert on siege warfare, and a siege at Yorktown is what he got (Sears 1992:31–45).

Although McClellan held a better than two-to-one manpower advantage over the Confederate defenders, the advance up the Peninsula quickly bogged down into a protracted assault. For the remainder of April 1862, Federal forces worked feverishly to bring heavy siege guns to bear on the beleaguered Confederate bastion. Meanwhile, the siege lapsed into a grinding daily routine of trench life made miserable by relentlessly wet weather and punctuated by desultory sniping and artillery fire. All involved soon perceived that the meticulous McClellan would not launch his final attack on Yorktown until all his heavy guns were in position. Confederate general Joseph Johnston recognized that the impending bombardment would devastate the fortifications, and in late April he issued the order for the Yorktown defenders to withdraw on the night of May 3, 1862. Johnston's strategy proved a complete success. Launching a spectacular cannonade to distract the Federals, the Yorktown defenders abandoned the works largely undetected. McClellan, who had planned to begin his assault only two days later, was taken completely by surprise. The following day, advance elements of the "victorious" Army of the Potomac entered Yorktown, whose deserted streets were riddled with deadly "torpedoes," a variety of lethal land mines and booby traps (Sears 1992:45–67).

In delaying McClellan's army at Yorktown, the Confederates stole valuable time in which to organize forces that would eventually defeat him at Richmond's doorstep. By the end of August 1862, McClellan and much of the Army of the Potomac had left the Peninsula. Much of the area remained in Union hands, however, and the 2nd Division of Erasmus D. Keyes' 4th Corps was posted at Yorktown. For the next two years Yorktown remained in Federal hands, its garrison characterized by a continued succession of units and nearly constant bureaucratic reorganization (Welcher 1989:153–54, 362–63).

The only known visual representation of Lot 16 during Yorktown's wartime occupation is an undated sketch by Thomas Place, Company H, 1st New York Mounted Rifles (figure 9.2). The image likely was made between September 1863 and April 1864, when Place's company was in the Williamsburg area

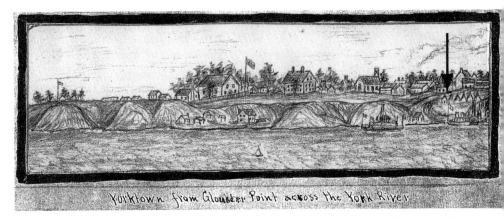

Figure 9.2. "Yorktown from Glouster [*sic*] Point across the York River" (Thomas Place Scrapbook n.d.:26, Mss5:7 P6902:1, Courtesy Virginia Historical Society, Richmond).

(Hewett 1997:167). The sketch depicts Yorktown under Union control as seen from Gloucester Point on the opposite side of the York River. At the extreme right, Place drew a row of five triangular tents (marked with arrow), at the end of which is a slightly different, vertical-walled shelter, which may represent a walled or "wedge" tent (see Nelson 1987:80–81). These tents/shelters are located just north of Ballard Street, at the point where the road descends from the bluffs to the waterfront. This position would put them either on or in the immediate vicinity of Lot 16. Although this rudimentary sketch certainly does not offer photographic realism, it does suggest that Union troops were occupying this part of town in the aftermath of the siege.

The Civil War's effect on Yorktown was considerable. Damage caused by the Confederate winter encampment of October–May 1861–62, the siege of April–May 1862, and the Federal garrisons that held the town from May 1862 to July 1864 has not been fully researched, but the available sources clearly indicate that many properties were damaged or destroyed during these years. In 1860, York County officials assessed tax on twenty-six structures; in 1865, the commissioner of the revenue reported that at least fourteen dwellings and other structures had been lost and five others damaged. While this damage was the inevitable result of military use, a spectacular accident during the Union occupation wrecked a number of properties. On December 16, 1863, a fire ignited munitions stored in the eighteenth-century Swan Tavern. The resulting explosion demolished the tavern and its outbuildings. Burning debris then triggered secondary blasts throughout the town, including one at the courthouse, which exploded with such force that it came off its foundations. The nearby jail and clerk's office were also leveled. As for Lot 16, documentary evidence sheds little light on who occupied the property during the war, and for how long. According to the county's tax records, it ended the war essentially as it had begun: in the hands of Robert Anderson's heirs, with no taxable buildings assessed (Hatch 1974:57; Richter 1998:29).

THE ARCHAEOLOGY OF FEATURE 311

Throughout 1989 JRIA archaeologists conducted comprehensive archaeological investigations of Lot 16, located between Buckner and Ballard streets (see figure 9.2). As work began, earthworks were visible on the back of the lot—evidently portions of the Yorktown defenses originally erected during the American Revolution and reworked by both armies during the Civil War. Recognizing the historical and archaeological significance of the property, a privately funded, nonprofit organization hired JRIA to fully excavate the lot and salvage all significant archaeological material before the construction of luxury condominiums. In August of that year, in the center of Lot 16, approximately ninety feet west of Ballard Street, archaeologists uncovered a roughly rectangular feature some eleven feet by six and a half feet in size (figure 9.3). Filled with dark brown and gray sandy loam that stood out against the surrounding orange clay subsoil,

Figure 9.3. Overview of Feature 311 prior to excavation, facing north toward the York River (photo by the author).

the feature was further defined during excavation as a small, semisubterranean "dug-out" dwelling no more than seven and a half feet long and six feet wide, with a partially intact brick chimney projecting from one end.

Dubbing this soil anomaly "Feature 311," archaeologists first used trowels to scrape it down and define the feature's edges for excavation. During this process a copper-alloy gilt sleeve button from a Virginia militia uniform was recovered. While all archaeological artifacts have the potential to provide information about the past, some artifacts can be more informative than others. An artifact's value often is dependent on where it is located in the archaeological record and how it got there—what is otherwise known as its "archaeological context." Although the button strongly suggested that the hut had been built and inhabited by Confederate soldiers in the winter of 1861–62, its archaeological context was suspect and its association with the hut was not ironclad.

Each artifact recovered from any site can be attributed to at least one of three general archaeological contexts. The most common is known in archaeological parlance as "secondary refuse" (Schiffer 1987:58–59). Most archaeological features, our hut included, were created in one of two ways: a feature could have been purposefully backfilled with soil obtained from the immediate environs, or it could have silted in naturally after abandonment. In both cases, the feature will contain redeposited soil mixed with random secondary refuse, meaning that whatever artifacts are mixed in the soil matrix have no direct association with the feature during its use. The Virginia sleeve button is secondary refuse and could not be confidently linked with the hut feature. It could have come from anywhere by chance and may have had nothing to do with the hut.

There are at least two other forms of archaeological deposition, known as "primary refuse" and "de facto refuse"; both have the potential to help investigators understand the past, although they occur less frequently than secondary refuse (Schiffer 1987:58–59, 89–90). Primary refuse is represented by those artifacts deposited into the archaeological record at the location of their use. For example, pieces of a bottle broken on the hut's floor would constitute primary refuse. However, a careful consideration of the context of the broken bottle pieces is necessary to determine whether the bottle was broken while resting on the hut's floor (primary refuse) or whether the glass fragments reached their destination when the hut was backfilled (secondary refuse). Similar to primary refuse, de facto refuse consists of useable artifacts that were left in place when the hut was abandoned and represent the most compelling form of archaeological data (Schiffer 1987:89–90). In the hut, any objects left in place—such as a

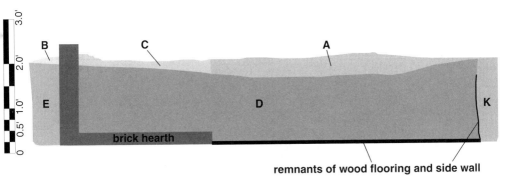

Figure 9.4. Profile drawing of Feature 311, facing south. Stratum A, B, C: upper fill layer (drawing by the author).

haversack stashed in the corner with its contents still intact or a cooking pot left on the hearth—would constitute de facto refuse.

As the archaeologists prepared to dig into the hut feature, they were aware that the key to identifying which army occupied it would largely depend upon archaeological context, particularly if primary and de facto artifacts could be found. Formal excavation began with the bisecting of the feature and removal of the north half layer by layer. To our disappointment, although nineteen discrete contexts were assigned to Feature 311, it became obvious that the hut had been backfilled almost entirely in one contiguous episode (figure 9.4). This enormous layer of rich brown and gray sandy loam was designated as Layer D. It spanned from the surface to the feature's floor (roughly 1.7 feet in depth) and was composed entirely of secondary refuse. Only 4 percent of the ceramic sherds in Layer 311D dated to the nineteenth century, meaning that a large percentage of the fill predated the Civil War. Because of the presence of a mid- eighteenth-century kitchen only a few dozen feet away and evidence of intensive use during the American Revolution, the abundance of eighteenth-century ceramics and wine bottle glass, English clay tobacco pipe stems, and other domestic refuse was not unexpected.

Within the hut, archaeologists encountered only minimal evidence of soil layers washing into it or any signs of a gradual accumulation of silt and sand. There was a small amount of siltation in the southeast and southwest corners, but this probably occurred during the hut's use or at abandonment. For the most part, the stratigraphy indicated that when the hut was abandoned, it was backfilled almost immediately.

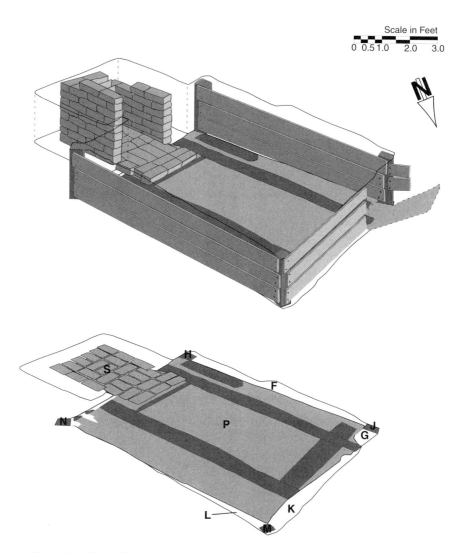

Figure 9.5. Plan of Feature 311 after removal of fill. Stratum F, K, and L: builder's trenches; features H, J, M, and N: corner post stains; stratum G: wash layer fronting entrance; stratum P: floor layer; features: base of brick hearth (drawing by Jamie May).

HUT ARCHITECTURE

If the hut remained open for any length of time, its brick hearth, wood floor, or wood walls would most likely not have survived prolonged exposure to the elements. However, backfilled soils helped preserve and protect the structure's interior to such a high degree that much of the method and mode of its construction can be deciphered (figure 9.5).

Firsthand accounts of Civil War–era winter huts from both sides of the Mason-Dixon line are not in short supply (see, for example, Billings 1993; Cowtan 1887; Craft 1885; Fiske 1866; Hitchcock 1904; Kepler 1886; Kirkland 1895; Santvoord 1894; Sprenger 1885; Thompson 1888; Wiley 1971, 1975). One that seems to come closest to potentially describing the construction stages of the Yorktown hut feature comes from Sergeant George F. Sprenger, 122nd Pennsylvania Regiment(3rd Division, III Corps), who recalled,

> In the first place, we dug out a hole in the ground about 10 feet long by nearly 6 feet wide, and 18 inches deep. Over and about this we erected a hut four feet high . . . making a doorway, or rather sort of a creep-hole, in the gable ends. We next put up a ridge-pole, over which we stretched our shelter-tents, to the height of about three feet above the walls, thus giving ample pitch and forming a neatly-proportioned hut; whereupon, through the acquisition of four mess-pork barrels . . . we were soon provided with an excellent flue or chimney. (Sprenger 1885:204)

Based on Feature 311's excavation, it appears that soldiers first dug a crude rectangular pit, at least two feet deep, but perhaps as much as three to three and a half feet below ground surface (gauged by modern grade). Wood planks were laid across the dirt floor, with two long planks running the length of the hut serving as makeshift joists onto which other planks were lapped (figures 9.5, 9.6). One square-cut wood post was placed into each corner, each approximately five to six inches in diameter. Horizontal sidewall planks then were nailed to the outside face of the corner posts on the south wall and on the inside face on the north wall to form interior walls.

The space between the horizontal planks and the dirt sidewalls formed builder's trenches. The north wall was relatively flush with the dirt sidewall, requiring very little backfilling behind the wall, thereby suggesting that this was the first wall built in the hut (figure 9.5). In fact, this wall appears to have been preassembled, with nails driven through the sidewall boards into the outer face of the northwest and northeast corner posts and then positioned into the open hole. The builder's trench for the south wall was much more prominent, indi-

Figure 9.6. View of wood planks and side walls of Feature 311, facing south (photo by the author).

Figure 9.7. View of hearth in Feature 311 with artifacts in place, facing east (photo by the author).

cating that it was the last wall fastened together. Here, the sidewall boards were attached to the inner face of the two corner posts, and soil was then packed behind it, around the posts and up against the boards. Except for two upright timbers the size of small slats along the east wall near the northeast corner post, no other framing members were noted.

During excavation, archaeologists noticed a breach in the west wall adjacent to the southwest corner post and found evidence of a board having been nailed to the south face of that post and projecting out of the hut (see figure 9.5). The breach was approximately two feet wide, just enough room to allow access into and out of the hut. A wash layer of soil appeared to be pooled on the floor, and as archaeologists probed the area, they determined that there had been a shallow ramp leading into the hut, either purposely cut out or worn down by use.

At the east end of the hut, opposite from the hut entrance, the builders used eighty-eight bricks to fashion a small, enclosed hearth (figure 9.7). A three-foot-by-four-foot hole had been dug off the east end, into which was built a brick box measuring two feet wide by two and a quarter feet long by slightly under two feet high. Soil was packed around the brick box to form a builder's trench. The bricks apparently had been scavenged from the town, and some had remnants of their original oyster-shell mortar adhering. The bricks were held together

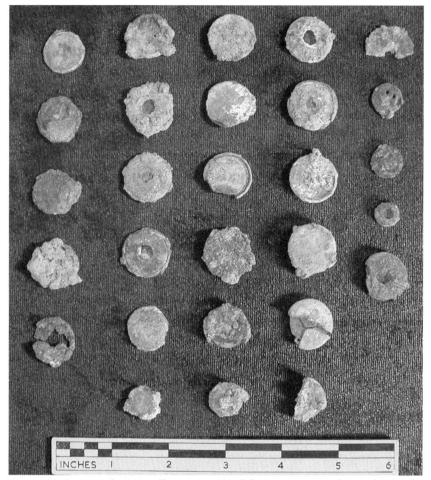

Figure 9.8. Iron tent button collection recovered from Feature 311 (photo by the author).

by makeshift mortar formed from brown and reddish sandy clay. As would be expected, this clay mortar was burned black on the inner walls and hearth floor. The hearth front projected out from the box by several courses of brick overlapping the plank floor slightly.

We can only surmise what the hut looked like aboveground—something like George Sprenger's description, perhaps (Sprenger 1885; see also Nelson 1987). However, some artifacts recovered from its fill provide clues. For example, twenty-eight iron buttons, almost surely used to attach canvas tents together, were recovered from the hut fill, including seventeen from the floor (figure 9.8). This evidence alone strongly suggests that the roof, and perhaps the hut's superstructure, consisted of several military-issue tents buttoned together. Soldiers usually were supplied with a canvas tent half, roughly five or six feet square, which allowed them to pair with another to form a full tent (Laird et al. 2000; Nelson 1987:80). Depending upon how high above the ground the hut sat, it may have required several tent pieces to cover it sufficiently.

While iron tent buttons indicate how it was covered, identifying what kind of walls, if any, the hut may have had is a more difficult undertaking. Archaeologists observed no direct evidence of walls outside the pit. The sides of the pit were lined with boards, but investigators could not ascertain whether those boards extended aboveground, although this is possible, based on descriptions and photographs (see Nelson 1987:81). The four corner posts were not seated in the ground, meaning that they were probably incapable of supporting aboveground walls of any height; a good gust of wind presumably could have toppled the structure unless the walls were reinforced with props or with mud or clay packed around the exterior. Whatever the case, if lumber could be procured, and it was probably more readily available in Yorktown compared with most places, the low board walls likely extended several feet aboveground.

A more labor-intensive alternative would have been to build walls by stacking and notching logs together up to a level several feet above the ground, in effect building a small log cabin. The use of logs would have depended on their availability, and whether or not there were nearby stands of pine or deciduous trees in the relatively urban setting of Yorktown is questionable, especially if the hut was built by Union soldiers after the winter of 1861–62. Given these scenarios, it is perhaps most likely that the builders fashioned low walls with milled boards (perhaps nailed to the corner posts), draped a tent over a ridgepole, and fastened the canvas over the tops of the walls.

The brick chimney likely projected aboveground only a few inches, whereupon wood barrels could have been stacked on top to serve as a flue. Old pork barrels were one common device used to convey smoke from winter huts (Nelson 1987:83, 87). In support of this interpretation, archaeologists retrieved an iron barrel band fragment jerry-rigged with a screw from the hut fill (311D), evidence that a recycled barrel may have been in use. Overall, two soldiers probably could have resided comfortably in the hut, and perhaps a third could have crammed in—making it a cramped but serviceable abode, one that may have been occupied for only a few winter months and then abruptly abandoned when the weather turned warm or soldiers were given orders to decamp.

Table 9.1. Total Artifacts from Hut Feature (44YO466/F.311)

Context	Number	Percentage
Intrusive artifacts predating the hut	628	24.5
Nondiagnostic artifacts	271	10.6
Camp life artifacts	1,588	61.9
Floor artifacts	78	3.0
Total	2,565	100.0

HUT ARTIFACTS

For purposes of discussion, we believe that the artifacts from Feature 311 can be divided into four main groupings: intrusive artifacts that predate the hut, nondiagnostic artifacts that cannot be reasonably attributed to any particular era, backfilled diagnostic artifacts from the hut's vicinity that represent camp life, and artifacts from the floor, the only context (primary refuse) directly associated with the inhabitants (table 9.1).

Nearly two-thirds (64.9 percent) of the artifacts relate to Civil War–era activity in and around the hut. Using a modified version of Stanley South's artifact classification system (see South 1977:92–93), we have divided the camp life and floor artifacts ($n=1,666$) into seven general groups (kitchen, architectural, arms, and so forth), partitioning these into twenty-one subset classes (ceramics, kitchenware, buckles, military equipment, and so forth) (table 9.2). The collection is dominated by kitchen and architectural artifacts that produced nearly 93 percent of the entire collection. In particular, iron nails comprised the single largest class of artifacts (39.0 percent), followed by glass bottle fragments (34.8 percent) and fragments of iron kitchenware (17.4 percent).

The counting of fragments overemphasizes the kitchen and architectural groups in the collection because of the number of broken glass shards and iron nails. A more reliable indicator of the makeup of the artifact collection is derived from a minimum vessel count. For example, the nine ceramic sherds can be confidently attributed to six vessels: three stoneware crocks or jugs, two ginger beer bottles, and a whiteware plate (table 9.2; figure 9.9). Based on the number of complete bases, necks, and rims, the minimum vessel count for dark green liquor bottles stands at eight, and light green case bottles at four, making a minimum tally of a dozen liquor bottles in the backfill of the hut feature (table 9.2; figure 9.9). Like bottle glass, the kitchenware class is skewed by fragments, in this case by 289 iron fragments, most of which appear to be from a

Table 9.2. Camp Life and Floor Artifacts from Hut Feature (by group and class)

Civil War–era artifacts	Fragment count	Fragment percentage	Object count	Object percentage
Kitchen artifact group	894	53.66	31	25.56
1. Ceramics	9	0.54	6	4.51
2. Glass bottle fragments	579	34.75	12	9.02
5. Pharm. bottle fragments	14	0.84	5	3.76
7. Tableware	2	0.12	2	1.50
8. Kitchenware	290	17.41	6	4.51
Architectural group	650	39.02	*	
11. Cut or wire nails	650	39.02	*	
Arms group	5	0.30	5	3.76
16. Shot, lead	3	0.19	3	2.26
16a. Minié ball	1	0.06	1	0.75
18. Percussion cap	1	0.06	1	0.75
Clothing group	46	2.76	46	34.59
19. Buckles	11	0.66	11	8.27
21. Buttons	32	1.92	32	24.06
Shoe grommet	1	0.06	1	0.75
Shoe heel	2	0.12	2	1.50
Personal group	4	0.24	4	3.01
29. Personal items	4	0.24	4	3.01
Tobacco pipe group	4	0.24	4	3.01
30. Reed stem pipes	4	0.24	4	3.01
Activities group	63	3.78	40	30.08
31. Construction tools	2	0.12	2	1.50
32. Farm tools	1	0.06	1	0.75
37. Storage items	4	0.24	4	3.01
40. Misc. hardware	2	0.12	2	1.50
41. Other	1	0.06	1	0.75
42. Military equipment	53	3.18	30	22.56
Total	1,666	100.00	133	100.01

* The 650 nails have been eliminated from any of the calculations involving objects.

few individual objects such as a coffee pot, a canister, a Dutch oven, and an iron plate (table 9.3). Thus, the number of minimum vessels among the kitchenware class probably consists of six cookware items or metal containers, one of which may be a coal scuttle. The military equipment class is the only other class that consists of fragments, including twenty-two iron bands that served as struts for a canteen and three iron foil fragments of the lining of a cartridge crate, which reduces the number of military equipment objects to thirty (table 9.2).

Table 9.3. Kitchenware Artifacts

Artifact	Number	Percentage
Bowl, iron	4	0.24
Can key	1	0.06
Canister fragments	50	3.00
Canister lid, complete	1	0.06
Coffee pot lid fragments	35	2.10
Coffee pot fragments	1	0.06
Container fragments	163	9.78
Dutch oven fragments	9	0.54
Plate, iron	26	1.56
Total	290	17.41

Figure 9.9. Liquor containers from Feature 311. *Left:* American brown stoneware jug, 11 inches high, capacity approximately 2 quarts, probably manufactured at the Old Bridge Pottery in New Jersey, ca. 1810 to 1823; *upper right:* close-up decoration on the shoulder of the stoneware jug, stamped "GIN" with an encircling stamped fish motif; *lower right:* glass liquor bottle, 9.75 inches high, capacity approximately 1 pint (photo by the author).

Figure 9.10. Confederate clothing buttons from Feature 311. *Left:* sleeve button, "VIRGINIA" on front, "EXTRA QUALITY" on reverse; *right,* tunic button, "VIRGINIA SIC SEMPER TYRANNIS" on front, "CANFIELD & BROTHER BALTIMORE" on reverse (photo by the author).

Although technically nails are individual objects, by subtracting out the 650 nails from the collection, we are left with 130 individual objects with which to interpret the material circumstances of life in Feature 311. In this manner, the clothing group comprises slightly more than one-third of the objects (35.38 percent), followed by the activities group (30.77 percent; primarily due to the military equipment class), and the kitchen group (23.85 percent) (table 9.2).

Aside from two Confederate uniform buttons with questionable contexts, no artifacts can be attributed to one army or the other (figure 9.10). All remaining clothing buttons are generic, primary from undergarments that soldiers on both sides wore (figure 9.11). The military equipment was available in varying degrees to a typical soldier in either army (figure 9.12), as were the domestic goods (figure 9.13). In fact, all 130 identified objects, sans the Confederate buttons, realistically could have been found in a Confederate or a Union camp. Even the two Confederate buttons could have been scavenged by a Union soldier and reused or kept as keepsakes that were eventually backfilled. Had one or both buttons been recovered from the floor level, we would have been able to categorically interpret the hut as a Confederate residence. However, given their uncertain context, the buttons have too many drawbacks to be considered irrefutable.

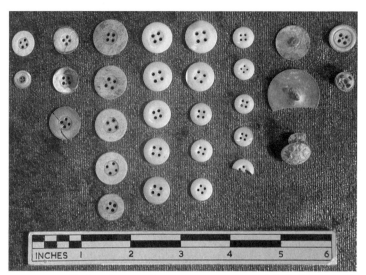

Figure 9.11. Clothing buttons from Feature 311. *From left,* shell buttons, burnished bone buttons, wooden buttons, Prosser glass buttons, one-piece brass buttons, iron hat button, animal horn button, brass clothing snap (photo by the author).

Figure 9.12. Military gear from Feature 311. *From left:* unfired .58-caliber lead shot, small lead shot, fired brass percussion cap, unfired Minié ball, iron hatband buckles and equipment buckles, bent belt-buckle tongue, brass waist belt buckle (photo by the author).

Figure 9.13. Miscellaneous personal goods from Feature 311. *Left: top row,* lead pipe fragment; *far left, center row:* iron spoon bowl; *middle, center row:* iron and bone utensil handle; *left, bottom row:* ceramic tobacco bowl base with green glaze finish and "PRESID . . ." embossed on one side and " . . . MORE" on the other [President Filmore]; *right, bottom row:* nearly complete reed-stem clay tobacco pipe; *far right, center row:* iron clasp knife with bone handle; *right, top row:* glass inkwell embossed with "JAMES S MASON & CO" on side panel (photo by the author).

Discussion

Feature 311 offers a glimpse, albeit brief, into Yorktown's military occupation. The goal of excavating and studying this feature was to glean as much information as possible concerning what life had been like in Civil War Yorktown, particularly for the soldiers occupying this particular dugout hut. However, as noted in the introduction, there were some preliminary nuts-and-bolts issues that first had to be addressed, namely, who built Feature 311, who occupied it, and who filled it in? In general, when a Civil War camp is excavated, there is little question as to which army occupied the site, as maps, documents, diaries, and occasionally even photographs can be employed to assist in the identification (see Laird et al. 2000). Feature 311 poses a unique problem of interpretation, however; given its setting in the contested and congested setting of 1860s Yorktown, a compelling case can be made for either Confederate or Union associations.

We believe there are two incontrovertible facts that apply to the hut, no matter which army occupied it. First, the hut was built expressly to keep its inhabitants warm over the course of the winter. The dugout hole provided an insulated space to efficiently use the heat from an elaborate hearth. Faced with the prospect of enduring a damp, cold Virginia winter, soldiers were willing to expend the effort to dig a sizeable hole, acquire wood and brick, and build a makeshift structure. As the temperature increased in the spring, summer, and fall, the hut's attractiveness as quarters would have diminished considerably. In fact, no one would likely have occupied the hut in the sweltering heat of a Virginia summer. Therefore, the hut was almost certainly built either by Confederate soldiers in the winter of 1861–62 or by Union soldiers in the subsequent two winters.

The second basic fact is that the hut was filled in immediately after its abandonment. Archaeologists detected no credible stratigraphic evidence that the hut remained open for any length of time once it was vacated; no wash layers were evident, the wood walls remained intact, and the hearth was in pristine condition with a few burned in situ artifacts still resting on its bricks. These archaeological facts underpin the central mystery of Feature 311: who would have been compelled to fill in a recently abandoned winter hut? Approaching the question chronologically backwards, if one could reasonably determine who filled in the hut and when, the answers might offer the best clue to who built and occupied it.

Confederate soldiers might very well have built Feature 311 in the winter of

1861–62. Several soldiers may have joined forces, pooled their resources and tent halves, and erected the hut in the waning months of 1861. Hunkered down until the early spring, the Confederate army abruptly evacuated Yorktown in early May. Although some identifiable artifacts were manufactured in the North, including one uniform button in Baltimore, there is no reason to believe that at this early stage of the war, goods from all regions of the country could not have found their way into the hands of Confederate troops. As such, stoneware jugs from New Jersey and glass bottles from Maryland might be accounted for by the still-fluid nature of supply. Certainly, the Union naval blockade at the mouth of the Chesapeake Bay had an effect on Confederate supply, and Confederate soldiers endured shortages, but the archaeological evidence is not nuanced enough to reveal an identifiable pattern of supply for either army.

It is highly unlikely that the Confederates would have taken the time or effort to fill the hut prior to abandoning Yorktown on May 3, 1862. However, Union soldiers may have had a compelling reason for backfilling it rapidly in May 1862. Although there is no concrete evidence to confirm this hypothesis, the fear of "torpedoes" (the lethal mines and booby traps left by the retreating Confederates) may have been the motivation behind its destruction. Union soldier narratives after the siege are rife with descriptions of the "infernal machines" left by their foes, which were considered "ungentlemanly" and beneath the standards of civilized warfare. "Torpedoes were planted in any place that was likely to be visited by our men," wrote Private Alfred Bellard, "on the walks by the forts and between the graves where rebel soldiers had been buried" (Donald 1975:64). Similarly, soldier-artist Robert Knox Sneden of the 40th New York Infantry recounted the hazards of postsiege Yorktown, which claimed the life of his regimental telegraphist and nearly his own. "The enemy had planted live shells with fuse attached in the main road leading into the works, and in houses, and buried them in the parapets and other places," he recalled. Booby traps were placed in tempting places, such as barrels of cornmeal or potatoes in abandoned houses (Bryan and Lankford 2000:59–60). Interestingly, a lead pipe was apparently left sitting on the hearth of Feature 311 before the hut was filled (figures 9.7 and 9.13). Under such conditions, it would not be surprising if cautious Union soldiers had simply filled in Feature 311 in fear of any potentially sinister object.

The sketch of Yorktown made by Thomas Place (figure 9.2) indicates that Union soldiers did, at some point, occupy the block encompassing Lot 16, though in his drawing, likely made in 1863–64, the troops were clearly under canvas. Notwithstanding the concern for hidden torpedoes, it is possible that Feature 311 was seen simply as a nuisance that impeded establishment of the orderly tent camp sketched by Place. Officers preferred organized encampments based on lines, rows, and uniformity, although this often was not possible given the vagaries of the landscape and circumstances (see Nelson 1987:79–80; Chapter 2). Hardly expecting to occupy Yorktown for two subsequent winters, Union officers may have ordered the hut backfilled as more of a "housekeeping" measure.

Finally, the hut may have been constructed and occupied by one of the procession of Federal units that garrisoned Yorktown between May 1862 and July 1864. Still, had the hut been built and occupied during the winters of 1862–63 or 1863–64, the question arises as to who would have backfilled the hut after Union troops finally left in 1864. Documentary evidence indicates that Lot 16 was vacant before and after the war, and it is difficult to imagine what aesthetic or functional purpose would have prompted someone to expend the effort to quickly fill an eleven-foot-by-six-foot hole when the landowner was long dead and his estate still in litigation.

Conclusion

If cities are messy places, then perhaps it is appropriate that all we can offer in the end is a messy answer. Feature 311 presents itself as a rather peculiar puzzle: who built and occupied this semisubterranean winter hut? To reach an answer, we have applied a form of historical and archaeological reasoning, an analytical process that interplays documentary and archaeological lines of evidence to deduce what we hope is a reasonably accurate assessment of the hut. Yet the frustrating fact remains that no single reading of the archaeological or documentary evidence can solve the question of who built and occupied the hut, and how and why it was finally backfilled and forgotten. Circumstantial evidence suggests that the most likely possibility may be that the hut was occupied by Confederate forces during the winter of 1861–62 and backfilled immediately by newly arrived Union troops, whether in fear of hidden "torpedoes" or through a more mundane military desire to impose order and regularity on a landscape already ravaged by war. Perhaps future investigations of similar Civil War features in Yorktown may offer a new perspective on Feature 311 and its history and significance, offering by extension a fuller insight into wartime life in this unique urban context. Until that time, however, any definitive answers concerning this single mysterious feature will remain tantalizingly out of reach.

ACKNOWLEDGMENTS

We would like to thank William Pittman of the Colonial Williamsburg Foundation Department of Archaeological Research, who lent an expert eye and helped us identify some of the artifacts in the collection. Jamie May of the Jamestown Rediscovery Project was kind enough to produce figure 9.5. Any errors, omissions, or mistakes are the responsibility of the coauthors.

REFERENCES CITED

Billings, John D.
1993   *Hardtack and Coffee.* University of Nebraska Press, Lincoln. (Originally published 1887.)

Bryan, Charles F., Jr., and Nelson D. Lankford (editors)
2000   *Eye of the Storm: A Civil War Odyssey.* Free Press, New York.

Cowtan, Charles W.
1887   *Services of the Tenth New York Volunteers (National Zouaves) in the War of the Rebellion.* C. H. Ludwig, New York.

Craft, David
1885   *History of the One Hundred Forty-First Regiment, Pennsylvania Volunteers, 1862–1865.* Reporter-Journal Printing Company, Towanda, Penn.

Donald, David Herbert (editor)
1975   *Gone for a Soldier: The Civil War Memoirs of Private Alfred Bellard.* Little, Brown, Boston.

Dubbs, Carol Kettenburg
2002   *Defend This Old Town: Williamsburg during the Civil War.* Louisiana State University Press, Baton Rouge.

Fiske, Samuel
1866   *Mr. Dunn Browne's Experiences in the Army.* Nichols and Noyes, Boston.

Grzymala, Elizabeth J.
1998   *Yorktown Archaeological/Historical Assessment.* Volume 1: *Archaeological Summary.* Colonial Williamsburg Foundation, Department of Archaeological Research, Williamsburg, Va.

Hastings, Early C., Jr., and David S. Hastings
1997   *A Pitiless Rain: The Battle of Williamsburg, 1862.* White Mane Publishing, Shippensburg, Penn.

Hatch, Charles E., Jr.
1973   *"York under the Hill": Yorktown's Waterfront.* National Park Service, Department of the Interior, Denver, Colo.

1974   *Yorktown's Main Street (from Secretary Nelson's to the Windmill) and Military Entrenchments Close In and Around the Town of York.* National Park Service, Department of the Interior, Denver, Colo.

Hewett, Janet B. (editor)
1997   *Supplement to the Official Records of the Union and Confederate Armies,* vol. 41. Broadfoot Publishing, Wilmington, N.C.

Hitchcock, Frederick L.
1904   *War from the Inside: The Story of the 132nd Regiment Pennsylvania Volunteer Infantry in the War for the Suppression of the Rebellion, 1862–63.* J. B. Lippincott, Philadelphia.

Kepler, William
1886   *History of the Three Months' and Three Years' Service of the Fourth Regiment Ohio Volunteer Infantry in the War for the Union.* Leader Printing, Cleveland, Ohio.

Kirkland, Frazar
1895   *Reminiscences of the Blue and Gray '61–'65.* Preston Publishing, Chicago.

Laird, Matthew R., Kimberly S. Zawacki, and Gregory LaBudde
2000   Recruiting the Landscape: Authority, Individuality, and the Archaeology of Camp French. Phase II and Phase III Archaeological Investigations at the Fredericksburg Auto Auction Property, Stafford County, Virginia. Report prepared by Cultural Resources, Inc., Fredericksburg, Va.

Nelson, Dean E.
1987   "Right Nice Little Houses": Impermanent Camp Architecture of the American Civil War. In *Perspectives in Vernacular Architecture.* Edited by Camille Wells, pp. 79–93. University of Missouri Press, Columbia.

Official Records of the Union and Confederate Armies (OR)
1972   *The War of the Rebellion: A Compilation of the Official Records of the Union and Confederate Armies.* United States War Department. Reprinted by the National Historical Society, Gettysburg, Penn.

Richter, Julie
1998   *Yorktown Archaeological/Historical Assessment.* Volume 2: *Historical Summary.* Colonial Williamsburg Foundation, Department of Archaeological Research, Williamsburg, Va.

Sandweiss, Eric
1996   Reading the Urban Landscape: An Approach to the History of American Cities. In *Historical Archaeology and the Study of American Culture.* Edited by Lu Ann De Cunzo and Bernard L. Herman, pp. 319–57. University of Tennessee Press, Knoxville.

Santvoord, C. Van
1894   *The One Hundred and Twentieth Regiment, New York State Volunteers: A Narrative of Its Services in the War for the Union.* Press of the Kingston Freeman, Rondout, N.Y.

Schiffer, Michael B.

1987   *Formation Processes of the Archaeological Record.* University of New Mexico Press, Albuquerque.

Sears, Stephen W.

1992 *To the Gates of Richmond: The Peninsula Campaign.* Ticknor and Fields, New York.

South, Stanley

1977   *Method and Theory in Historical Archaeology.* Academic Press, San Diego, Calif.

Sprenger, George F.

1885   *Concise History of the Camp and Field Life of the 122d Regiment, Penn'a Volunteers.* New Era Steam Book Print, Lancaster, Penn.

Thompson, Millett S.

1888   *Thirteenth Regiment of New Hampshire Volunteer Infantry in the War of the Rebellion, 1861–1865.* Houghton, Mifflin, Boston.

Welcher, Frank J.

1989   *The Union Army, 1861–1865, Organization and Operations.* Volume 1: *The Eastern Theater.* Indiana University Press, Bloomington.

Wiley, Bell Irvin

1971   *The Life of Billy Yank: The Common Soldier of the Union.* Doubleday, Garden City, N.Y.

1975   *The Common Soldier of the Civil War.* Scribners, New York.

York County Circuit Court

1860–65 Land Tax Records. Yorktown, Va.

10

Cabin in Command

The City Point Headquarters of Ulysses S. Grant

DAVID G. ORR

City Point, Virginia, situated on a bluff overlooking the juncture of the James and Appomattox rivers, was an extremely attractive site for human occupation over many millennia (Orr et al. 1984:64). During the American Civil War, the headquarters for the Union armies during the Petersburg campaign of 1864–65 was located here, and the choice proved to be particularly advantageous. It was within easy water communication of both Fort Monroe and Washington and the Union forces arrayed before Petersburg and Richmond. In the words of Horace Porter, a lieutenant colonel on Grant's staff, the City Point headquarters "was destined to become historic and to be the scene of some of the most memorable events of the war" (Porter 1961:211). Here, on the City Point bluff, near the dwelling of Dr. Richard Eppes, General Ulysses S. Grant established his headquarters, first in tents located just over a hundred feet from the bluff, and then in more commodious log huts, which appeared in November 1864 (Butowsky 1978). Since Grant was the commander of all the Union armies, his log hut was the hub of the complex, a material witness to the great events that terminated the conflict. Alone of all its kind, it has endured to the present as an important legacy of the Civil War.

The Cabin in Situ at City Point

By mid-December 1864, the headquarters staff had abandoned their tents for simple log structures. General Marsena Patrick, provost marshall general of the Army of the Potomac, left a diary record of his own movement from tents to more permanent quarters: "Soon after breakfast we began to move and it has taken most of the day to get settled. I think I shall like these quarters better than the other, when we get fairly settled in them. The tents of the Construction Corps are not yet struck and I expect but little peace tonight" (Patrick 1864–65:341, entry for December 14, 1864).

Patrick later (on December 15) remarked that he had "slept very well" in his new quarters although his bed was "not softer" although wider (Patrick 1864–65:342). In fact, the construction corps had been hard at work since October 1864, and Grant's complex was probably finished by early November (Badeau 1865). Adam Badeau's letter to George H. Stuart gives the best concise history of the cabin's role at City Point (Badeau 1865). Grant spent the war's last four months directing army activities from this structure. The two-room cabin occupied the center of the twenty-two-building complex adjacent to Dr. Eppes' dwelling (figure 10.1) (Lossing 1866:333). The front room was utilized as an office, with the back portion of the T-shaped cabin serving as Grant's private quarters. His wife, Julia, and son, Jesse, probably shared this space in January 1865 when they joined Grant in the field. Badeau provided good accounts of the momentous events that took place here and the role this simple structure played as the conflict finally came to an end. Badeau was a lieutenant colonel when he served as military secretary to General Grant at City Point.

On March 25, 1865, President Lincoln met Grant at the headquarters cabin to discuss his possible visit to the front. During this visit Lincoln was accompanied by a distinguished assemblage of naval officers led by Rear Admiral David D. Porter (Pfanz 1989:7). Grant, initially hesitant about the president's desire to visit the battle lines, acceded to the commander-in-chief's wishes and ordered a special train that took them to the front lines (Pfanz 1989:7). Lincoln returned to the headquarters complex the next day and even visited the adjacent telegraph station, where he exchanged remarks with the soldiers working there. Grant's meetings with various military leaders in the cabin are well known and can be recounted by numerous eyewitnesses and primary sources.

The cabin as it originally stood on the bluff has been well described and photographed (figure 10.2). The logs were erected in the "stockade" pattern; subsequent archaeology has confirmed that they were not driven deep into the earth but rested instead on a wooden sill plank. The front room was approximately fourteen feet square with the back room twenty-five by nine feet in overall extent (*Philadelphia Inquirer* 1865). The logs were described as Virginia pine (confirmed by analysis), with about two hundred used to enclose the cabin. The principal entrance—facing the river—had logs that were squared off and planed, while the other logs were left with their bark still attached. One source claimed that the cabin cost 2,800 dollars and required four days to be constructed (*Philadelphia Inquirer* 1865). Forty men were used, including blacks who were paid as civilian laborers.

The interior of the cabin was very well described. The front room had two

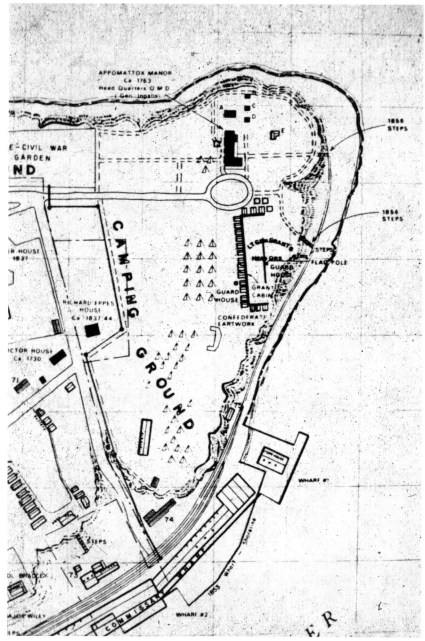

Figure 10.1. The City Point headquarters complex of General Ulysses S. Grant, 1864–65. (Detail, Historical Base Map, City Point 1864–65, National Park Service).

Figure 10.2. Grant's cabin complex, 1865. Richard Eppes' house is at far right, with Grant's cabin at far left (Library of Congress).

windows and one door, and the bedroom was provided with two windows and one door. There was a partition between the two rooms made of milled lumber. A brick chimney served the open front room fireplace with andirons constructed from contemporary muskets made by a Union soldier and presented to Grant (Inquirer 1865). The *Philadelphia Inquirer's* (1865) description continues by adding, "The [fireplace] fender, made of sheet iron, is punctured with the letters "U.S.G.," with a star on either side of the initials." The cabin was simply furnished: eyewitness accounts describe a few tables, chairs, and a chest of paper (Pfanz 1988:8–9). A few charts and maps covered the walls. The ceiling consisted of canvas cloth tacked securely to the rafters. One armchair—an ornately carved Victorian one used by U. S. Grant in a Matthew Brady photograph (figure 10.3)—was probably in the cabin as well and may have been borrowed from Eppes' dwelling. Again, Badeau (1881:136) gives us a fine vignette of how the cabin's interior might have looked during its life at City Point: "There was a flooring of plank, a deal table for maps and writing materials, a wooden chair or two, and, in the inner division [back room], a camp bed and an iron washstand: this was the provision made for the general of the armies." A letter from Badeau

Figure 10.3. Grant's cabin, April 12, 1965. Grant seated in center, surrounded by staff. Photograph by Matthew Brady (Library of Congress).

(1889) to Russell Thayer, the chief engineer and superintendent of Fairmount Park, gives a picturesque quality to the interior:

> Sometimes the door remained open, and the candle flickered in its iron frame. I can see him now in his light blue soldier's overcoat and his broad-brimmed hat, cigar in mouth, leaning over the table and writing an order to one of his great generals. . . . One or two maps always lay on the table, and as he got news from Sherman on his great marches, or a report from Sheridan after a victory in the Valley, he often entered to look for the exact spot where the manoeuvres or the battle had occurred.

The overall impression of these descriptions creates the image of Grant living in simple surroundings, capable of experiencing the discomfort many of his soldiers endured in similar lodgings.

Dramatically, the last significant event in which the cabin took part was a "grand" photograph of Grant and his staff taken by Matthew Brady on April 12, 1865; according to General Patrick, the staff posed for the photograph between two and four in the afternoon (figure 10.3) (Frassanito 1983:413; Sparks 1964:494). The Union staff had newly returned to their old headquarters, just after the surrender of Lee's army at Appomattox Court House. Ulysses S. Grant walked away from this photograph and never returned to City Point or, for that matter, visited his old cabin again.

ON TO PHILADELPHIA

After the departure of Grant's staff from the City Point bluff, Dr. Richard Eppes returned to his property. He described what he saw on his estate grounds in his journal entry for September 1, 1865: "The grounds around my dwelling house were filled with many little huts having been the Headquarters of General Grant during the campaign around Petersburg, all of shrubbery fruit trees and garden had been nearly destroyed and that along the river banks also much injured though most of the large shade ornamental trees were still standing" (Eppes journal, September 1, 1865; Turk and Willis 1982:20).

The cabins themselves were United States property, and many were sold at auction. Dr. Eppes actually purchased some of these cabins for his own use as utility buildings, offices, and even to house his newly freed former slaves. One structure, used by Eppes as an office, survived until the early twentieth century, when it was torn down (Elise Cutchin, personal communication, July 10, 1982). A diary entry in Richard Eppes' journal makes the following observations: "chimneys finished in log houses moved to pasture" (Eppes journal, March 1, 1866). Earlier Richard Eppes had decided to rent cabins with a small piece of ground to freedmen and to remove sixteen others from his grounds to the Appomattox plantation (Eppes journal, January 4, 1866). Another structure, presumably also part of the headquarters complex, was loaded on a barge and floated up the Appomattox River to Pocohontas Island (Smith et al. n.d.:37–38). The building and a lot on the island were deeded to Jack Fisher and his wife on August 18, 1866, and the cabin was converted into a school/chapel for the black residents of Pocohontas. The deed was remitted to the Fishers by Francis C. Shaw, agent for the New York Freedman's Society, the site being donated by "benevolent individuals in Petersburg and elsewhere" (Smith et al. n.d.:37; Deed Book, Number 29:661, Petersburg Clerk's Office). This building has not survived. Fortunately, this was not the only headquarters building shipped from the site on a barge.

Grant's headquarters cabin was not sold or demolished. It was presented by him to George H. Stuart of Philadelphia in recognition of Stuart's service during the war. After the conclusion of hostilities, Stuart wrote Grant asking for the donation of the cabin to Philadelphia in token of the city's support for the Union cause during the conflict. Grant agreed, and Stuart received a letter from Lieutenant Colonel Badeau informing him that the general was "perfectly willing" to place the cabin wherever "you or the citizens of Philadelphia" preferred (Badeau 1865).

During the Civil War, Stuart was president of the U.S. Christian Commission and earlier had presided over the international conventions of the YMCA in 1859 and 1861. A successful businessman, Stuart sponsored the sanitary fairs that raised money supporting the soldiers in the field. Later, he twice declined cabinet positions in the Grant administration (Wilson and Fiske 1888:"Stuart, George Hay"; Stuart 1890).

The cabin was dismantled and re-erected in Fairmount Park, where the *Philadelphia Inquirer* article of August 1865 describes its move as being such that it was rebuilt on its new site "exactly as it was erected at City Point." The article adds that the cabin "is now being placed in a conspicuous position in the park. . . . The logs, planks, and other material were all numbered when it was taken down, and the cabin is being rebuilt with strict reference to these numbers." The cabin's roof was sawn into six sections to accommodate the move. The rebuilt cabin also contained as much original furniture as could be acquired, although the article complains of "relic hunters" who had carried off many important pieces. The article adds that the building would be open within ten days for free public inspection. A stereocard photograph shows the cabin in August of 1865, a revenue stamp on the back of the card bearing the cancellation date of August 31, 1865 (figure 10.4).

Mr. Stuart received the accolades of a grateful city in the form of a "Resolution of Thanks" from the Philadelphia Select and Common Council for his generosity. From 1865 until 1981 the cabin stood in Fairmount Park, although it was moved a short distance in 1876 to avoid centennial landscaping and construction (Ingle 1988:75; Magee 1876:3) (figure 10.5). In 1898 Stuart's son, George H. Stuart II, formally transferred ownership to the Fairmount Park Commission.

A remarkable development occurred between 1914 and 1917 as the cabin became the focus of an extraordinary preservation effort. A letter from the younger Stuart to the Fairmount Park Commission president, Edward T. Stotesbury, supported an idea by Civil War captain S. Emlen Meigs to enclose the entire structure in a glass casing, which would protect the hallowed relic from further deterioration (*Philadelphia Ledger* 1914; Stuart 1914a). Meigs' plan was endorsed by other veterans, the park commission receiving approval from Post 2 Hall, Grand Army of the Republic (Roop 1916). A newspaper article documents the deterioration of the cabin itself and comments that when a reporter visited it, the cabin had no visitors, the site was deserted, and there were no guards (*Philadelphia Ledger* 1914). The writer of the article observed, "No flag was flying in front of the cabin, but not very far away was to be seen

Figure 10.4. Stereocard of Grant's Cabin in Fairmount Park, Philadelphia, dated August 31, 1865 (Lossing Collection, Virginia Historical Society).

Figure 10.5. Postcard view of Grant's Cabin, early twentieth century (author's collection).

a tall pole, with a large flag, which I was told was flying over the Park Guard House. I saw numbers of persons passing by, but none turned to notice the cabin, which had been used as The Nation's Guard House" (*Philadelphia Ledger* 1914).

George Stuart II later wrote to the president of the park commission praising the decision to "place an outer glass covering over this historic structure" and even recommending that a tablet honoring S. Emlen Meigs be attached in honor of his efforts (Stuart 1914b). However, in 1917, testimony was presented to the park commission by Zantzinger and Boris, architects, that such an enclosure would accelerate the cabin's deterioration, and the commission voted down the glass-covering proposal and agreed to more conventional preservation methods (Ingle 1988:76). In the 1920s the Dames of the Loyal Legion of Pennsylvania placed wreaths and erected a memorial tablet at the cabin site. During one wreath-laying ceremony commemorating the "sixth annual pilgrimage" on June 2, 1921, the *Philadelphia Bulletin* reported that the cabin was Grant's birthplace rather than the City Point headquarters (Ingle 1988:77)! The cabin was beginning a period of increasing neglect, which would lead to its ultimate removal. Union veterans kept the memory of the structure alive, but as they began to succumb to the exigencies of age the cabin also began to crumble (Fairmount Park 1917). Never an especially monumental edifice, the little office was obviously not built to endure such a long passage of time, and the northern winters had an extremely negative effect on its condition. Various attempts were made to arrest the cabin's gradual destruction, but none of them was equal to the task. Although the cabin in the mid-1920s is described by one account as still in fairly good condition, its best years were definitely behind it (Barton 1928:259). In the 1940s and 1950s, the cabin barely survived the threats of fire and vandalism; by the 1970s, correspondence between the National Park Service and the City of Philadelphia began, which culminated in a letter requesting the transfer of Grant's Cabin to the National Park Service to relocate it to its original City Point site (Ingle 1988:79).

The cabin had played out a number of important roles while it stood in Philadelphia. It obviously was a focus for remembering the valiant efforts of the Union cause during the Civil War (figure 10.5). Yet we should remember that such sites can also reflect other things, as the cabin survived into the twentieth century. Grant's Cabin, sitting serenely in Fairmount Park, gave us many perceptions of past time as present meanings, and future perceptions arose with each passing generation (Orr 2003:2; Shackel 2003).

Questions arise as we ponder the cabin's peregrinations and existence. It served as a symbol of Union power, logistical and strategic superiority, and Federal patriotism during its time at City Point. It reflected personal devotion and sacrifice and the memory of Union victory while it stood in Fairmount Park during its pre-1930 years. Conversely it mirrored the neglect of that effort as the veterans passed away and the "colors faded." It reemerged from relative obscurity because of the rekindled interest in the Civil War created by the 1961–65 centennial and the war's repercussions in the 1970s. But why did its principal occupant, Ulysses S. Grant, not visit the cabin while it was in Fairmount Park? He did not use the cabin in 1876 during the centennial celebrations held in Philadelphia. Did he not wish to fuel the fires of recent Civil War enmities? Was it a material enemy of the great reunion occurring between the North and the South during the period 1870–1920? Grant's masterfully written memoirs clearly promoted the reconciliation of the North and South, and his views on reunion have been discussed (Blight 2001:212–16). More research is necessary to adequately address these questions. Yet the cabin probably was used by many different publics, and its "relic" status from another time and place doubtless responded to other questions of collective and individual identity as well.

DISCOVERY

Only one detail was unknown when the cabin was given to the National Park Service: where did it stand during the Civil War? The first step was the acquisition of the site, Appomattox Manor, and this was finalized by the formal acquisition of the property from the Eppes family in late 1979 (Development Concept Plan 1986:1). The first archaeological survey at City Point was an extensive geophysical mapping of the cabin site and its environs. This survey utilized ground-penetrating radar and magnetometry. The preliminary results were somewhat disappointing; very little of Grant's headquarters complex remained (Bevan 1981:1), and according to the radar, the approximate area occupied by Grant's cabin had been trenched to a depth of four feet. Although commenting that there would probably be no intact evidence left of any Civil War cabins, geophysicist Bruce Bevan stated, "However, while it appears that this soil disturbance occurred after the Civil War, the geophysical evidence is not completely definite on this point" (Bevan 1981:10).

The geophysical survey did locate post–Civil War features such as late deposits of iron and paths but was cautious on the dating of the cabin site soil disturbance. As it turned out, the soil disturbance occurred *before* the Civil War, and the subsequent excavation of the cabin site demonstrated conclusively not only that the cabin foundations were preserved intact but also that they lay at an average depth of about eight inches. Bevan stated that most of the features began at a depth "within two feet of the surface" (Bevan 1981:10). Thus, they could easily be interpreted as pre–Civil War, and the cabin's remains could rest on top of the large geophysical anomaly. Additionally, the area of Grant's cabin was subject to drainage activities after the war. Richard Eppes' diary entry for April 9, 1895, speaks of a cloudburst that "caused the valley hillside [river bluff?] to cave." Yet

Figure 10.6. Sill board in foundation trench (National Park Service).

Figure 10.7. Foundation trench detail. This illustration shows the front of the cabin facing the James River to the north. Just beyond the range pole (outside of the foundation trench) was the approximate location of Grant's seated staff members as seen in figure 10.3 (National Park Service).

the cabin site was spared any serious disturbance. This activity continues to the present day, with severe erosion on the City Point "hillside" and bluff posing a preservation challenge for contemporary National Park Service management.

During the summer of 1982, excavations began in the Grant's cabin area previously surveyed by Bevan (*Courier* 1982:3). After some initial field problems the cabin site was located and its chief features exposed. Our pessimistic predictions were unconfirmed; the foundations of the structure were remarkable for both their clarity and their preservation! Some units exposed intact sill boards (figure 10.6), while others contained a dark brownish stain documenting the sill's presence. The cabin had not been constructed by driving posts into the ground, as we once had believed. Rather, it had been built of logs strung together in groups and then fastened to the wooden sill with large nails. The sill itself had been placed in a shallow footing excavation, which had been almost completely filled with the mortar chinking left by the cabin's disassembly (figure 10.7). The original sill was analyzed and found to be eastern white pine. Few artifacts were found in the "destruction" phase, since the footing itself had not been robbed and had been quickly covered over with soil after the structure's re-

Figure 10.8. Ink bottle in situ in foundation trench (National Park Service).

Figure 10.9. Foundation outlined by rope. Virtually all of the original foundation still is preserved under the unexcavated sections marked by the rope (National Park Service).

moval. One exception was an intact octagonal mold blown ink bottle recovered in situ well within the fill created by the cabin's removal (figure 10.8). Great care was taken to preserve in situ as much as possible of the original footing trench and its associated matrices (figure 10.9).

CARRY ME BACK TO OLD VIRGINNY: THE RETURN OF THE CABIN TO CITY POINT

The final stage of the National Park Service project was to dismantle the cabin in Fairmount Park and move it to City Point, where it was carefully reassembled on the original site. To protect the original foundation still resting in situ, the "restored" cabin was re-erected slightly askew of the archaeological remnants of the cabin (Ingle 1988). Although admittedly possessing a fraction of its original fabric, Grant's Cabin proudly stands today on its original site—a great symbol of both the Unionist effort to maintain the nation's integrity and, correspondingly, the last of its kind still surviving aboveground.

Conclusion

Ironically, Grant's headquarters cabin at City Point was not the only Grant building subjected to such a dramatic peregrination. The farm that Grant established southwest of St. Louis, Missouri—called "Hardscrabble"—also experienced some assembly and reassembly. Originally built in 1855 and later, the cabin was moved twice more to accommodate other uses and exhibitions! It too was constructed of logs, which gave it an important niche in the hierarchy of Grant buildings, an important story for another study. Back at City Point, Grant's Cabin resolutely stands, reminding all of us of many different stories indeed. Archaeological survey indicated that other cabins to the west and south of Grant's are important goals for future archaeological work to better contextualize the present anomalous isolation of the restored structure.

Anthropologically, the site in its broadest configuration over time and space gives the cabin its proper context, a brief moment in the continuum of the bluff's long human occupational epoch (Blades 1988; Campana 1989). Yet for us who seek to understand the challenges and experiences of those who fought in one of America's most costly struggles, the cabin's almost monumental role as one of the few surviving standing ephemeral structures of the American Civil War is impressive and ongoing.

References Cited

Badeau, Adam

1865   Letter to George H. Stuart, Esq., July 21, 1865. Fairmount Park Commission, Philadelphia.

1881   *Military History of Ulysses S. Grant, from April 1861, to April 1865,* vol. 3. D. Appleton, New York.

1889   Letter to Russell Thayer, Esq., February 12, 1889. Fairmount Park Commission, Philadelphia.

Barton, George

1928   *Walks and Talks about Old Philadelphia.* Peter Reilly, Philadelphia.

Bevan, Bruce

1981   A Geophysical Survey at Appomattox Manor. Report on file, Northeast Regional Office, National Park Service, Philadelphia.

Blades, Brooke S.

1988   An Archaeological Survey of Historic Occupation at City Point, Virginia. Report on file, Northeast Regional Office, National Park Service, Philadelphia.

Blight, David W.

2001 *Race and Reunion: The Civil War in American Memory.* Harvard University Press, Cambridge, Mass.

Butowsky, Harry

1978 Appomattox Manor—City Point: A History. Report on file, Northeast Regional Office, National Park Service, Philadelphia.

Campana, Douglas V.

1989 A Survey of the Prehistoric Occupation of City Point, Virginia. Report on file, Northeast Regional Office, National Park Service, Philadelphia.

Courier, The

1982 "Student Archeologists Assist NPS," October 1982. National Park Service, Washington, D.C.

Development Concept Plan

1986 City Point Unit, Petersburg National Battlefield, Virginia. Report on file, Northeast Regional Office, National Park Service, Philadelphia.

Eppes, Dr. Richard

n.d. Journals. Virginia Historical Society, Richmond.

Fairmount Park

1917 Descriptive Souvenir of Fairmount Park. Fairmount Park Guard Pension Fund, Philadelphia.

Frassanito, William A.

1983 *Grant and Lee: The Virginia Campaigns, 1864–65.* Charles Scribner and Sons, New York.

1981 Historical Base Map, City Point 1864–65. Petersburg National Battlefield. Hopewell, Virginia. USDOI-NPS 325-20007—September 1981—Denver Service Center. Map on file, Northeast Regional Office, National Park Service, Philadelphia.

Ingle, John

1988 Report on Relocation and Restoration of Grant's Cabin. Report on file, Northeast Regional Office, National Park Service, Philadelphia.

Lossing, Benson J.

1866 *Pictorial History of the Civil War in the United States of America,* vol. 3. David McKay, Philadelphia.

Magee, Richard

1876 *Magee's Centennial Guide of Philadelphia.* Richard Magee and Sons, Philadelphia.

Meigs, S. Emlen

1914 Grant's Log-Cabin in Fairmount Park. In *The Philadelphia Public Ledger,* January 9.

Orr, David G.

1983 The City Point Headquarters Cabin of Ulysses S. Grant. In *Perspectives in Vernac-*

ular Architecture. Edited by Camille Wells, pp. 195–200. Vernacular Architecture Forum, Annapolis, Md.

1994   The Archaeology of Trauma: An Introduction to the Historical Archaeology of the American Civil War. In *Look to the Earth: Historical Archaeology and the American Civil War*. Edited by Clarence R. Geier Jr. and Susan E. Winter, pp. 21–35. The University of Tennessee Press, Knoxville.

2003   Preface: Landscapes of Conflict. In Remembering Landscapes of Conflict. Edited by Paul A. Shackel. *Historical Archaeology* 37(3):1–2.

Orr, David G., Brooke S. Blades, and Douglas V. Campana

1984   Uncovering Early Colonial City Point, Virginia. *Archaeology* 38(3):64–65, 78.

Patrick, Marsena Rudolph

1864–65 Diary. Library of Congress.

Pfanz, Donald C.

1988   Historic Furnishings Report on Grant's Cabin, City Point Unit, Petersburg National Battlefield. Report on file, Petersburg National Battlefield, Petersburg, Va.

1989   *The Petersburg Campaign: Abraham Lincoln at City Point, March 20–April 9, 1865*. H. E. Howard, Lynchburg, Va.

Philadelphia Inquirer

1865   Relics of the War-General Grant's Log Cabin. August 4.

Philadelphia Ledger

1914   Grants Cabin. January 9.

Porter, Horace

1961   *Campaigning with Grant*. Edited by Wayne C. Temple. Indiana University Press, Bloomington.

Roop, Washington

1916 Letter to Col. Thomas S. Martin, secretary, Park Commission, Philadelphia, April 6, 1916. Fairmount Park Archives, Philadelphia.

Shackel, Paul A.

2003   Introduction: Archaeology, Memory, and Landscapes of Conflict. In Remembering Landscapes of Conflict. Edited by Paul A. Shackel. *Historical Archaeology* 37(3):3–13.

Smith, James W, Martha S. Dance, and the L. R. Valentine Youth Group

n.d.   The History and Legend of Pocohontas Island. Unpublished manuscript. Teacher's Professional Library, Petersburg Public Schools, Petersburg, Va.

Sparks, David S.

1964   *Inside Lincoln's Army: The Diary of Marsena Rudolf Patrick*. Thomas Yoseloff, New York.

Stuart, George H.

1890   *The Life of George H. Stuart, Written by Himself*. Edited by Robert Ellis Thompson, DD. J. M. Stoddart, Philadelphia.

Stuart, George H., II

1914a Letter to E. T. Stotesbury, president of the Fairmount Park Commission, City Hall, Philadelphia, January 14, 1914. Fairmount Park Archives, Philadelphia.

1914b Letter to E. T. Stotesbury, president of the Fairmount Park Commission, City Hall, Philadelphia, June 24, 1914. Fairmount Park Archives, Philadelphia.

Turk, Richard G., and G. Frank Willis

1982 Historic Structure Report: Physical History and Analysis Section, Appomattox Manor. Denver Service Center, National Park Service, Denver.

Wilson, James Grant, and John Fiske, editors

1888 *Appleton's Cyclopaedia of American Biography,* vol. 5. D. Appleton and Company, New York.

Part V

Conclusions and Beginnings

DAVID G. ORR AND CLARENCE R. GEIER

Caesar himself resolved to remain in Gaul until he knew the legions had secured and fortified their several cantonments.
Moses Hadas, ed., *The Gallic War and Other Writings of Julius Caesar*, p. 107

Gaius Julius Caesar was very familiar with the problem of military encampments and their significant role in any successful martial campaign. Throughout history, armies similar to Caesar's legions in their winter quarters in Gaul have gone into well-ordered camps as they continued their operations against enemy forces. Like Caesar's legions over two millennia ago, the field armies of the American Civil War were kept close to the theater of operations during the winter months. This volume's discussion of these encampments leads us to the broader issues and questions that have faced armies throughout time and which can be asked of many differing cultures. Some are only significant to postindustrial conflicts, like the American Civil War, while others are valid throughout time and across wide technological differences and possibilities. In this larger area of inquiry the topics and themes of this work can be effectively summarized.

The American Civil War, because of its scope, its visible footprint on vast areas of what was the mid-nineteenth-century United States, and its impact on all parts of American society, acts as a large synthesis for the examination of encampment issues. All this remains to be the subject of further scrutiny and analysis, but the results of such investigations would be indeed revealing. Certainly, however, the importance of the study of encampment to understanding the lives and social constructs of soldiers is not limited to that period of American history or, as noted above, to the American theater of action. Examinations of the American Revolutionary War, for example, provide excellent examples for encampment life and the resultant study of the American soldier. The deployment of the Continental Army at Valley Forge, 1777–78, serves as a powerful instance in which these same issues are clearly demonstrated. The handbooks that led to the orderly planning of camp layouts and designs for the Civil War were strongly influenced by the manual of Baron Von Steuben and his French and English predecessors (see chapter 2). We have presented examples of how such planned camps can show idiosyncratic variations based on local topography, availability of supplies, threat of attack, and so forth—all factors that were faced by the Revolutionary War armies as well. Archaeological work at the site of the Virginia Brigade encampment in Valley Forge produced data that in the future can be used to show the continuum of military thought and planning that has reached into our own time. The themes of this book, then, can be used to generate and shape a study of encampments over a much longer period of time and incorporating a much larger spatial purview.

This work has given an introductory evaluation of how important encampment sites are for the study of the American military experience. Each of our section introductions has enumerated the many ways in which such archaeological and historic data can and must be used to present a holistic picture of soldier life. Unlike the battlefields, the encampments give us the opportunity to examine material culture that was generated over a longer duration of time and in a more definable closed space. A host of scholarly inquiries can be posited by the data generated in these camps. How is the social and political character of these mobile military societies reflected in the plan and differential material culture of their encampment footprint? What were the diets of the soldiers on both sides? How were discipline and regimentation mirrored by camp architecture and planning? How did the individual huts and quarters mitigate against such self-consciously imposed regimens of behavior? How were issues of rank and status reflected by the material evidence? Every camp was different, yet at the same time certain values appeared in all encampment structures. These are the kinds of studies that we hope will take some inspiration from our efforts.

This book also has a poignant reminder for all who labor in the attempt to understand and interpret the life of the Civil War soldier. Unlike the battlefields—which, albeit imperfectly, are represented in the preservation efforts of our cultural resource management institutions—campsites have been largely overlooked. The result is that sites that have the most significant data to be brought to bear on understanding the everyday problems of the Civil War soldier are being destroyed at an alarming rate. We hope that this book will raise the national consciousness as to the true significance of these campsites and will lead to appropriate actions in which this data can be left for scientific study.

While the issue of cultural and historical significance is of preeminent importance if significant examples of this vanishing cultural resource are to be protected, discussions in this text also generate challenges to the professional community of archaeologists and historical archaeologists. Over and over again, traditional methodologies established within the professional community have been found lacking when dealing with military sites and, specifically for this text, encampments. Not only does this create a methodological challenge to members of the discipline that is being addressed, but the implications for the study of more traditionally investigated site types may be significant as well. In an era when the domestic implications for landscape archaeology to anthropological interpretation are of increasing import, the ability to identify often small, scattered, ephemeral yet interpretively significant support structures such as sheds, stables, barns, slave quarters, and so forth may require applications of methods of a type comparable to those used on military sites.

If the goals of historical archaeologists, historians, and preservationists include the management, interpretation, and protection of military sites, including encampments, it is clear that no one group can, or should, do it by themselves. The discussion generated in chapters 4 and 5 illustrates clearly that scholars, cultural resource managers, archaeologists, and preservation advocates must seek alliances with like-minded individuals also interested in the material remains of the Civil War. In the foreword to this volume, Robert Krick eloquently reminds us of the necessity to be vigilant and fully aware of the crises facing American Civil War battlefields. Yet those who share our belief that all citizens have an interest in the interpretation of the archaeological resources represented in these camps are welcome partners in future preservation efforts. It has not been the dedication of scholars or the wisdom of politicians that has established the legal preservation guidelines of this nation or that has brought widespread popular attention to the American Civil War and its players. It has been demands made by the American public—as reflected in historical societies, preservation groups, and Civil War and other types of roundtables—that have shaped the debates on historic preservation at the local and national level.

The material world of the American Civil War encampment has been assessed and evaluated in a preliminary fashion. Several case studies have indicated how important these sites are for the issues raised above. But there are even broader issues as well. Camp life and experience was an important source for the subsequent social and political life of the American republic. Camp iconography dominated the images projected by national elections for over half a century. Edmund Wilson has argued that the war was a most literate one, with almost every veteran desiring to present his views about his military experience (Wilson 1962:ix—xi). Camp life was at the heart of many of these reminiscences, and the material record emerges as an important data source in this respect. Even if Walt Whitman's assurance that the "real war would never get into the books" might be true, he assuredly did not have the benefit of the archaeological record (Whitman 1982:481). Does the archaeological record match up with many of these memoirs? Camp life represents an important theme in the memories of a good many participants. As we have seen in this book, the soldiers many times regarded their semipermanent quarters with some affection and looked back at them in later years as an important part of their military experience. Camps were even used as metaphors for graveyards, as in Walt Whitman's "Camps of Green" (Whitman 1982:606–607). We are just beginning to understand just how important camp life was for the soldiers of the Civil War, many of whom never previously endured such quarters for such an extended period of time and in so many different circumstances.

Very significantly, the above discussion of material culture and camp life identifies another area of necessary collaboration with the scholarly and amateur communities. There can be little argument that the greater number of professional archaeologists in the United States are newcomers to the study of the vast body of military architecture and artifacts of all types. In contrast, scholars from the ranks of amateur historians and relic hunters have created a vast resource of data on these issues; largely through their efforts, professional archaeology has begun to find a footing upon which it can build and address many of the topics noted.

Like the archaeological record of Valley Forge's winter camp, the American Civil War's material legacy mostly speaks to everyday ritual and ennui. The anxiety of imminent death in battle is postponed as the soldiers seek a respite from this violent world. Constant drilling reminds them of the next campaign, but there is a common identity shared by all of their comrades in arms: the "right nice little house" that sheltered them and sustained them during a grim time in their lives. They forged new friendships and learned about different regions of their own country. It is this anonymous but collective identity that we seek in the archaeological assemblages of military camps. On both sides the survivors of the war returned home to a different life and awareness. Like all veterans of all wars, the occupants of these camps faced new challenges and experiences in civilian life. How important was the memory of camp life for the veterans who sought to adjust to the growing pains of a reunified nation?

REFERENCES CITED

Caesar, Julius
1957   *The Gallic War and Other Writings of Julius Caesar.* Edited and translated by Moses Hadas. Modern Library, New York.
Whitman, Walt
1982   *Complete Poetry and Collected Prose.* Library of America, New York.
Wilson, Edmund
1962   *Patriotic Gore: Studies in the Literature of the American Civil War.* Oxford University Press, New York.

Contributors

Joseph F. Balicki is a senior archaeologist with John Milner Associates. He is a highly regarded field archaeologist with a lengthy history of work in the American Civil War in the Middle Atlantic region, particularly Virginia. He was an important contributor to Clarence R. Geier and Stephen R. Potter's *Archaeological Perspectives on the American Civil War* (University Press of Florida, 2003).

Brandon S. Bies received a Master's of Applied Anthropology from the University of Maryland, College Park, in 2003. He presently works as a cultural resource specialist with the National Park Service at the George Washington Memorial Parkway, which includes a number of Civil War sites and fortifications. He has worked at several historic sites, ranging from a contact-period Native American village to Civil War encampments. The majority of his research and fieldwork has focused on the Battle of Monocacy, and he has also conducted work at other Civil War sites, such as Antietam, Petersburg, Fort Delaware, and the Defenses of Washington.

Bryan L. Corle is an archaeologist with John Milner Associates. He has contributed to such projects as the Fairfax County Civil War Sites Inventory and the 2000 surface exploration of Camp Security, as well as the excavation of Site 18CH664 in Charles County, Maryland.

Garrett R. Fesler, Matthew R. Laird, and Hank D. Lutton at the James River Institute for Archaeology of Williamsburg, Virginia, have extensive experience in identifying, documenting, and excavating Civil War resources across Virginia. In the course of their cultural resource management studies they have investigated a wide variety of military landscapes and archaeological sites, including battlefields, fortifications, earthen defenses, and encampments. They have also drafted management plans for preserving and protecting Civil War resources and have produced exhibits and other materials for public interpretation programs.

Clarence R. Geier is professor of anthropology at James Madison University. He is coeditor of and contributing author to two previous texts on the historical archaeology of the American Civil War, one of which was published by the University Press of Florida and has just gone into paperback. His experiences have dealt with Civil War–period military and domestic sites in the Shenandoah Valley, including the battlefields of Cool Spring, Third Winchester, and Cedar Creek. His most recent research has been on domestic, industrial, and military sites on the battlefields of Fredericksburg, Chancellorsville, Wilderness, and Spotsylvania Court House.

Robert K. Krick is the author of fourteen books and more than a hundred articles on the Civil War in Virginia. His *Stonewall Jackson at Cedar Mountain* won three national awards, including the Douglas Southall Freeman Prize for best book in Southern history, which was a main selection of the History Book Club and a selection of the Book of the Month Club. He was chief historian of Fredericksburg and Spotsylvania National Military Park for thirty years.

Kim A. McBride is a historical archaeologist specializing in the military history of the French and Indian War and American Civil War; she received her Ph.D. from Michigan State University. She has worked on such excavations as those at Fort Edwards in West Virginia and Logan's Fort in Kentucky. She has also contributed to several books, including *Archaeological Perspectives on the American Civil War,* edited by Clarence R. Geier and Stephen R. Potter (University Press of Florida, 2003), and *Look to the Earth: An Archaeology of the Civil War,* edited by Clarence R. Geier and Susan Winter (1994). She is also an editor of *Historic Archaeology in Kentucky* (Kentucky Heritage Council).

Stephen W. McBride is the director of Camp Nelson Heritage Park. He received his doctoral degree from Michigan State University and is a historical archaeologist who has extensively researched the military history of the French and Indian War and the American Civil War. He has excavated such sites as Arbuckle's Fort in West Virginia and the Pope House in Kentucky. He has contributed to several books, including *Archaeological Perspectives on the American Civil War,* edited by Clarence R. Geier and Stephen R. Potter (University Press of Florida, 2003), and *Look to the Earth: An Archaeology of the Civil War,* edited by Clarence R. Geier and Susan Winter (1994). He is also an editor of *Historic Archaeology in Kentucky* (Kentucky Heritage Council).

Dean E. Nelson, a well-recognized student of encampment architecture and a highly regarded historian, is museum administrator at the Museum of Connecticut History at the Connecticut State Library. He has acted as a special consultant on such projects as Connecticut Public Television's "New England in the Civil War" and is a participant in the North-South Skirmish Association.

David G. Orr was educated at Ohio University and the University of Maryland, where he received a Ph.D. in classical history. He won the Prix-de-Rome in Classics at the American Academy in Rome for 1971–73. Orr has taught at the University of Maryland, Thomas Jefferson University, the University of Pennsylvania, and the University of Delaware. He entered the National Park Service in 1977 and has worked for that agency ever since. He has held NEH grants for exemplary teaching at Hagley Museum in Delaware and has codirected two Earthwatch projects in Italy. Orr has coedited two anthologies and has published numerous articles and book chapters on popular culture, archaeology, Pompeii, and Roman religion. He has directed excavations at Valley Forge, Gettysburg, Fredericksburg, Petersburg, Independence National Historical Park, and many other national park sites, as well as both Cuma and Pompeii, Italy. Currently he is a research professor in the Department of Anthropology at Temple University and the senior regional archeologist for the National Park Service's Northeast Region.

Matthew B. Reeves is director of archaeology at the Montpelier Foundation. While most of his expertise involves plantation archaeology (he has conducted surveys and excavations on plantation sites in Jamaica, Maryland, and Virginia), over the past five years he has become actively involved with the archaeology of the Civil War. In his research he has dealt with Civil War encampments and battle sites in Piedmont Virginia, including surveys of battlefield sites related to the first and second battles of Manassas and Confederate encampment in central Virginia associated with the 1864 overland campaign. He has published a monograph on the archaeology of the Civil War at Manassas National Battlefield Park and articles dealing with the Civil War and emancipation.

Joseph W. A. Whitehorne is a retired United States Army officer who served as a staff historian in the United States and Europe. His last assignment was on the staff of the secretary of the army. His duties included primary research, battlefield interpretation, archives development, and support to archaeological and casualty recovery operations. One of his last military projects was historian to the Snake Hill excavation at Fort Erie, Ontario—a War of 1812 site. Since retiring in 1989, he has been a professor of history at Lord Fairfax Community College and historical consultant to the Department of Anthropology and Sociology at James Madison University. In the latter capacity, he has written the history portions of six major reports on Civil War military sites in the Shenandoah Valley.

Index